APPROACHING GOD

About the Author

 Steve Brown is a radio broadcaster, seminary professor, and author. He previously served as a pastor for over twenty-five years and now devotes much of his time to the radio broadcasts *Key Life* and *Steve Brown Etc.*

With such varied experience and unique perspective on life, Steve is an original. He refuses to be a "guru," doesn't want to be anyone's mother, and gives in his teaching, the freedom to think. Overall, Steve has become known for his refreshing and practical biblical applications.

Steve serves as professor of preaching at Reformed Theological Seminary in Orlando, Florida. He sits on the board of the National Religious Broadcasters and Harvest USA. Traveling extensively, Steve is a much-in-demand speaker.

Steve is the author of numerous books including *What Was I Thinking?*, *A Scandalous Freedom*, *Born Free*, *When Being Good Isn't Good Enough*, and *When Your Rope Breaks*. His articles appear in such magazines and journals as *Leadership*, *Decision*, *Plain Truth*, and *Today's Christian Woman*.

APPROACHING GOD

Accepting the Invitation to Stand
in the Presence of God

STEVE BROWN

HOWARD BOOKS
A DIVISION OF SIMON & SCHUSTER
New York   London   Toronto   Sydney

Our purpose at Howard Books is to:
- *Increase faith* in the hearts of growing Christians
- *Inspire holiness* in the lives of believers
- *Instill hope* in the hearts of struggling people everywhere
Because He's coming again!

Published by Howard Books, a division of Simon & Schuster, Inc.
1230 Avenue of the Americas, New York, NY 10020
www.howardpublishing.com

Approaching God © 2008 by Steve Brown

Library of Congress Cataloging-in-Publication Data
Brown, Steve.
Approaching God : accepting the invitation to stand in the presence of God / by Steve Brown.
p. cm.
Includes bibliographical references.
1. Prayer—Christianity. 2. Spirituality. 3. Spiritual life—Christianity. I. Title.
BV210.3B77 2008
248.3'2—dc22
2008005018

ISBN-13: 978-1-4165-6733-2
ISBN-10:   1-4165-6733-X

1   3   5   7   9   10   8   6   4   2

HOWARD and colophon are registered trademarks of Simon & Schuster, Inc.

Manufactured in the United States of America

For information regarding special discounts for bulk purchases, please contact:
Simon & Schuster Special Sales at 1-800-456-6798 or
business@simonandschuster.com

Cover design by LUCAS Art & Design, Jenison, MI
Interior design by Davina Mock-Maniscalco

Contents

Acknowledgments

MANY THANKS TO . . .

Robin DeMurga (our daughter), Lonnie Hull DuPont, and Philis Boultinghouse for their editorial work . . .

The staff at Key Life for their comments and for making it possible for me to write . . .

My colleagues at Reformed Theological Seminary in Orlando who keep me from becoming a heretic . . .

And to my wife, Anna, whose encouragement, support, and prayers make my ministry possible and who models the principles of this book.

Introduction

I'M AN EXPERT ON religion. It's what I do.

In fact, I'm probably one of the most religious people you know. I write religious books, do religious broadcasts, speak at religious conferences, and teach in a religious graduate school . . . where I teach religious students to be more religious and how to teach other religious people to be more religious.

(A friend of mine says that religion is for people who don't want to go to hell, and the Christian faith is for people who've already been there.)

While I am an expert on religion, I'm not an expert on God. Nobody is.

God confuses me, and when it comes to what he's doing, why he's doing it, and why it hurts so much, I'm long on questions and short on answers. Paul asked the rhetorical questions: "Who has known the mind of the Lord, or who has been his counselor? Or who has given a gift to him that he might be repaid?" (Rom. 11:34–35 ESV).

The answer is, of course, "Nobody here!"

That doesn't mean that I don't know anything about God. He has, for some reason I've never understood, called me to be his servant and friend. For some reason, he has asked me to talk about him to others. I wouldn't do it for anybody else but him. I have too many sins and too many doubts, and I'm way too cynical about myself and about lots of other things.

That's why it was such a surprise when I was asked to write a book on prayer. The original publisher made the proposal and offered a fairly large cash advance to write it.

I laughed at him.

(I didn't laugh at the advance because I'm so spiritual. The advances and royalties from all my books go to Key Life Network, the ministry with which I'm associated. Not only that, they aren't that big anyway. Howard Books, take note.)

"You're kidding," I said, pointing to my library shelves filled with books on prayer. "We don't have enough books on prayer?"

"Plenty," he responded, "but they're written by experts."

He thought he was making a joke (well, maybe not), but his words were the only reason a flawed, sinful, and sometimes wrong old preacher like me would ever write a book on prayer. In fact, the more I thought about it, the more I realized there really was a need for an honest book on prayer written by someone who wasn't an expert but was a "man of prayer."

A friend of mine told me once that he thought God had called me to be a teacher so that others could say, "If Steve can do it, anybody can!"

Anybody can!

That's the reason for this book. It's from a man (me) who has been there, tried that, and is telling you about what he discovered.

One of the good things about a publisher's publishing a rewrite of a book (as Howard Books is doing) is that the author gets a reality check. I've often said to conferences and congregations, "Half of what I just taught you is wrong. I'm just not sure which half. So you're going to have to do some checking for yourself."

That's not true with this book.

I've made some changes here and there. I've expanded the book with some things I've learned since I wrote the first one. And I've added some of your own prayer stories. But, believe it or not, I haven't discovered anything majorly wrong with the first book.

So, if you've read the first one, you don't have to buy this book. The first one still works.

Uh . . . erase that. Buy the book. Key Life needs the money.

ONE

Prayer 101

*Our prayers must mean something to us
if they are to mean anything to God.*
—Maltbie D. Babcock

The best prayers have often more groans than words.
—John Bunyan

*God has not always answered my prayers. If he had,
I would have married the wrong man—several times!*
—Ruth Bell Graham

JOHN OWEN, THE SEVENTEENTH-CENTURY Puritan theologian, wrote that we should have mutual communion with God and in "total giving up of ourselves to him, resting in him as our utmost end . . . [that we] walk together in a covenant of peace."[1]

Does that make you feel guilty?

Mark Harris, in his book *Companions for Your Spiritual Journey*, writes, "Being a Christian means setting out on an inner journey—a journey of following Jesus. Along the way we learn to obey him and imitate him. Above all we become his intimate friends, and our lives are transformed by that friendship."[2]

How does that make you feel? Still guilty?

A. W. Tozer wrote: "The universal Presence is a fact. God

1

is here. . . . And always He is trying to get our attention, to reveal Himself to us, to communicate with us. We have within us the ability to know Him if we will but respond to His overtures. We will know Him in increasing degree as our receptivity becomes more perfect by faith and love and practice."[3]

Still feeling guilty?

If you aren't, you should stop reading this book right now.

On the other hand, if you do feel guilty and at the same time wish you knew the reality described in the above quotes but have had your hope destroyed so often that you hesitate to go any further, don't stop reading.

I understand, and I think I can help. I've been there, done that, and still wear the T-shirt on occasion. Let me begin by telling you my story.

A number of years ago I came to the awareness that God wasn't very real to me. Perhaps that would be no big deal to you, but for me it was very important. You see, I was a pastor and my job was God. I was the leader of a congregation, and those people looked to me for information about God that was something other than hearsay. God was what I was about—and God was someone with whom I was not on familiar terms.

Don't get me wrong. I had long before this time determined that my faith was true. I had gone through a period of agnosticism and doubt and would not have remained a pastor had I not discovered the theological and doctrinal truth of the things I taught and believed. The Christian faith had become true to me in the same way the multiplication tables were true, and once I had seen the truth, I couldn't "unsee" it. But have you ever been comforted by the multiplication tables? Have you ever tried to find hope in a doctrine?

I knew a lot about God, but I didn't know God in anything other than the most superficial way. I had come to believe that the Bible was true, that Jesus Christ was truly the

Son of God, that the Resurrection really happened, and that Christ would come back to clean up the mess. That in itself is no mean thing. Once we discover those truths, there are certain implications about those truths that we ignore only at our peril.

If I find out that two plus two equals four instead of five or three, there are certain implications of that truth for my life, my grocery price list, and my checkbook. Just so, if we discover truths in the spiritual and theological realm, there are also implications. I did my best to live out those implications. I wrote books on the implications. I lectured and preached on the implications. I knew that the Ten Commandments were from God and were not the Ten Suggestions. I knew there was a right and a wrong way to live, and I tried to live the right way. If God had revealed himself in Christ, then there were certain implications to be garnered from that truth: meaning and hope and forgiveness. If God was not a monster, then I could trust in his truth and act on his Word. The discovery of the truth was a major gift of grace in my life, and I will be eternally grateful for it.

However, I was only a tourist describing a country I had never visited. I was convinced that the country was there, I had read the travel brochures, and I had worked hard at learning the language of that country. I had even met people who lived there, and I had listened to everything they said about the country. The problem was that I had become an expert on a country I had never visited.

Do you know the story about the young man who wanted, more than anything in the world, to be a lion trainer? He read books on lion training, he talked to lion trainers, and every chance he got, he visited the zoo to look at the lions. Then one night he decided to test his knowledge. After the zoo closed, he climbed over the fence and into the lion section of the zoo.

The next morning they found some bones, bits and pieces of clothing, and a torn-up book on lion training.

My experience with the Lion of Judah was not dissimilar. I had gone about as far as I could with the book. I was tired of knowing a lot about the Lion. I wanted to *know* the Lion.

But the difference between my experience and the experience of the boy in the story was that I knew that lions could be quite dangerous. I knew enough about my subject to know that one doesn't go flippantly into the presence of a lion. Lions are not to be treated casually.

But there was more than fear that came from my knowledge of God and the truth he had revealed in Scripture. There was a longing.

I can remember the longing. I would be teaching the truths I found in the Bible and would look at the congregation and see people who were deeply moved by those truths.

Sometimes I even saw tears. I didn't understand that. I would wonder what was wrong with those who cried. One doesn't get emotional about truth. Truth is just truth. One doesn't shed tears over the multiplication tables.

You say, "Steve, you're a hard man."

You have no idea how hard. But I was not so hard that I failed to see in those tears a reality that simply was not my reality. When you don't have something or you're faking it and you meet the "real thing," it can be devastating.

So I got on my knees and I prayed. I knew the words and the formulas. I had learned those words from books, from my tradition, and from my experience. But this time I put aside the words and was honest before the Lion. I prayed:

Father, my sin is more real to me than you are. I believe that you have asked me to teach your people, to lead them, and to be their pastor. You have been gracious to me, and I have no complaint. If you are never more real to me than what I have discovered in your book and in the words of others, it will be enough, and I will be grateful for that much. I'm not going to leave, because there is no truth more important than your truth.

But Father, I want to know you. I want to speak from the depth of my experience of you, not my knowledge about you. I want our relationship to be more than a formal relationship. I desire intimacy with you more than anything else. I ask that, whatever it takes, you would reveal yourself to me and that you would allow me to be close to you and to trust you more than I trust a doctrine or a religious formula.

Up to that time, I had never understood the emotional and relational side of the Christian faith. Truth was true, and I taught that truth as best I could. I listened when people talked about the intimacy they had with God, but it was not my experience. I was a teacher of truth, not a creator of "warm fuzzy" experiences. A member of the church where I was serving at the time put it in a way that was sobering. He told me that he had been angry at me because of my lack of love. Referring to another minister in the church, he said, "I have decided that it is okay. Cliff loves us, and Steve teaches us." Another member of the church, a college student, was complaining to a friend about the coldness of the church. The friend told him within my hearing, "You don't understand. We don't come here to be loved, we come to be taught."

So I prayed. Not the cold, formal prayer of the liturgy but the prayer of a child in pain reaching out to Daddy. It was the cry of my soul for intimacy with the God of my life. I didn't bargain, I didn't pretend (I did enough of that with people), I didn't come with preconceived ideas of what God would do, and I made no demands. I simply came and asked to know him.

And that is how I began the journey that eventually led me to become the spiritual giant you see before you today . . . and if you believe that, you will believe anything. But let me tell you what happened. He *came*. God didn't come when I demanded it, but he came. On the other side of the silence, I encountered the God who is really there. It took me a long time to still the other voices in my mind, a long time to turn down the fires that had burned out my soul, a long time to learn to be quiet—but he did come.

Sometimes—not all the time, but sometimes—I can stand before a congregation, a seminary class, or a conference and say, "This morning I was with the Father," and mean that in the most literal way. Sometimes—not all the time, but sometimes—I can speak more boldly to others about God because I have spoken to God about others and have heard his concern and known his love for them.

For those of you who are afraid to pray because you are afraid he might not be there, I have some very good news: I've checked, and he's really there. For those of you who won't pray because you are afraid he might be there, I have some rather disturbing news: You have every reason to be disturbed—and overjoyed. He's there, he's really there!

No, I'm not a spiritual giant. I suspect that you, with me, find it hard to identify with spiritual giants. I'm not a contemplative. I wish I could claim the insight of Spanish mystics Saint Teresa of Ávila and Saint John of the Cross, and I wish I could walk the paths of English poet and pastor John Donne. I wish I had the facility with spiritual words of Bible translator Lancelot Andrews, the clarity of Puritan preacher Richard Baxter, or the ability to communicate with the winsomeness of writer and monk Thomas Merton. But I don't. I'm just a man who wanted to be serious with God, and God took me as seriously as I took him—and more. I'm just a traveler on the road who would point out some sights you will encounter if you decide to walk the same road. I am, if you will, one beggar telling another beggar where he found bread.

I once received a catalog titled *Things You Never Knew Existed.*[4] It had ads for a Hocus-Pocus Card Deck and T-shirts with slogans like "Will play golf for food," "I'm not as think as you drunk I am," and "I don't suffer from stress, I'm a carrier," along with books exposing freemasonry and bottles of shark cartilage. In the midst of all this, I found an offer for a book on prayer. Given the fact that I was working on this book and looking for scholarly information on prayer, I read the advertisement.

It read: *"Formula for Successful Prayer* . . . Realize the spirit of God within you. Become one with God through successful prayer. Famous book tells you when to pray, how to pray, and what to pray for, so you get what you need. Also contains the magic formulas for health, success, money, luck, influencing others, and overcoming fear. Learn the secrets that have given thousands serenity and peace of mind."

A Story of Answered Prayer

Fighting Angels

On August 22, 2006, I was diagnosed with transformed follicular non-Hodgkin's lymphoma. I'd had my tonsils out the week before, and a *"cyst"* was removed. Turned out it wasn't a cyst, but a tumor.

I was so scared. I didn't think the cancer was going to kill me, but I thought the treatment would. I prayed and prayed. One time I closed my eyes, feeling the peace that passes understanding. While my eyes were closed and I was praying, I saw in my room two very large, white beings. One sat on my bed at my feet and the other stood by my window. The one on my bed spoke: *We are ready to fight.* The being at the window was dressed in a breastplate of armor and held a long spear in his right hand. He stood erect like a soldier.

As time passed, my head told me it didn't happen. I've even "tried to make it happen" again the way it happened that day in August, but I just couldn't do it. I have stopped trying to discount this experience and have accepted that I am truly loved by God. There have been other prayer incidents during this journey of cancer, but I will stop with this one.

—Jane C.

Prozac and Magic Formulas

What in the world is prayer? Is it "magic formulas" whereby we can manipulate God and get what we want? Is it "getting in touch" with the God in you? Is it a psychological trick whereby we can feel better about ourselves? Is it a cheaper way to find serenity than Prozac? Definition is important, so let's start there.

At its most basic, prayer is simply the communion, the communication, and the contact between the creature and the Creator. It is the expression of a relationship between two persons, One who is infinite and one who is finite. Prayer is what happens when the soul cries out to its Maker. No matter what the words, no matter what the feelings, no matter what the method, when it happens, it is prayer.

Before we turn to some of the details about prayer, I think it is important to lay out some presuppositions regarding prayer. One of the reasons it took me so many years to find the joy of prayer is that people assumed that because I was a Mature Christian, trained in theological and philosophical truth, and a clergyman, I already knew about prayer. So at the risk of saying the obvious, let me give you those presuppositions.

First, *prayer begins with God.* I'm going to have a lot to say about prayer in this book, but the starting point is that God is . . . well . . . God. He is sovereign, he is all-powerful, all-present, and all-knowing. If we ever know anything about him or have any relationship with him, it must originate from his side. Scripture says, "'My thoughts are not your thoughts, nor are your ways My ways,' says the LORD. 'For as the heavens are higher than the earth, so are My ways higher than your ways, and My thoughts than your thoughts'" (Isa. 55:8–9).

The late A. W. Tozer, one of the most insightful Christians of the twentieth century, wrote:

> We pursue God because, and only because, He has first put an urge within us that spurs us to the pursuit. "No man can come to me," said our Lord, "except the Father which hath sent me draw him," and it is by this prevenient drawing that God takes from us every vestige of credit for the act of coming. The impulse to pursue God originates with God, but the outworking of that impulse is our following hard after Him. All the time we are pursuing Him we are already in His hand: "Thy right hand upholdeth me."[5]

Blaise Pascal prayed, "I would not have searched for Thee, had Thou not already found me." In other words, prayer is the natural response of the creature to the Creator who calls. It's like that old-fashioned saying: "I chased her and chased her until she finally caught me." It applies to our coming to God in prayer. We really did chase him and chase him until he finally caught us.

The second presupposition is this: *before God calls us to a conversation, he calls us to a relationship.* Jesus said, "You do not believe, because you are not of My sheep, as I said to you. My sheep hear My voice, and I know them, and they follow Me" (John 10:26–27). In other words, a conversation follows a relationship.

Of course, I would not suggest that God only listens to the prayers of believers. I suspect that God does whatever he wants, and for some reason he has never checked with me about hardly anything. However, I do know that if *your* children approach me, my reaction to them will be quite different than if *my* children approach me.

There is a wonderful story about a young man during the Civil War who wanted to return to the family farm to help his mother with the harvest. He had lost two brothers and his father in the war, and there was no one to help his mother. He went to his captain and asked for permission to return home during harvest time. The captain said that he did not have the authority to grant that kind of request. "It must," he said, "come from a higher authority." Then the captain gave the young man some time to seek out those who could grant his request.

The young man, with the presumption of youth, decided to go to the highest authority, the president of the United States, Abraham Lincoln. He journeyed to Washington and boldly made his way to the steps of the White House. He was stopped by an officer in the army who was serving as a guard there. The guard asked the reason he had come, and the young man told him his story.

"Son," said the guard, "don't you know that there is a war on? This is not the time to leave. Lots of us have lost those we loved, and many face hardship. You are a soldier. Go back to your unit and serve your mother and your country by fighting for freedom."

The young man was devastated. He turned and walked away. He was walking through the streets of Washington when a little boy saw him, noticed the depression on his face, and asked if he could help. The young man needed to tell someone, so he told the little boy the story.

"Sir," said the little boy, "I think I can help."

With that, the little boy took the soldier's hand and proceeded back to the White House, past the guard, up the steps, and directly to the office of the president. They walked into the office without knocking, and Lincoln, working at his desk, looked up and said, "Yes, Tad, what can I do for you?"

The point, of course, is that a son or daughter can make more headway with a father than can a stranger. That is true in prayer too.

I'm not an evangelist. Early in my ministry I asked God to allow me to have the kind of ministry Billy Graham had. I wanted to issue a spoken invitation to thousands and see them come to a knowledge of God. God told me that I was, as the late Episcopal priest and author Sam Shoemaker said, "to stand by the door" and help people find their way inside the house. I've done that as best I could.

But I still do like, on occasion, to issue an invitation, and right now is a good time. Jesus said, "Come to Me, all you who labor and are heavy laden, and I will give you rest. Take My yoke upon you and learn from Me, for I am gentle and lowly in heart, and you will find rest for your souls. For My yoke is easy and My burden is light" (Matt. 11:28–30). Jesus said some very amazing things like, "Those who are well have no need of a physician, but those who are sick. . . . For I did not come to call the righteous, but sinners" (Matt. 9:12–13). He was called a friend of tax collectors and sinners—and he was.

Scripture says, "When we were still without strength, in due time Christ died for [that is, in the place of] the ungodly. For scarcely for a righteous man will one die; yet perhaps for a good man someone would even dare to die. But God demonstrates His own love toward us, in that while we were still sinners, Christ died for us" (Rom. 5:6–8).

This is the bottom line: just as prayer is initiated by God, relationship is initiated by God too. He came to us when we couldn't come to him. He loved us when we couldn't love him. He reached out to us when we couldn't reach out to him. In other words, the only qualification for being in a relationship with God is to be unqualified.

I live in Orlando, Florida, which is near Daytona Beach; and Daytona Beach is the place where every year there's "Bike Week." Motorcyclists come from all over the nation and, for that week, there are motorcycles everywhere. (You know you are going to have a bad day when your horn sticks and you are behind a group of Hell's Angels.) At Bike Week some believers have been giving out a little pamphlet titled, "He Would Have Ridden a Harley." The text reads in part:

> He was a lot like you and me. The government didn't like Him. The church thought He was weird. His friends were few. What friends He had denied Him. He was persecuted by hypocrites. He hung around people like you and me, not the goody-two-shoes Pharisees. Yes, if Jesus were on this earth in the flesh, He would be next to you on His Harley telling you He loved you . . . enough to die for you.

Whether or not you are a motorcyclist, he has come to where you are emotionally, spiritually, and existentially. He knows who you are, what you have done, and what you need. And—this is the best part—all you have to do is come to him in your need. Don't let the simplicity fool you. This stuff is deep enough for elephants to swim in, but it is also shallow enough for children to play in. It is profound but, like most profound truths, it is simple. Just go to him. That's all. Tell him that you know you aren't qualified, and ask him to accept you on the basis of Christ's sacrifice on the cross in your place.

He will do that. And as an old friend of mine, the apostle

John, says, "As many as received Him, to them He gave the right to become children of God, to those who believe in His name" (John 1:12). That's it. Just go to him, recognizing that you have nothing with which to commend yourself to him, and he will accept you. You will then be in a relationship with him. Don't listen to the "religious" people who tell you that you have to be a "better person" or that you have to "try hard." They are wrong. Just go to him, and he will welcome you.

The third presupposition concerns truth: *if a finite being is going to communicate with an infinite God, there need to be parameters whereby we know that "real" prayer is taking place.* We need to know when prayer is not some vain and silly exercise in delusion. Those parameters are found in Scripture.

This is not a book on the authority of Scripture, but I do want to say that I believe that the Bible is revealed truth and that it is the source of everything I *know* about God. My volitional decision about Scripture is not made in a vacuum or without clear, rational, and cogent reasons. I have dealt with those in other places and will only give you the bottom line here: all truth is built on presuppositions that are accepted as true. The presumption of this book is this: I know nothing about God on my own. Nature helps, but even that which is revealed in nature isn't very helpful if I am seeking intimacy with God. Not only that, my perception of nature is distorted. I can understand something of God's sovereignty, of his power, and of his rule from nature, but when I want to know something about him, his nature, and his plans for me and for others, he must tell me those things.

I believe that he has done that in the Bible. The Bible will tell you who God is, what he thinks, and what he requires. If, for instance, you believe God is a monster, you have gotten that from some place other than the Bible. If your prayer causes you to become angry, critical, and judgmental of others who don't always see things the way you see them, you need to go back to the God revealed in the Bible. If you, from your prayers, find no hope, no love, and no understanding, then you aren't praying to the God of the Bible. Just as the truths of mathematics will allow you to check out the accuracy of the profit-and-loss statement of your business, the truths of the Bible will allow you to check out the truths of your life of prayer.

And while we are on this subject, I must say one other thing that is important about the Bible. The psychologist Carl Jung said some things, in regard to prayer, that are horribly wrong. However, he was right about this: in the supernatural world, there is supernatural good, and there is supernatural evil.

If you are going to be a woman or man of prayer, you will be entering into a world where, without the Bible, there is no map. The demonic element is always a danger in prayer. There is really more to this thing than is "dreamt of in your philosophy" (as Shakespeare's Hamlet puts it), and it is important that you have some way to discern that which is demonic from that which is of God. You will find, if you are serious about prayer, that you have decided to engage in a supernatural battle. Paul says, "We do not wrestle against flesh and blood, but against principalities, against powers, against the rulers of the darkness of this age, against spiritual hosts of wickedness in the heavenly places" (Eph. 6:12).

I believe that prayer can be dangerous. It takes us to a place where there are all sorts of beings—some good and some evil. There are great opportunities for error and for horrible actions based on that error. That is why the Bible is so important. Let it be your guide.

The fourth presupposition concerns the way we come to prayer: *we approach God in helplessness.* In O. Hallesby's classic work *Prayer,* he made a recognition of our helplessness a key element of prayer. He wrote,

> In the first place, helplessness. This is unquestionably the first and the surest indication of a praying heart. As far as I can see, prayer has been ordained only for the helpless. It is the last resort of the helpless. Indeed, the very last way out. We try everything before we finally resort to prayer. . . . Listen, my friend! Your helplessness is your best prayer. It calls from your heart to the heart of God with greater effect than all your uttered pleas. He hears it from the very moment that you are seized with helplessness, and He becomes actively engaged at once in hearing and answering the prayer of your helplessness.[6]

When talking about prayer, what does it mean to be helpless?

To be helpless means that in prayer we can make no demands. Every once in a while someone will tell me they don't believe in God, and in answer to my query as to why, they tell me they asked God to do something for them (e.g., prevent the death of a mother or child, grant protection in a difficult situation, ameliorate the pain of cancer, etc.), and God didn't do what they asked. They will say something like, "I just can't believe that a loving God would do that to me, and I don't believe in him."

It is dangerous to set up the parameters of how one will come to God and what one will expect from the encounter. To bring one's own agenda before God and to define his existence, his character, and the efficacy of prayer by whether or not he accepts and affirms that agenda is not only silly, it is sinful.

Now, don't get me wrong here. I'm not saying that one who prays out of great pain should not take that pain to the Father in prayer. I am not saying that there isn't great disappointment when the prayer for help seems to meet deaf ears or that it is silly or sinful to express that disappointment to God. I'm simply saying that God is God, and the most basic understanding of our requests is that they are just that—requests. One must be very careful about making our belief in the efficacy of prayer dependent on whether or not God does what we want him to do. I know the pain of unanswered prayer, and I have also been tempted to say with Huck Finn, "There ain't nothin' to it." But that is a dead-end road, and it misses the point of prayer—that God is God, and we aren't.

Let me move from what can be a very painful experience of unanswered prayer to a less painful illustration of the point I'm making. I once received a letter from a listener to my *Key Life* radio broadcast (and I've changed the names),

> Dear friends at Key Life:
> Each year my friend Bill and I have a little contest based on the National Hockey League. Each of us selects teams in certain categories, and the player whose team performs best in the most categories wins the contest. The loser is required to make a $100 donation to Key Life.
> We also select teams on behalf of Steve, and we have pledged that, if Steve's selections win the contest, both Bill and I would make a $100 donation.
> Well, this year Steve won! As a result, enclosed are two checks for $100 to be used to spread the good news. Good luck, Steve, in the coming hockey season.

I responded:

> Dear Jack and Bill, Sara and Judy:
> Sara and Judy, I do hope you know about your husbands' involvement in this less-than-godly enterprise. The money your husbands have given to Key Life is tainted money. . . . 'Tain't enough!
> Does your pastor know?
> For double, I'll keep quiet. Of course, having accepted the money, I am now culpable in this unsavory venture, and we have what can be described as a "Mexican standoff." I'll keep quiet if you guys keep quiet, and we won't hurt each other.
> For an old cynical preacher to laugh as hard as I have is probably sinful too. I only wish I could share the whole thing on the air.
> Now, some serious business. If you will send me the names of the hockey teams you have picked for me during the coming season, the entire Key Life staff and I will pray for their success.

Do you know something? The hockey teams that were mine didn't win. I don't think I believe in God anymore. I think that a loving God would know how much the ministry of Key Life needs the money for his work and would have granted our wish. I'm not ever going to pray again. It's all a sham.

It's sort of like the fly on the cow's tail that informed the cow that he was leaving. The cow replied, "Oh, really? I didn't even know you were there."

Silly? Of course it's silly. But take the silly illustration and apply it to some of the very serious work of prayer. God is God, and demands are inappropriate. One simply comes to him, understanding that his agenda is the only relevant agenda.

Does that mean he doesn't love us? Does it mean he wants to make us miserable? Does it mean he never says yes to our requests? Of course not, and we are going to say a lot about that later. But one must start properly, and the proper place to start is in the realization that God is God, and we aren't.

F. W. Faber said:

We must wait for God, long, meekly, in the wind and wet, in the thunder and lightning, in the cold and the dark. Wait, and He will come. He never comes to those who do not wait. When He comes, go with Him, but go slowly, fall a little behind; when He quickens His pace, be sure of it before you quicken yours. But when He slackens, slacken at once and do not be slow only, but silent, very silent, for He is God.[7]

To be helpless is to be humble and broken before God. The psalmist said, "The sacrifices of God are a broken spirit, a broken and a contrite heart—these, O God, You will not despise" (Ps. 51:17).

Do you remember the story Jesus told about the clergyman and the abortionist who went to God in prayer? (Actually, it was a Pharisee and a tax collector, but I understand the story better my way.) The clergyman told God that he was thankful that he wasn't like the abortionist, and then he told God all that he had done for God. The abortionist could scarcely look up. In fact, he knew that he was in the presence of a holy and righteous God. He could only cry out for mercy. Jesus said that the abortionist went away having pleased God. Then Jesus said something that anyone who tries to pray needs to remember. He said, "Everyone who exalts himself will be humbled, and he who humbles himself will be exalted" (Luke 18:14).

To be helpless is to know that you can't do much for yourself and to trust in the mercy and the goodness of the One before whom one goes for help. We are going to talk a lot more about God's nature in the book, but it is necessary that we say something here. It is not enough to believe in God. If God is malevolent, then I don't want to pray. Praying to a malevolent God is like trying to pet a snake or caress a scorpion. If God is malevolent, my prayer will operate under the rubric of "I'll leave you alone if you leave me alone." Prayer presupposes not only that God is there, but that God is in some sense a God who is benevolent.

There is one other presupposition: *form follows and defines function.* In other words, don't worry so much about the posture of prayer, the words of your prayer, or the form of your prayer. Some of the best praying I have ever done sounded more like a moan than a prayer. One rabbi, when asked about the proper position for prayer, commented that he had once fallen down a well and that the best praying he ever did was standing on his head.

For many years I was a swimming and diving instructor. I remember teaching one little boy about diving. I explained that if his head was right, everything else would be fine, that the body would follow the head as he entered the water. The boy would try it but still manage only to belly flop. Coming up sputtering, he would ask, "Mr. Brown, did I keep my feet together?" Once again I would explain about the head, and once again he would make a mess of it. He would ask, "Mr. Brown, did I keep my hands aimed right?" I would explain that the trick was not in the hands or the feet and that if he got his head right, he wouldn't have to worry about the rest.

Prayer is sort of like that. Going to God, knowing that he is God and that you aren't, feeling the helplessness, and making no demands before God—in other words, bringing the cry of your soul to God—will eventually find its form. To start with form is to play the part of one who prays—it is not to pray.

I have a friend who had just joined a church and was anxious to learn how to pray. He tried and he tried, but he felt his prayers weren't getting much higher than the ceiling. Someone gave him a book on prayer, and he was excited. He said to me, "Steve, now I know the problem. I just didn't know the rules. Now that I know the rules and now that I understand the system, I'll finally be able to pray."

A few days later I saw him and asked him about his experiments in prayer. His face fell, and he said, "I followed all the rules, and my prayers were deader than ever. I threw the book away." I affirmed him in his choice of what books to throw away.

A number of months later, this same friend was in a horrible and painful situation. There was a chance that his business would go down the drain. He said to me, "The only good thing about this, is that my prayer life is dynamite."

I asked him what rules he had followed.

"No rules," he said. "I was too scared to remember the rules, and I told God that."

A Story of Answered Prayer

Prayer Theology

When I was young, my dad was my hero, and I wanted to be just like him. He was the son of missionaries in central Africa and spent much of his childhood there. As I grew up, my dad's luster dulled. He seemed smaller, pettier, and fraught with inconsistencies and shortcomings. We began to argue—about everything.

The situation became so bad that when my wife and I would visit my parents, my dad would withdraw in stony silence. I said to my wife after one of these visits, "If this is how it's going to be, I wish he would just die and get it over with, because it feels like he's dead already."

That sentence jarred me. Had I really said that? Did I really mean it?

Those questions repeated themselves in my mind again and again over the next few weeks.

Then one day as I was listening to Chuck Swindoll on the radio, the Lord impressed upon me that, although I had prayed about the situation with my dad, I hadn't really laid it all on the line. My prayers were weak because I really didn't expect God to do anything about these problems with my dad. A crazy thought entered my mind: what if I asked something specific of God and gave him a deadline? My mind raced with the implications of that thought: Was that good theology? What if nothing happened? I can't tell God what to do! But finally, I came to this conclusion: I'm his child. If it's wrong to pray like this, he'll tell me.

So I prayed, *Lord, you know this situation with my dad tears me apart. I know you want us to have a relationship. I don't know what to do anymore. It's Wednesday night. Would you have my dad call me within this next week? Amen.*

Almost a week passed. On Tuesday night, I was nervous. Tomorrow was Wednesday and no phone call yet. I prayed on the way home from work. I walked in the door, and within five minutes, the phone rang. My dad invited me to breakfast. He said there were too many things between us and that we should talk them out. We met the next morning and talked for about two hours. I told him the story I just told you. We both cried. The waitresses at the diner probably thought we were nuts! That was March of 2003, and since then, my relationship with my dad has been transformed. We're close again.

—Russell W.

Throw Away Your Checklist

I often counsel men on how to treat their wives. I used to give them a list of things a sensitive man should do for his wife. I told them to say "I love you" at least three times a day, to buy flowers at least once every two weeks, and to take their wives out to dinner without the kids at least once a week. I told them to give their wives a break every few days by watching the children.

I don't tell men that anymore. Do you know why? A wife told me, "Steve, I can't stand it anymore. When he does nice things, he does those things because you told him to. I've become a checklist. Once the list is completed, he gets a beer and, as always, vegetates in front of the television set."

Now I tell men to love their wives. That's all. I find that when they act from the base of love, they become sensitive husbands.

I learned that from God, who was glad when I threw away the checklist with which I went to him.

I'm going to devote a later chapter to some techniques of prayer. I'll tell you about the importance of forms and patterns—what some call liturgy—and I'll give you some suggestions on how to pray and what to say. We will discuss what some of the great contemplatives have said about the methodology of prayer. But never confuse the form with the reality. The function will make the form proper.

A friend of mine, after a few years away from God, told me she had started praying again. I asked her about her prayers, expecting to hear a description of how she had spent hours repenting, confessing, adoring, praising, and petitioning God. She said, "Steve, you aren't going to think it is much of a prayer. I just say to him before I go to sleep, 'Good night, Jesus.'"

In the silence of my surprise I thought I heard the laughter of a God who was pleased.

A Story of Answered Prayer

Special-Delivery Baby

My wife and I tried to have children. We tried infertility doctors, two surgeries, many exploratory procedures, fourteen artificial inseminations, and two in vitro procedures that did not work.

My wife was later diagnosed with a fibroid tumor and had to have a hysterectomy. This meant the end of even the hope of having our own children.

Then God began working in our lives, and the subject of adoption kept coming up. I told my wife that I was going to pray for God to lead us. I prayed like I've never prayed before and said to God, *I'm not that smart, Lord. If you are speaking to us, let us know in no uncertain terms.*

The next day a pediatrician who attends our church called and said, "Would you like a baby?"

We interviewed with the grandparents of the baby at the hospital that day and then with their daughter, the baby's mother.

After getting all the legalities in order, we picked up our baby . . . one day from the initial call from the pediatrician and two days from the prayer!

He is the most beautiful child—fun and very loving. Our lives turned upside down for the better. God moved everything around. Be careful what you pray for, because God can be very loud when he speaks into our lives!

—Tom P.

TWO

Hugging a Dirty Kid

If Jupiter hurled his thunderbolt as often as men sinned,
he would soon be out of thunderbolts.
—Ovid

Be a sinner and sin mightily,
but more mightily believe and rejoice in Christ.
—Martin Luther

A NUMBER OF YEARS AGO a young woman came into my study without knocking. No respect for the clergy. I looked up from the book I was reading and asked her if I could help her.

"No," she said, grinning, "I'm going to help you. I have something that you will use in a sermon sometime. Last night I went to a Bible study, and the Bible teacher said something that you will like. She said, 'It is hard to hug a stiff kid.'"

"That's good," I said, remembering how difficult it was to hug our teenage daughters, especially when they were angry and sullen—sort of like hugging a telephone pole.

"But that's not all. Last night after the Bible study, I went to baby-sit a two-year-old boy. He had been playing in the dirt all day and was the dirtiest kid I've ever seen. When I went into his room, he lifted up his arms to be hugged. Do you know," she asked, "what I learned?"

"What?"

"That it is easier to hug a dirty kid than it is to hug a stiff kid."

Almost always when I talk to people about prayer, they tell me they don't pray because they aren't good enough and that God doesn't want to hear from people as sinful as they are.

Listen to me, and never forget what I'm going to tell you: it isn't your sin that causes God to be far away. The vicarious atonement of Christ takes care of sin. But stiffness—now that will kill your prayer life every time. You say, "But you don't know what I've done." I don't care what you've done. That is never the problem.

I've been a pastor for a whole bunch of years, and there isn't much (if anything) you can tell me that I haven't heard before or that will shock me. I've heard it all. I've cleaned up after more suicides than I can remember and listened to more confessions than a district attorney, and sin is hardly ever the real problem. The real problem is stiffness.

I have noticed that those who would like to pray but can't have something like cosmic claustrophobia: they believe that God is holy and righteous (and he is) and that going into his presence requires that they be holy and righteous (also true). But they feel extremely uncomfortable as they approach God in prayer. You can fool your friends, your wife, or your husband but not God. God knows. He knows your actions, your thoughts, and your secrets—and that is pretty scary.

Some, because of their guilt, decide to become unbelievers. Those are the folks who, because of the discomfort in the presence of a holy and righteous God, say they doubt that God exists. Others, who have tried and tried to be holy and righteous, have stopped praying because they have decided that whatever it is that makes people righteous and holy, they don't have. They think, *I've asked God to forgive me and change me so many times that he is getting tired of hearing from me. I'm ashamed to go into his presence again with the same old stuff so I'm not going to do it anymore.*

Or we pray to God and we feel uncomfortable in his presence because he is holy and righteous, and so sometimes we simply make another god who is more comfortable. God ceases to be the God revealed in the Bible and becomes a sort of cosmic Santa who would never be angry, never question, and never make us feel uncomfortable. It is a way to deal with guilt, but a very superficial way.

I once went skiing with some friends in Switzerland. They grew up on skis and just assumed that anybody could do it. They put me on a major ski slope, without my ever having a lesson. I remember thinking as I sped down that slope going much faster than human beings are supposed to go, *Lord, if you get me down alive, I promise I won't do this again.*

He did and I haven't.

But if I ever decide to ski again, let me tell you something that is an absolute commitment: I will learn from someone who has been as scared as I was the first time I went skiing, who had to learn the hard way and has the bruises to prove it, and who knows that skiing is hard.

Just so you know, when we talk about prayer, I've experienced, at some level, every one of the issues I described above. I know the darkness and the games, the doubts and the denial. I've experienced cosmic claustrophobia, because I'm not nearly as spiritual and good as people—because of my job—think I am. I've tried to be good so God would listen to my prayers, but I just couldn't pull it off. I've run from God because he frightened me, and I've tried to find some rest in the spurious belief that he didn't exist. I've created my own god who was far easier to deal with than the real one.

I was desperate. And to my way of thinking, desperate is a good place to be. My desperation and helplessness opened doors that my efforts could never open. If it had not been for my desperation, I wouldn't be able to tell you what I'm writing in this book.

Some of you remember the "God is dead" movement of a number of years ago. *Time* magazine ran a special edition titled "God on Trial." A group of nitwits suggested that now that God was dead, human beings needed to produce a sort of self-help "religionless Christianity." God, of course, threw his head back and gave a big belly laugh. He probably suggested that someone ought to check the coffin.

But there are gods we worship that ought to be dead. They deserve to be buried. Prayer, if it is in any sense to be meaningful, must be an encounter with the real God. The real God can be frightening. If you have never stood before God and been terribly afraid, then you have never stood before God. He isn't safe, he isn't always nice, he isn't accommodating, and he isn't in the business of making us feel comfortable with our rebellion. I have a friend who says he has a deal with God: "God likes to forgive, and I like to sin." Someday he is going to meet the real thing, and it is going to be a frightening experience.

Cosmic claustrophobia is, in fact, a legitimate reaction to God. The psychiatrist who told his patient that the reason he had an inferiority complex was because he was inferior may not have made the patient feel any better, but at least his assessment of the patient was without sugar. The reason we feel guilty before the God of the universe is because we are guilty and because God is really God. So, if you feel guilty, you've made a very good start. At least you are beginning at the right place. Properly understood, that is the bridge you cross that will get you to God in prayer.

But we are getting ahead of ourselves. Let's talk about guilt.

When our guilt is the factor that prevents our praying or

praying beyond anything but a cursory way, it is because we have misunderstood three things: human nature, God's nature, and the purpose of guilt. Before we talk about stiffness, let's talk about those three misunderstandings.

A Story of Answered Prayer

A Flash of Light

I was waiting for my son to come home one night. It was getting very late, and his cell phone was going right to voice mail. I was getting a very uneasy feeling in my stomach. I started to pray as my anxiety increased, "Lord, please keep him safe."

About half an hour later, the phone rang. Our son had had an accident and needed our help. We rushed out to the location, about a mile from the house. When we arrived, we saw a sea of flashing lights. (I didn't know our town had that many emergency vehicles.) The paramedic checked out my son and said he was going to be fine. My son told me he was "very banged up, but okay."

He told us how he had fallen asleep at the wheel and crashed. His foot must have pressed the gas pedal, because the car careened about thirty feet up onto a stone wall, clipping many small trees, smashed into a large pine tree, and finally came to rest on the other side of the stone wall. The car's engine was pushed into the fire wall, the frame was twisted, and there was no spot on the car that did not have damage. Even the steering wheel was broken, and the interior window handles came off. Everyone at the scene said they were amazed that my son was alive, let alone walking around.

My son said he was awakened with a loud banging noise when the car hit the wall and that just before he hit the tree, a bright white light was all around him. He did not remember hitting the tree itself. After the crash, he got out of the car, and it was totally dark outside (we live in the country and there are no street lights). He did not know which way to go and could not make out anything. There were trees all around him. He heard a voice in his head telling him to follow the lights. The light led him to the road and down the street. He then stopped and rang the doorbell of a neighbor.

I can't explain the lights or how he survived the crash. I strongly believe that God intervened.

—Bob K.

GETTING WHAT WE DON'T DESERVE

Most folks believe that human beings are good and that if they work hard at it, they can become even better. Everything, including our view of prayer, is built on the premise that good things come to those who *earn* them. We learned as children that if we were nice, we would be loved and affirmed by authority figures. If we worked hard in academics, we would earn good grades. As adults, we believe that if we are hardworking employees and produce good work, we will be rewarded by employment security and financial remuneration. If we are good neighbors or good citizens, then other good neighbors and good citizens will accept us and like us. If we obey all the rules, then everything will work out right.

Needless to say, simple observation makes clear that some of the above beliefs are patently untrue. The observations of the writer of the book of Ecclesiastes are not always pleasant, but they wash away the easy and foolish assumptions of human wisdom and our impossible demand for fairness. "The race is not to the swift, nor the battle to the strong, nor bread to the wise, nor riches to men of understanding, nor favor to men of skill; but time and chance happen to them all" (Eccles. 9:11).

The spurious nature of the view that human beings are basically good can be illustrated in a variety of human situations. One could, for instance, point out that the educational philosophy built on the belief in human goodness has, almost without exception, been a failure when applied to educational practice. One could show the monumental failure of the penal institutions in America to alter human behavior or government's failure to eliminate dysfunctional behavior by instituting laws. But perhaps the clearest example of failure as a result of a wrong view of human nature can be found in the welfare system in America.

Marvin Olasky, in his very good book *The Tragedy of American Compassion,* shows how the view that human beings are innately good has almost destroyed recipients of welfare in America.[1] Horace Greeley, the founder an editor of the *New York Tribune* (1841), was one of the theoretical "lights" for much of modern welfare. He believed that human beings were not evil—human institutions were evil. If the institutions were changed, then the innate goodness in human beings would manifest itself in altruism and justice.[2]

Years later Greeley changed his position, but not until that position had already become the basis of much of modern welfare. And its dismal failure. The view that human being are by nature good, pure, and innocent has been the basis of the failure of much of modern education, religion, and government; more important for our consideration here, it has been the cause of major failure in our efforts to have meaningful prayer lives.

Ted Peters, in his study of evil (*Sin: Radical Evil in Soul and Society*) says,

> During the period in which I have been studying the matter seriously, a number of things have become clear. First, mainline Protestant and Roman Catholic theologians of our present generation seem to have lost the ability to talk about topics such as sin. . . . The

evils of our world have been consigned to social forces beyond the scope of our own personal responsibility. Deep down, however, it seems to me that each of us is at least dimly aware of our personal responsibility. But when our theological leaders abandon the task of helping us to understand the experiential dynamics of sin, we are left with a symbolic or conceptual void.[3]

Prayer is sort of like a mirror in the sense that we can't live in the denial of our essential evil and remain in the presence of One whose essential characteristics are holiness, righteousness, and purity. If we are arrogant, elitist, and sure of our own goodness, we haven't been with God. As a matter of fact, those who have been with God are those who have been exposed and torn from every prevarication, every excuse, every denial, and every rationalization. The universal cry of all who have stood before the white-hot fire of God's purity and holiness is the cry of Isaiah: "Woe is me, for I am undone! Because I am a man of unclean lips, and I dwell in the midst of a people of unclean lips" (Isa. 6:5).

When we go to God, the Bible teaches, it is because we are looking for rescue, salvation. Salvation is built on the premise that everyone needs to be saved. The Bible teaches that "the heart is deceitful above all things, and desperately wicked" (Jer. 17:9) and that a deceitful and corrupt heart is what drives us to a holy God, looking for relief.

The problem with our doctrine of salvation is that we have this spurious view that once our sin has been revealed and we have turned to Christ for salvation, everything is settled. The truth is that nothing but salvation is settled. Everything else—living the Christian life, learning the truth about ourselves, reaching out to others with humility, learning that we can hardly throw rocks at anyone—is just beginning. My salvation was acquired because I was aware of my sin and my need of a redeemer. However, now that I've been "saved" for a whole lot of years, I am far more aware of the evil in my heart than I ever was when I first came to my Redeemer. The truth is that I have reached the point where I hardly ever feel worthy to criticize anybody about anything. I now realize there is no evil of which I am not capable.

You're thinking, *Well, you must have a fine self-image.* Yes, as a matter of fact, I do. You see, self-image that is built on a lie will one day destroy you. I'm important, valuable, and significant not because I am good but because I am loved—incredibly loved. The realization that I am unconditionally loved is the very thing that has led to psychological security. I have a very good self-image, thank you.

There is a church near where I live. I have to pass it every day on my way home. The church has a new pastor and, while I don't know him, I like him. How do I know? Three weeks ago the church sign read: "Hang in there" and the next week it read, "No, we really don't know!" This week the message read, "It's hard to be forgiven!"

When I saw that third sign, I was confused at first. Then I realized that it really is tough to be forgiven. Do you know why? Because in order to get there, you have to face the stuff for which you need to be forgiven. It is tough to be forgiven because we don't want to owe anyone anything, and if we are forgiven, God is one up on us. It is tough to be forgiven because when one has been forgiven, it is hard to look down one's arrogant nose at anybody else.

I'm a Bible teacher, and I believe I've been called to tell people that God isn't angry at them. That's not my idea; it's God's. The Bible teaches a wonderful doctrine called the imputation of Christ's righteousness (see Rom. 4:23–24 and James 2:23). That means that when Christ died for our sins, God gave us (i.e., "imputed" or "counted" to our account) the goodness, the purity, the perfection and the righteousness of Jesus Christ. Every time God looks at us, we are clothed in the righteousness of his Son.

That means that he isn't angry at us.

I've never understood why believers get so angry at me when I say that God isn't angry at them. You should see the letters I receive.

I was talking to my friend Tony Campolo the other day about why people get so angry at me when I talk about God's love and grace. He laughed and said, "They know that God loves them and gives them grace . . . it's those *other* people." That could be true. We may think, *I'm working so hard at this, I've achieved so much goodness with my discipline, and I've been faithful. Of course God isn't angry at me . . . but he is at them. They don't even care.*

Jesus told a story about a man who owned a farm and hired laborers to go into the field (see Matt. 20:1–16). Some of them worked long, hard hours, others worked less, and some were hired just before closing time. The owner of the farm paid all of them the same—a very good wage. The ones who had worked the hardest were quite angry.

In order to understand great grace, you have to understand your great need. In order to understand God's lack of anger, you have to understand how much you deserve the anger of a holy God. In order to understand great mercy, you have to know that you need it.

As I have deepened in my understanding of God in prayer, I have found that the last thing in the world I want to do is look with judgment upon others. I have found myself blushing before the throne about things I thought made me good and pure. I have cringed as the Father has shown me my selfishness, my bitterness, my lust, my hate, my jealousy, and my empty and shallow piousness. The hardest thing about prayer is to stand next to the One before whom I cannot hide.

A Story of Answered Prayer

Beautiful Bones!

A cancer diagnosis or any other significant event (and there are plenty of other crummy diseases and really painful things that enter our lives), allows God to be glorified because He alone is worthy! Through my struggles with cancer, he grew my relationship with Him, he grew my faith, he grew my trust, He continues to give and give Himself to me . . .

Recently, our gentle Shepherd was guarding me as I had entered a bone scan test. Placed horizontal one more time for another test in another cold hospital room before my surgery, a tiny tear trickled out of my right eye, as I whispered to him, "Lord Jesus, precious Shepherd, I know that you will never leave me or forsake me, and I know that you do not want to be here any more than I want to be here. Please, please, please help me!"

At that exact moment, the nurse watching the bone scan monitor pronounced, "Beautiful bones!" If you have ever had any kind of testing done for cancer in a hospital, you know that no one ever makes any comment whatsoever about any test results.

So, thank you Jesus, for answering prayer in your perfect timing.

—Kathy C.

GOING FAR ENOUGH FOR THE FUN

Our misunderstanding doesn't stop with this idea about human goodness in general and our goodness in particular.

Our misunderstanding is compounded because we have misunderstood the nature of God.

They lied to us about who God is. Those who lied thought they were helping, but they weren't. They didn't mean to lie. I suppose others lied to them, and then they tried to cope with it the best they could. And when it came time to tell others, they just reverted to what they thought was true. The lies about God have been believed for so long and by so many people that it has become a horrible "disease" in the church, and it's killing us.

If God were only holy and righteous—if his essential and defining nature were that of a "standard giver" and he were a judge of our impurity—prayer would be useless for anyone except those with masochistic tendencies. The good news from those who have encountered God is that his revelations are always in the context of such an amazing love that one can hardly accept it. And therein is the central tenet of biblical prayer. In fact, most people never "go far enough for the fun," because the horror of revelation becomes the wall beyond which they will not go.

So I've got some good news. Don't stop. For God's sake and yours, please don't stop at the wall.

Not too long ago I conducted a funeral for the spouse of a very old and dear friend of mine. The spouse died of AIDS. My friends moved in a very fast crowd, and the funeral service in their home was quite informal. There was a keyboard artist playing jazz and plenty of booze and balloons. The people who came to the service were not the kind of people who are generally found sitting on the front row at the First Church by the Gas Station. In fact, most of the folks who were at the service had long since given up on religion. I could understand that. I've almost given up myself on several occasions.

I went to the keyboard artist and said to him, "Son, when you finish this piece, bring it to an end because I'm going to say something religious." When he stopped playing and there was silence, I decided to follow Jesus' example. He would probably (judging the report of the gospel writers who chronicled his life) be more comfortable with people like this than with the normal folks who attend normal funeral services. So, after saying a quick silent prayer, I said to the folks there:

"I don't do many funerals with balloons and booze. But it's okay because that's the way _____ would have wanted it. The balloons are appropriate because this is not a funeral service, it's a graduation service. Our friend isn't here. She's in another place where there isn't any more pain. She's in heaven, and I'm going to tell you why."

I told them about the people Jesus loved. I told them that their friend wasn't in heaven because she was a "good" person (they knew better than that) but because she knew she wasn't and had turned to One who loved her enough to die on a cross in her place.

"I'm here," I went on, "for only one reason. You needed someone to tell you the truth. I'm just one bad person telling other bad people the most important thing you will ever hear: God is God, and you should remember that. But if you go to him, he won't be angry with you. In fact, he'll love you. Our friend found that out, and we wanted to make sure you knew."

As I looked around the room, there was hardly a dry eye. I didn't have to tell them they were guilty. At least they had that right. They needed someone to tell them about a God who would love them and forgive them if they would only go to him.

That's what I do: I tell people about God's love. Some people want to go to him but are afraid he will be angry, so I tell them about God's nature, which goes beyond judgment to grace and mercy. God has called me to tell people that if they go to him, he won't be angry. "'Come now, and let us reason together,' says the LORD. 'Though your sins are like scarlet, they shall be as white as snow; though they are red like crimson, they shall be as wool'" (Isa. 1:18).

Now, don't get me wrong here. I'm not telling you that God is simply nice and safe and will pat you on the back and tell you how wonderful you are and how all you have done that is evil, hateful, and sinful doesn't matter. It does matter. It mattered enough for God to give us his Son to die on a cross, bearing our penalty for the rebellion. He is still holy and righteous, and justice is always exacted. But in the case of those who go to him, justice and mercy have met on a hill in Palestine in the shape of a skull—Golgotha. That's where God's Son died, between two thieves, that we might go boldly to a God whose face is love.

The whole story of history is God searching for us. He came to us, the apostle John says, because we couldn't come to him; he loved us when we were incapable of loving him (see 1 John 4:10). Love, unless it is manifested, isn't love. The Bible says that God is not just a loving person or one who acts in a loving way. The Bible says that God's essence, his definition, is love—that "God *is* love" (1 John 4:8).

A Story of Answered Prayer

A Visit from Gabriel

I baby-sit two of my grandsons Monday through Friday, so I prayed and asked the Lord for opportunities to serve him from home. One day, shortly after I prayed, I was using my son's computer when one of my son's friends sent him an instant message. I replied and told the young man that I was Mike's mom, and we had a short conversation.

Later, my son told me that the young man was twenty-one years old and had brain cancer as a boy. After recovering and living a somewhat restricted life (with short-term memory disabilities), the cancer was back, and he had gone to the hospital to have surgery.

This boy (Adam) became a prayer obsession in my life. I prayed for him day and night, every day. I could not get him off my mind. I brought this prayer concern to church and asked everyone there to pray. I also sent a card to Adam and his family telling them that we were all praying.

One day, Adam's sister called me and said that he was in the hospital again, and though no one in their family was "religious," she felt they really needed to "think about it" because Adam's cancer was metastasizing.

His condition kept deteriorating, and through emails I did my best to give the gospel to the sister. I prayed constantly that the Lord would send someone to Adam before it was too late. Then Adam's sister emailed. Adam was in a coma. The doctor said the cancer had spread throughout his brain and body, and he was on hospice care.

In the middle of one night, as I prayed, I said, "Lord, no one but you can reach Adam now, unless you wake him and send someone." Then I suddenly had a thought that I had never had before. I prayed, "Lord, please, Adam is still breathing, so he is still alive. We cannot reach him—but you can! Remember how you sent the angel Gabriel to Mary to tell her about the coming of baby Jesus? Well, then you could send Gabriel to tell Adam about your being our Savior."

Then one day, I received an email from the sister, saying that Adam had died about ten days before. He had opened his eyes for a couple of minutes before he died, and they had been able to tell him good-bye.

I read the email and cried my eyes out for a boy I had never met, but who had been a burden on my soul for several months. I asked the Lord to tell me that Adam was safe with Him.

After supper that night, I went into the computer room to read my

Bible. I looked up on the shelf and saw a Bible that has the scriptures for each day to read the Bible in a year. I remember thinking, *I really need to do my reading that way.* So I reached up, took the Bible, and when I opened it to read, it fell open to March 14. I looked and thought, *Strange—that would be the day Adam died!* I looked down, and the words for that day struck my eyes: "And the Lord sent the angel Gabriel . . ." Needless to say, I was in shock—and then the psalm for that day read, "And he was rescued from trouble."

God did it. He sent Gabriel. Adam accepted and was saved!

Does God answer what seem to us impossible prayers? You know he does!

—Vicki A.

WHERE GRACE ABOUNDS

Now the question is this: *if God is love, why all this talk about sin and rebellion?* Why doesn't God just love us and forget about all this sin stuff? There are two answers to that. *The first answer is justice.* God really is righteous and holy, and justice demands that books be balanced and sin be destroyed. There is a moral element built into the nature of the universe, and there is always the requirement that actions have consequences. Justice requires that everything be balanced, and violations of the laws of God mean something is out of balance. When Napoleon and Hitler were finally defeated, it wasn't because they were weak or because leadership skills were lacking. They were defeated because something was out of kilter in the universe. They had violated the balance, and God demanded justice.

But there is another reason for the reality of sin and evil on this side of God's love: *it is only through sin that we see his grace and his love.* Let me give you a wonderful passage of Scripture from the Gospel of Luke. Jesus is at a dinner party for religious folks, and a prostitute crashes the party. Before anybody can get to her, she falls at the feet of Jesus and begins kissing his feet. Luke tells the story:

> Now when the Pharisee who had invited Him saw this, he spoke to himself, saying, "This Man, if He were a prophet, would know who and what manner of woman this is who is touching Him, for she is a sinner."
>
> And Jesus answered and said to him, "Simon, I have something to say to you."
>
> So he said, "Teacher, say it."
>
> "There was a certain creditor who had two debtors. One owed five hundred denarii, and the other fifty. And when they had nothing with which to repay, he freely forgave them both. Tell Me, therefore, which of them will love him more?"
>
> Simon answered and said, "I suppose the one whom he forgave more."
>
> And He said to him, "You have rightly judged." Then He turned to the woman and said to Simon, "Do you see this woman? I entered your house; you gave Me no water for My feet, but she has washed My feet with her tears and wiped them with the hair of her head. You gave Me no kiss, but this woman has not ceased to kiss My feet since the time I came in. You did not anoint My head with oil, but this woman has anointed My feet with fragrant oil. Therefore I say to you, her sins, which are many, are forgiven, for she loved much. But to whom little is forgiven, the same loves little."
> (Luke 7:39–47)

Let that phrase "to whom little is forgiven, the same loves little" ring in your mind until the excitement of it begins to become a part of how you define yourself. It means that the pain of revelation from God about our evil is matched by the joy of his forgiveness and grace. And out of that realization, one should never again have to fear standing before a holy God.

Let me tell you about my dad and then give you a principle.

My father was not a "good" man in the sense that most people define it. He was an alcoholic, and he did some very bad things. But my father taught me about love—unconditional love. When other boys did something wrong, they would say, "If my father finds out, he'll kill me." My father wasn't like that. I used to think, *If my father finds out, he'll love me, and that's worse.*

Now the principle: love in response to goodness is not love; it is reward.

I have wonderful grown children. They were a delight when they were kids, but they were not perfect. I'm glad my children weren't. If they had been perfect, they would have thought that my love for them was based on their perfection. It was only when they were disobedient and rebellious that they were able to see my love. That is true with God too. When the Bible says, "Where sin abounded, grace abounded much more" (Rom. 5:20), it means that God used our rebellion (it was a part of his plan) to be the very thing that would bring us to himself.

Why?

Because he likes us.

The Good of Guilt

And that brings us to the third misunderstanding about guilt that hurts our understanding and practice of prayer: a misunderstanding about the purpose of our guilt. Our proper guilt is God's methodology of bringing us to himself. Just as sickness sends us to a physician, guilt sends us to God—and keeps us there. In fact, it is both guilt and the feeling of guilt (and here I use the word *guilt* in its broadest possible understanding of "helplessness," "discomfort," "emptiness," "disunity," "fear," "shame," and "embarrassment") that is the impetus for prayer. It is guilt that builds a fire of love in our hearts. It is guilt that makes us more like Christ. It is that guilt that becomes our greatest blessing.

Something happens when we come to God for his grace and mercy—something so radical and so amazing that it can only be described as death to our old selves. It is the overwhelming desire to please the One who has loved us with such amazing and unconditional love.

Reinhold Niebuhr, whose insights into radical evil dominated Christian thought in the middle years of the twentieth century, was lecturing in England on the doctrine of human depravity. Some of the students who were there on that occasion composed a limerick:

> *At Stanwick, when Niebuhr had quit it,*
> *Said a young man: "At last I have hit it.*
> *Since I cannot do right,*
> *I must find out tonight*
> *The best sin to commit—and commit it."*

No, that isn't the implication that flows from an understanding of radical evil. However, when we find that God is in the business of hugging dirty kids, we see a new spin on the matter. I may not get better overnight; I may not be the fine, upstanding, and wonderful Christian I thought I was; but I now have a desire to please the One who loved me that much. That desire is the soil in which goodness grows—not perfectly, by any means, but it does grow. And the cycle of the guilt, the pain, the forgiveness, the love and grace, and the growth becomes the ongoing and lasting impetus for prayer.

In 1758, Robert Robinson wrote one of the most beloved hymns of the church, "Come, Thou Fount." The words have moved Christians from the time he wrote it.

> *Come, Thou Fount of every blessing,*
> *Tune my heart to sing Thy grace;*
> *Streams of mercy, never ceasing,*
> *Call for songs of loudest praise.*
> *Teach me some melodious sonnet,*
> *Sung by flaming tongues above;*
> *Praise the mount—I'm fixed upon it—*
> *Mount of Thy redeeming love. . . .*
>
> *Prone to wander, Lord, I feel it,*
> *Prone to leave the God I love;*
> *Here's my heart, O take and seal it;*
> *Seal it for Thy courts above.*

A lot of people don't know that, after writing that hymn, Robinson left the faith about which he had written. It was not that he no longer believed. He believed in the doctrine, but his own failure and sin caused him to lose his belief that God could love him. Years later, on a summer evening, he was riding in a carriage with a lady friend. They rode past a church and heard the strains of the hymn Robinson had written so many years before coming from the open windows of the church.

Robinson began to cry. His friend asked him the reason for his tears, and he told her that the hymn was his. "I would give everything I own," he said, "to know the peace that I knew when I wrote that hymn."

I wish I could have talked to Robert Robinson. I would

have told him, "Don't you understand? Nothing you could ever do, or think, or say would ever cause God to unseal what he has sealed. It is not your sin that has broken off the 'soft place' of your relationship with him. It's your stiffness, man, it's your stiffness. Go to him. Don't waste time. Go to him! He won't be angry. He'll love you, and it will be as if you had never left!"

Healing Our Stiffness

Now let's talk about stiffness.

In the first volume of Calvin Miller's wonderful Singer trilogy, the Singer (Christ) sings his song to the world, and people are changed and healed. The Singer encounters a miller with a hand that is badly scarred and crippled. The miller describes how his hand had come to be deformed. He had dropped his broom on the stone floor, and when he reached to get it, the grinding stone caught his arm and hand.

The Singer says that he will heal the hand and make it useful once again. The miller is angry and accuses the Singer of mocking him in his pain and deformity. The Singer says:

> *There is power within the Melody*
> *I know to make you well. Please,*
> *Miller, trust and let me sing and*
> *you will run the mill alone*
> *with two good hands.*[4]

The miller refuses the help and falls on his knees, crying out to God in his pain.

It was, you see, the Miller's stiffness that prevented the healing. It is our stiffness that kills our prayers.

The Scriptures assure us: "A bruised reed He will not break, and smoking flax He will not quench" (Isa. 42:3). David, in the midst of the most horrible of sins, understood that "a broken and a contrite heart—these, O God, You will not despise" (Ps. 51:17).

What does it mean to be stiff before God?

First, of course, it means that we think we bring to God the qualifications of goodness, purity, and ability. It means that we suppose that God has need of our goodness, our purity, and our ability.

Let me give you both some good news and some bad news. The bad news first: God doesn't need us. He was doing fine before we came along, and he will do fine long after we have left the world's scene. Ever wonder what people think about you? The truth is that most of them aren't thinking about you at all. Paranoia is the false assumption that we are important enough for people to organize their lives around destroying us. Cosmic paranoia assumes that God has organized his life around his need for us and that his wrath is the result of our refusal to meet his need.

I teach at a seminary, and it is a joy. But when I first started teaching, I was flying to the seminary campus from my home in Miami one day a week and lecturing for some seven hours. Then, so tired I could hardly climb onto the plane, I would fly back home in the evening. It was a terribly tiring experience, and I suspect that there were times when I was quite hostile. I said to the students when I first started teaching: "I don't want to be here. My schedule is already busy, and I don't have time for this. I'm not your mother, and I'm not your friend. I'm here for one reason, and that is to teach you how to talk so people will listen. You've been given some very important truths in this seminary, and I'm going to teach you how to teach those truths to others so they can understand."

Then, after a few months, those students got "under my skin." I have come to love them, to learn from them, and to have my cynical soul washed out with the freshness of their commitment and the joy of their calling. However, there is a bit of arrogance in seminary students. They rarely see any "gray" anywhere, and they tend to be quite disapproving of any aberration in what they consider God's standard of human behavior or wavering on what they consider orthodox doctrine.

Sometimes, after a particularly scathing attack by a student on some individual whose doctrinal position is not orthodox or whose lifestyle seems less than Christian, I will say, "Ladies and gentlemen, you haven't lived long enough or sinned big enough to even have an opinion on that subject." When I say something like that, the students often become silent. In the silence there is an understanding that this old guy might be right.

How do they know what I said was true? They have been before God, and although they are young in years and often young in the faith, they are learning that arrogance is the stiffness that would destroy their ministry. It was an arrogant priest who prayed when he was in his twenties: "Lord, enable me to save the world." It was a humbled priest who prayed in his forties: "Lord, enable me to save my church." It was a wise priest who prayed in his sixties: "Lord, help me not to lose too many."

God's Agenda—and Ours

Stiffness is made up of the agenda we bring to God. I have learned that God really does know better than I do. It was the confessor of Augustine's mother who told her not to worry so much about her son. "The child of so many prayers," he said, "cannot be lost." But she continued to pray and tell God exactly what he should do about her son.

One of the great fears that Monica had for her son was that he would visit Rome. She was afraid that her son would fall to the fleshly and theological temptations of that city. But regardless of the fervency of her prayers, Augustine went to Rome. And it was there that Augustine fell under the influence of Ambrose and committed his life to Christ.

Thousands of illustrations could be given of God's love and the bounties given to those who know their agendas are unimportant in comparison to God's agenda. I'm often asked about the purpose of prayer before a sovereign God. "If God knows what I'm going to ask before I ask it, why pray?" It's a good question, but it misses the point. We pray not to get what we want, but to want what God wants, and we do that with the awareness that he is sovereign and that he knows best.

Not too long ago I was flying back from a Canadian Key Life board meeting in Toronto. Our plane landed in Pittsburgh one week after another plane (the same airline) had crashed in Pittsburgh. We went through some of the most horrible turbulence I've ever experienced. I thought we were going to die. In fact, I was sure of it. Now that kind of experience has a tendency to make one's prayers intense. The irritating part about my praying on that occasion was the snores of the sleeping woman next to me. When we finally landed safely, she woke up and stretched. I said to her, "Lady, we almost died, and you were sleeping. It seems to me that a person ought to be awake for her death."

She laughed and said, "Mister, I can't fly this plane!"

Profound point about flying . . . and about life too.

God likes to say yes to our requests, but he never accedes to demands. "As a father pities his children, so the LORD pities those who fear Him. For He knows our frame; He remembers that we are dust" (Ps. 103:13–14). When the stiffness of our agendas is brought before God, he laughs.

Finally, stiffness is often the mark of an adult who has been educated in the school of hard knocks. A lack of stiffness is the mark of a child. Jesus said, "Assuredly, I say to you, unless you are converted and become as little children, you will by no means enter the kingdom of heaven. Therefore whoever humbles himself as this little child is the greatest in the kingdom of heaven" (Matt. 18:3–4).

Those who are seniors in the school of prayer aren't usually those who pray the best prayers, who understand the doctrinal truths surrounding prayer, or who have spent a lifetime in monasteries. Those who "have God's ear" are often the children, as well as those who have learned to "grow down" and become childlike.

I have a friend whose father, when my friend was a small boy, placed him on top of a kitchen counter and said, "Son, jump and I'll catch you." When my friend jumped, his father turned his back and let him hit the floor. Then his father said, "Son, you have just learned an important lesson. Never trust anybody . . . ever."

God says, "Jump and I'll catch you." When we do, we find that we are caught in the arms of a Father who has never broken a promise, never abused his children, never let us go.

A friend of mine gave me the text of a blessing offered by Brennan Manning. Let me give it to you:

May all your expectations be frustrated
May all your plans be thwarted
May all your desires be withered into nothingness . . .
That you may experience the powerlessness and poverty
of a child and sing and dance
in the compassion of God Who is
Father, Son, and Spirit. Amen.[5]

THREE

Tying the Trusses Down

LORD, make me to know my end,
and what is the measure of my days,
that I may know how frail I am.
—Psalm 39:4

I have had more trouble with myself
than with any other man.
—D. L. Moody

A NUMBER OF YEARS AGO we went through the horror of hurricane Andrew. In fact, we drove back from the mountains of North Carolina to go through the hurricane. Is that stupid, or what? As we were driving back to Miami the evening of the hurricane, we noted with some nervousness the thousands of cars going north.

I don't think I have ever been so frightened as I was the night of the hurricane. It was one of those defining life experiences. We went from room to room as the roof started falling. Eventually we ended up in a closet, and the roof in the closet started to leak. Talk about being scared. The experience did wonders for my prayer life.

Because Key Life Network (the daily radio/media/internet ministry with which I work) was the only national media ministry in South Florida, I ended up doing dozens of interviews with radio stations all over the country. I was asked to describe the devastation, to talk about how Christians responded to the tragedy and how people survived, about the churches, and more.

But the question I was asked in almost every interview was this: "After all of the loss and the pain, what spiritual lessons could you share with us?" Those who asked that question certainly expected my answer to be more spiritual than it was. They expected that I would talk about God's faithfulness (and he was and is faithful), about the peace that passed understanding (and there was, believe it or not, a strange peace through it all), or about how God was putting the pieces back together (and he has done that). However, the answer I gave more often than any other was this: "The greatest spiritual lesson I learned in the hurricane was to always tie the trusses down."

Sometimes the most spiritual thing we can do is the practical. You'll remember that I told you how much I "know" about God, prayer, and theology. It's what I do. But if knowledge doesn't have "legs," the knowledge doesn't mean a thing, and, not only that—it doesn't matter.

I often tell my students at Reformed Theological Seminary, where I teach, that they know far more than they think they do. The academic training at RTS is as rigorous as any in America. But, I often tell them, all the knowledge they possess—while good and true knowledge—isn't of any value if they don't know God deeply and intimately.

I teach practical theology at the seminary. My friend and colleague there, John Frame, says that if theology isn't practical, it isn't real. He, of course, is right. If theology doesn't have "dirt under its fingernails," it is a silly discipline.

In this chapter I want to talk about prayer in a practical way . . . trusses, as it were. I want to talk about those architectural brackets that provide the framework of the bridge of prayer. That is, I want to talk about practical stuff.

Someone tells the story of a young soldier who had attended church on Sunday. When he got back to the barracks, he was asked about the sermon. He said, "The preacher talked about salvation, about its need and its importance. But he never told us how to get it."

I started to leave this chapter out because some of what follows is so simple I thought it might offend you. But I remembered a friend of mine whose neighbor had just become a Christian. My friend, a Christian of many years, consented to have a weekly Bible study with her neighbor and to teach her some of the basics of the Christian faith. One scripture she *didn't* share was John 3:16—one of the Bible's most quoted and best-loved verses ("For God so loved the world that He gave His only begotten Son, that whoever believes in Him should not perish but have everlasting life"). My friend thought everybody already knew John 3:16.

One afternoon my friend's neighbor came running across the street and through the back door of my friend's house. "Mary! Mary!" she shouted, waving her Bible. "Look at what I've found. It's so wonderful. Listen to this: 'For God so loved the world . . . '" My friend, of course, rejoiced with her neighbor at this diamond that had been mined from Scripture. She told me later, "I have learned not to assume anything."

I'm not assuming anything either.

Now, before we begin, I need to say two important things regarding your method of prayer.

First, if Satan exists (and he does), it stands to reason that his priority for your life is to keep you from prayer, from taking God too seriously, and from any kind of intimate relationship with him.

C. S. Lewis—in his wonderful book of letters between Screwtape, a senior demon, and his nephew, Wormwood—has Screwtape say this about prayer: "The best thing, where it is possible, is to keep the patient from serious intention of praying altogether."[1] The mere act of prayer is abhorrent to the forces of evil, and you will find that there will be all sorts of hindrances (depression, doubt, frustrations, and so on). Many of those hindrances will have the smell of sulfur smoke about them.

But, second, even if Satan doesn't exist (or you don't believe that he exists), there is plenty in you that will keep you from praying. You might assume that because you have thought a lot about prayer, have planned prayers, and have studied the subject of prayer, that you have actually prayed.

A college professor invited a friend to dinner. The professor, forgetting that he had issued the invitation, prepared his own meal. When he was unexpectedly called away from his home, he left his dinner on the table. His friend arrived, noticed the dinner, and thinking it had been left for him, ate it. When the professor came home, he noticed the empty plate and said, "If it weren't for that empty plate, I would swear that I had not had dinner."

We are sort of like that about prayer. The signs are there, but the reality isn't. We know a lot about prayer and have even composed prayers, but we haven't prayed.

There is also the natural frustration that follows a serious commitment to prayer. Prayer is not easy. It requires time, effort, and commitment. There will be times when you think God has gone away on vacation, that your prayers will never bear fruit, and that it is all useless. When that happens, many give up the effort.

There are natural human emotions that hurt our prayer lives. When we are depressed, we feel that prayer is useless; when we are elated, we think prayer isn't necessary. We wait for inspiration before we pray, forgetting that inspiration is the result of prayer and not usually the cause of it. We have feelings of anger and bitterness that rob us of the peace necessary for prayer. And then there is that fear that he won't be there. Or that he will.

And we must not forget about doubt. Our nature is to give credence to that which we can see, feel, and touch. Prayer moves us from the world of sense to the world of the Spirit. There are times when we may feel we are simply playing a game, using a psychological trick and calling it prayer. And sometimes we have the sensation that our prayers aren't real and that we are silly for even trying.

Again, I've been to all those places.

Do you remember when Jesus told his disciples about the bad things that were going to happen? He then made this comment: "These things I have spoken to you, that you should not be made to stumble" (John 16:1). In other words, if you don't know the bad stuff will happen, the bad stuff will kill you.

I've learned from Jesus. When your emotions start coming into play, when you're worried that prayer is just a game of pretend, when the "demons" of doubt visit you, when you want to run, just remember that I told you about all of that. As the golfers say, "lean on my ball." I've been there and can't tell you the number of times I almost gave up. With Churchill and Jesus, let me say, "Don't give up! Never give up!"

A former president of Wheaton College told a group of pastors, "At Wheaton, we don't encourage dating—we don't have to." Well, in prayer one must do everything one can do to encourage prayer because there are so many things that will discourage us and derail our good intentions. The fact that you are reading this book is a sign that you are interested in pursuing prayer. And it sounds so exciting and so real while one is reading about it in a book. Remember, however, that the actual "doing" of prayer takes discipline.

There is a need for practical methodologies of prayer that will enable us to pursue God (or to allow him to pursue us) even when we have run out of the spiritual gasoline necessary for the effort. While what follows will be practical and, I hope, helpful, remember that systems and methodologies are not reality. There is a great danger that forms will be mistaken for reality, a danger that God will somehow get lost in the ways of approaching God. There will, of course, be dry times in your prayer life, sometimes lengthy ones. During those times it is important to continue, to persevere, and to prevail. However, even during those times of feeling the absence of God, we must lift our cold hearts before him, asking that he will build the fire, that he will come, that he will lift the veil of blindness, and that he will take our methodologies and systems and make them real.

Let's tie some trusses down.

A Story of Answered Prayer

An Angelic Rescue

When my brother, Charlie, and I were teenagers, he was diagnosed with schizophrenia. My mother told me, when I was eighteen, that I would have to take care of my brother. She cared for him as long as she was able. Our father died in 1966. After my mother died, I became Charlie's guardian.

When I developed cancer, my brother began to worry, wondering what would happen to him when his sister died. I prayed that God would let me outlive Charlie if it be his will.

In April of 2000, Charlie, our friend Bob, and I were walking our dogs on the levee near Chickamauga Creek in Chattanooga. All of a sudden, Charlie fell over in front of us. I thought he had just fallen, but then he didn't respond to Bob's CPR. I called 911. At the hospital, Charlie was pronounced dead.

Charlie was with Jesus! He loved the Lord more than anything, and everyone he met soon found out who Charlie loved!

We had Charlie's body shipped to Illinois. The next day, I called Bob's daughter, who told us that the night before Charlie died, her daughter Kristi (who has cerebral palsy and who thought a lot of Charlie) had had a vision of angels taking Charlie off rocks to heaven.

Subsequently, some painful incidents occurred, like serious surgery with me when I was close to death, and like Charlie's dog breaking his leg. Charlie would have been upset. God has been so good and allowed me to outlive Charlie. I am grateful to God for that and for answering my prayer.

—Naomi F.

Flying Without Parachutes

First, before you begin the hard work of prayer, you must make a commitment to prayer, no matter what, so that it becomes an essential part of your life. When the Bible's Daniel was commanded to pray to the king instead of to the true God, he was threatened with death. This is what he did: "When Daniel knew that the writing was signed, he went home. And in his upper room, with his windows open toward Jerusalem, he knelt down on his knees three times that day, and prayed and gave thanks before his God, *as was his custom since early days*" (Dan. 6:10). Jesus talked about the importance of "persevering" prayer in his parable about the woman who continued to persist in her request to the judge. Luke prefaces that parable by saying, "He spoke a parable to them, that men always ought to pray and not lose heart" (Luke 18:1).

We once had a problem with raccoons in our backyard.

Our daughter Jennifer (who is wont to bring home strays of the human and animal variety) had taken in a pregnant cat. The cat had kittens, and the kittens had kittens, and pretty soon I felt like Pharaoh and his frogs—only my plague was cats. We fed them in the backyard, and the raccoons, seeing a good thing, decided to horn in on the meals.

One evening I came on a plan to get rid of the raccoons. A very large raccoon came across the backyard and climbed up on the picnic table to help himself to the cats' food. I had a hose nearby with a nozzle that produced a very focused and strong stream of water. I let the raccoon have it. The raccoon ran but within five minutes was back on the table eating the food. I hit him again with the hose, and once again he ran, this time only a little way down the yard. Then he turned, my hose following him all the way, and ignoring the water, walked calmly back to the table, climbed up on it, turned to me, and stood up on his back legs, the spray from my hose still drenching him. He just stood there looking at me with scorn, as if he were saying: "I don't care what you do to me, I'm going to eat that food. When you get tired and the food is as wet as I am right now; when you have finished and go into your house, I will still be here, and I *will* eat that food."

That raccoon illustrates the kind of commitment we must have before we start experimenting with prayer. We must say that no matter what Satan does, no matter how depressed we become, no matter what doubts we have, no matter how tired we get, or how long it takes, we are going to pray. Unless the commitment is made, the prayers will eventually die on our lips.

I've never written a book on marriage for a couple of reasons. I have a happy marriage and have no idea why it's happy except that God was gracious in giving me a wife who has the ability to live with a twit. Aside from that, when I was a pastor,

I noticed that in spite of all the new books on how to have a happy marriage, the divorce rate still went up in the congregation. I suppose that upon reading such books, the people decided that their marriages were far worse than they supposed and that it would be impossible to fix them.

But the most important reason I haven't written a book on marriage is because it is hard to make a book out of one word. That word is *commitment*. Underneath all the bad stuff, if there is a commitment to the marriage, there probably won't be a divorce. And you can't teach commitment.

Eddie Rickenbacker, World War I flying ace and one of the major figures in the early days of the airline industry in America, used to talk about how pilots during the war flew without parachutes because parachutes were too tempting. Often the first Europeans who sailed to the Americas burned their boats on the American beach lest they be tempted to return when the times got hard. Prayer, if one is going to be successful at it, must constitute a major commitment. If that absolute commitment isn't there, you will (trust me on this) give it up.

How much time should one devote to prayer? I believe that one should devote no more than that which is necessary. I've noticed that many people, with very good intentions, devote themselves to a "season" of prayer each day. They set aside an hour or two for the sole purpose of being with God. But most people simply don't know what to do with an hour of prayer. They read the Bible, pray the Lord's Prayer, and offer their petitions in the first three minutes. Then they don't know what to do after that.

False expectations, I have found, account for more failure at prayer than almost anything else. For years people have complained to me about how hard it was to be faithful with their "quiet time" with God. One of the men in my Bible study told me, "I really want to have that time, but I've tried to start and have quit even more times than I've tried to quit smoking. Can you help me?"

I told him that his problem was that, in his enthusiasm for having a time of prayer, he was overcommitting himself. I suggested that he take no more than five or ten minutes each morning to read a passage of Scripture, to tell God how wonderful he is and thank him for all he has done, to confess all the sins he could remember, to pray the Lord's Prayer, and to pray about the things that bothered him. "Then quit," I said. "Don't increase the time you spend until it is absolutely necessary that you increase it. Don't go beyond the ten minutes until you simply can't stay within the ten minutes." That simple advice absolutely changed his walk with God. Now he can accurately be described as a man of prayer.

Later we are going to talk about contemplative prayer and meditation, and I'm going to show you some approaches to prayer that will put some meat on the bones of the prayer life you have begun. It is, however, very important that you start and be faithful with the simple act of prayer and that you start in a helpful way. It is very easy to bite off more than you can chew as you begin what, hopefully, will be a lifetime of walking with God in prayer.

A Story of Answered Prayer

Real Prayer

As a young man, years after being reconciled to the Lord, I was still distant from him. Of course, prayers were reserved for a last resort. I worked in a place where sometimes I had to retrieve numbered envelopes from piles of envelopes laid out on dimly lit shelves. When frustrated, I would think, *Lord, where is it?*

My hand was always led to the right one.

Over time, I realized that God was answering real prayer. That refueled my interest in his Word.

—Tim B.

PRAYER'S NUTS AND BOLTS

A prayer time need not be long, but it does need consistency and a commitment to that consistency. Don't cover your need for prayer by combining it with something else like driving to work, or waiting for a bus, or walking to lunch. Make the time you pray specific and regular, even if it is short.

What about posture in prayer? I suggest, particularly at the beginning of your journey in prayer, that you pray in the posture that is the most comfortable. It is the attitude of your heart more than the attitude of your body that is important. There will be occasions, especially as the length and the depth of your prayers increase, that you will be constrained to fall on your knees before the reality that you have discovered. There might even be times when the only appropriate posture in prayer will be prostrate on the floor "before the throne." However, none of that should be forced. Start by being comfortable.

When is a good time to pray? As I have gotten older, the Lord has given me a gift that I had asked for, but never received, when I was a young pastor. I had read where John Wesley got up each morning at 4:00 a.m., and I decided that if I was going to be a giant of the faith, I needed to do that too. The problem was that I discovered that God wasn't up at that hour. As someone else has commented, I am an atheist until I have my first cup of coffee. Aside from being sleepy all the time, I found myself falling asleep during my own sermons. That can cost a preacher his job. So I found another time to pray and used the early morning for what I thought it was created for, namely, sleep.

But in the last few years, as my schedule increased, I found myself waking up early and feeling refreshed. I decided that it was the Father calling me to spend some time with him. I can't tell you how good the early morning has been. Without staff around, without phone calls and appointments, it is amazing how good it is to be with the Father.

Perhaps you are still a spiritual Philistine and just can't abide the morning. If that is the case, find a time when you are least distracted, and set aside that time for your special time of prayer. Find a special place, and go to that place—perhaps a room in your home, your office, the front porch, etc.—where you can set aside the time to be still before God.

What about the form of prayer? It is important, at the beginning, that one have a form to get you through your beginning steps in intimacy with God. Later we are going to talk about the prayer of silence, but here let me suggest a couple of things that were suggested to me as I began my walk of prayer.

A number of people like to use the Lord's Prayer (see Matt. 6:9–13) as the form of their prayer time. The disciples of Jesus, you will remember, asked him to teach them to pray, and in response to that request, he gave them a prayer that has been used by Christians ever since. Let me show you how you can use that prayer as the form for your own prayers.

Pray: Our Father in heaven . . .

Think of God and all his power and greatness. Remember that he is really there and that you are directing your prayers to him. Address him as Father, and thank him that he has allowed you to address him that way.

Pray: Hallowed be Your name. . . .

The word *hallowed* means that someone is holy, pure, and sacred. Praise God for his holiness and his greatness. Thank him for his kindness to you and his showing himself to you. Praise him for all that he is.

Pray: *Your kingdom come. . . .*

Think about what it would mean if God's kingdom should be the reality in our world. Think of the love, the compassion, and the order that would be present. Think of the freedom from war and famine. Pray for the leaders of your nation and the people in authority, that they would conform their plans to his plans.

Pray: *Your will be done on earth as it is in heaven. . . .*

This is an affirmation that God is God and you aren't. When praying these words, you submit to him all that you are and all that you want to be. You are telling God that he knows best and that you relinquish all your plans, all your goods, and all your hopes to his will.

Pray: *Give us this day our daily bread . . .*

The Father, Jesus said, knows our needs, but we feel better telling him about them. Bring before the throne of God all the things that concern you. Make your requests and your petitions. Don't worry about praying about little things; all things are little with God.

Pray: *And forgive us our debts . . .*

Ask God to reveal to you those places in your life where you have been disobedient, where you have gone your way instead of his way, when you have acted in ways that you knew were wrong and sinful. Lift before him your sinful thought life and your angry words, and ask for his forgiveness.

Pray: *As we forgive our debtors. . . .*

Jesus made a very big issue out of the need to forgive others and of asking God to forgive us in the same way we forgive others. Forgiveness is not an action—it is a process. This is the place to at least begin the process. Ask God—even if you don't really want him to—to bless those who have harmed you, lied about you, and tried to destroy you. Then ask him to conform your heart to that request.

Pray: *And do not lead us into temptation . . .*

This is the place where you can tell God about your weakness, your foolishness, and your unwillingness to be obedient and godly. Confess your weakness before him and remind him (and mostly yourself) that your boat is very small and the ocean is very big.

Pray: *But deliver us from the evil one. . . .*

The Greek word Jesus uses here can mean evil, and it can also mean the personification of evil, Satan. Ask God to give you the courage and the strength to stand against evil, whatever its source. Ask him to put a protective hedge around you and to be your protector from evil people and their evil intentions.

While the following words are not in the original text of Jesus' prayer, they have become the traditional way for many Christians to end the prayer:

Pray: *For Yours is the kingdom and the power and the glory forever. Amen.*

Thank God for the time of prayer, and confess him again as God, worthy of all praise and adoration.

There are other forms of prayer that you might find helpful. Some believers like to use the ACTS method of prayer. ACTS is an acrostic pointing to the four main elements of verbal prayer: Adoration (when we praise God), Confession (when we admit our failures), Thanksgiving (when we express gratitude), and Supplication (when we ask for ourselves or others). Make those the four sections of your prayer.

Others like to take a psalm or other passage of Scripture and use it as a basis for prayer just as we did with the Lord's Prayer. For instance, you can use the familiar Twenty-third Psalm and pray through it, pausing after each phrase to think and pray about what it says. Sometimes it is helpful to substitute your name for the pronouns in the passage of Scripture.

Early in my own fledgling efforts at praying, and on the advice of a friend, I started a prayer list, and I continue using that method today. There are studies that say most pastors pray far less than we might think, less than five minutes a day. For many years that was true of me. Over and over again, people would ask me to pray for them, and I would assure them of my prayers, and then I would forget. I hate a lot of things, but hypocrisy is right near the top of my list. So I started writing down the names and the requests of people who asked me to pray. I added to that list my family, some close friends, and a list of the leaders of the church. *Then I told each person that I was praying daily for them.*

(I know, I know. There is an element of self-righteousness in telling them. I know that and asked God about it. He said that it was better I be a bit self-righteous, pray, and repent of it than to eliminate the self-righteousness and not pray. He told me that he was perfectly capable of dealing with my self-righteousness, but not my absence.)

Then, the next morning, when I thought about prayer and remembered my busy schedule and wanted to put the prayer time off, I remembered the promises I had made. Reluctantly, I stopped whatever plans I had and prayed for those people for whom I had promised to pray. They say that you are getting old when you bend down to get something and say to yourself, *Now, is there anything else I can do while I'm down here?* I suspect that those early times of prayer were like that. I would pray for the people for whom I had promised to pray and then think, *Well, since I'm already on my knees, I might as well pray a little longer.* Praying for others was a major "truss" in my prayer life and continues to be so today.

With a bit of pride and self-righteousness, let me tell you that I am now praying for hundreds of people every morning, and I have told them so. The reason I'm telling you and the reason I tell them isn't because I want you to think I'm really spiritual. Well, maybe a little bit. But those who know me would laugh at the thought. The reason is that tomorrow morning when I have decided that I'm too busy to pray, I'll remember the telling and will decide that it is better to pray than to be a hypocrite. I need that sort of thing.

Another good way to pray is to write your prayers in the form of letters to God. I have found that "writing to God" helps me focus my prayers. When I am under pressure, and my mind has a tendency to wander off to the pressure points instead of sticking to the prayer, I find that writing my prayers in the form of a letter is helpful. I sometimes type my prayers on a computer, always being careful to erase them when I'm finished, because there are certain things that I talk to God about that I don't want others to see or hear.

Now a word about failure: you will sometimes fail. You may say, "Well, thanks for the encouragement!" It really is encouraging, because people who try but fail in prayer must always be mindful of two things: first, everyone who has ever gotten serious with prayer has had times of failure; second, in times of failure it is important that you remember, as Jesus did in a different context, that I told you about them so you might not be discouraged.

After my first automobile accident as a teenager, my father forced me right back into the driver's seat of the family car. I asked him why, and he told me that if I didn't get up soon after I had fallen, I would want to stay on the ground, and if I didn't drive after messing up, there was a chance that I would never drive again.

A Story of Answered Prayer

A Nudge from the Spirit

One night I was on the phone with my mother. She had a serious sinus infection and had had it for two weeks. She figured she had let it go long enough and said she was going to see the doctor the next day.

As she was telling me, suddenly her voice became distant. I could hear her talking, but I couldn't decipher what she was saying. The Holy Spirit nudged me to pray for my mother right then. So I did, silently. As this was happening, I remember thinking, *Okay, I'll pray for her, but I really don't understand this.*

Mom and I finished our conversation and, as I hung up the phone, I thought, *What was that all about?*

The next day I phoned my mom and asked her if she had gone to the doctor. She said, "No, I didn't. It was the strangest thing, but I started to feel a lot better as I was talking to you on the phone last night."

My jaw dropped. He had done it!

—Amy N.

WHY METHODS AREN'T THE POINT

While I hope that some of the material in this chapter will help tie the trusses down for you and get you started, don't—and I must say this again—don't put your faith in methods and directions. Prayer is the natural cry of a child for a parent. Like breathing, it is not a problem to be worked out but an experience to savor. Birds sing simply because they have a song. Prayer isn't something one does because it is a good thing to do. Prayer, like the song, is sung because that is why we were created.

I suspect the reason you're reading this book is because of a desire. The desire is from God. We were created that way. God, as Augustine said, made us for himself and there is something in us that drives us to God in the same way that there is something in a child that drives him or her to the arms of his or her mother . . . or father.

There is a wonderful story about a man in Scotland who was on his deathbed. He was not worried about death and had prepared for it properly, but he was having serious trouble praying. His pastor visited one day, and the man told his pastor about the problem. "It's just not very real to me," he said.

"Why don't you place a chair next to your bed," the pastor suggested, "and imagine that Jesus is sitting in the chair. Then talk to him the same way you are talking to me."

Two days later, the pastor received a call from the daughter of the man he had visited. She had been nursing her father during his last days. "Pastor," she said on the phone, "I wanted you to know that my father passed away this afternoon. I had just finished fixing his lunch and went in to check on him, and he was gone. Nothing had changed since I left him . . . except that his hand was resting on the chair beside his bed."

That man had finally understood prayer.

——

FOUR

Growing Down

Children need love, especially when they don't deserve it.
—Harold Hulbert

How different is the man you are from the child you were!
—Ovid

Let the little children come to Me, and do not forbid them;
for of such is the kingdom of God.
—Mark 10:14

O NE OF THE MAJOR reasons so many people don't have fulfilling prayer lives is because they haven't understood that the essential nature of prayer is communication between a child and its father. Prayer is not a theological treatise.

I have a friend who went through a terrible time with drugs. During that time she did some appalling things for which she was ashamed. Once, we were talking, and my friend pulled out an old and worn picture of herself as a child. The little girl in the picture was pretty and was laughing as if she didn't have a care in the world. My friend started crying and through the sobs said to me, "What have I done to that little girl?"

We do all sorts of bad things to the child in us. In our efforts at maturing (which are often only efforts to conform to what others say is maturity) and in the process of socializing (which is often the way the world robs us of our childhood), we lose an essential element of prayer. That essential is the understanding that if you want to grow up in prayer, you have to grow down.

In this chapter I want to talk to you about childlikeness and what it means to be childlike in prayer. I am, of course, not going to talk about child*ish*ness. That is something else altogether. Too many people are childish—characterized by immaturity—when they think they are being childlike.

The Christian faith is by no means simple. Before we deal with more profound and difficult subjects in the area of prayer, it is important that we examine the basic and simple truth of the biblical requirement for childlikeness. Someone has said that simplicity on this side of complexity is not "worth a fig." I agree with that. But simplicity on the far side of complexity is, at least in the area of prayer, worth everything.

Karl Barth was once asked what he had learned after a lifetime of study and writing multiple volumes that had changed the face of modern theology. He said, "I have learned, 'Jesus loves me, this I know, for the Bible tells me so.'"

When Jesus was asked about who would be the greatest in the kingdom of heaven, to the surprise of everyone listening, he called a little child to him and said, "Assuredly, I say to you, unless you are converted and become as little children, you will by no means enter the kingdom of heaven. Therefore whoever humbles himself as this little child is the greatest in the kingdom of heaven" (Matt. 18:3–4).

The nature of prayer is such that childlikeness is one of the primary requirements for effective prayer. If you get everything else right but miss that, prayer will be a dull and boring experience. If you get how to be childlike right, even if everything else is wrong, your prayers will soar. Prayer is the recognition that one is speaking to one's heavenly Father. It has about it a lack of sophistication and slickness.

Now, before we get serious about not being so serious—that is, being childlike—I want to say a word to those for whom the word *father* does not solicit an altogether positive image. Perhaps you had a father who abused you or betrayed you. I understand. But I think it is important that you not miss what Jesus said about our heavenly Father. Rather than try to find another image of God, why not take the revealed one, "Father," and invest in it the proper qualities of a good father? Think of what it would be like to have a father who personified all the good qualities you would like in a father.

What Jesus did when he defined God as *Father* was define the word properly. He said, "If you then, being evil, know how to give good gifts to your children, how much more will your Father who is in heaven give good things to those who ask Him!" (Matt. 7:11). He portrayed God as a Father who cares, who oversees his own with love, and who is never an abuser of his children. Scripture teaches that we are to call God "Abba," a term of endearment that could be translated as "Daddy" or, as my granddaughters call me, "Pops." Perhaps we need to back away from our more adult images and inhibitions and get familiar. God is a Father who really likes to spend time with his children.

A Story of Answered Prayer

The Beginnings of Faith

When I was six years old, I climbed to the top of a six-foot chain-link fence. On the top of the fence were three strands of barbed wire. I attempted to go through the bottom two strands. My cutoff shorts got stuck on the barbed wire, and I could not move up or down or sideways.

I prayed for the Lord's help, and within a very short time, my mom came out to check on me. She got a step ladder and helped me get unstuck and down from the barbed wire.

From that day forward, I have had great faith in prayer.

—Joseph W.

Acting Like a Child

What does it mean to be childlike? First, childlikeness, at its heart, is a quality of trust. It is the recognition that God is not only in control but that he really is our heavenly Father. Jesus said, "Do not fear, little flock, for it is your Father's good pleasure to give you the kingdom" (Luke 12:32). The psalmist wrote, "Trust in Him at all times, you people; pour out your heart before Him; God is a refuge for us" (Ps. 62:8).

I have spent most of my life as a professional "religionist." I have read thousands of books on religion, theology, and prayer. I teach at a theological seminary and love to pursue questions of philosophical and theological truth. But I learned a lot about prayer from my dog, Quincy. Let me explain.

During hurricane Andrew, when we were hiding in the closet and the roof was falling into the house, our dog, Quincy the Wonder Dog, came running into the closet with a ball in his mouth. He dropped it on my lap and started wagging his tail. I said, harshly I'm afraid, "Quincy, you stupid dog! The house is falling apart. We are going to die! This is not the time to play catch!"

Quincy didn't understand that. As long as I was there, as long as the source of all his security was there, as long as he trusted me, the hurricane didn't matter. Once the hurricane was over, I thought about his wanting to play ball. I prayed, "Father, make me like that. Teach me to have that kind of trust."

Let me tell you about another incident. Quincy was the sole survivor of his litter and even as a puppy had trouble with his hips. Hip problems are common in German shepherds, and we figured there was nothing to be done about it. However, our vet said that if it could be done early, it was possible that his hips could be removed. He told us that cartilage and muscle would grow and, while the dog might have a slight limp, many dogs were able to function fully after the operation.

But, you see, Quincy didn't know about his displacement, muscle, and cartilage. He was just a dog. As far as he was concerned, he was fine. When I took him to the veterinarian where he would go through the considerable pain of surgery, I suspected he would never trust me again. After the surgery, Quincy could barely walk, and when he did, the cries of pain nearly broke my heart. I had to pick him up and put him in the backseat of the car to bring him home. I was sure I had lost the trust of my dog, and when a man's dog doesn't like him, that man is in serious trouble. I figured that Quincy, aware that I was the one who took him to the place where he had received so much pain, would turn from me to a master who was kinder and more loving than I had been.

I took Quincy to our family room and put him on a blanket in the corner of the room. I got the paper and sat down to read. After a couple of minutes I felt something moving my paper. Quincy nudged his nose under the paper, whined, and placed his head in my lap.

Lord, I prayed, *make me like that. Teach me to trust you, even when it hurts.*

I know that it is hard to trust. If you, like me, are from a dysfunctional background, one of the priorities you have in your life is control. By the way, I believe that one of the results of Adam and Eve's fall is that almost everyone is from a dysfunctional family in one form or another. A psychologist friend of mine has a cartoon that shows a very large auditorium with only three people in it. The caption reads: "The annual convention of children of normal parents." For most of us, life or family or difficult situations have taught us that every time things get out of control, we get hurt. So in order to keep from getting hurt, we try in every way possible to exercise control over our emotions, our physical environment, and those with whom we have relationships.

But God simply will not allow that kind of control in your life if you want to walk with him. In fact, those areas where you can't exert much control are those very areas where God will teach you about himself and about prayer. The woman whose carriage ran away and who said to the hero who finally rescued her, "I trusted God until the reins broke," did not trust God. She trusted the reins and didn't know that until they broke. God, I believe, takes delight in taking reins away, in putting those he loves in places where control is not an option, and then allowing us to see his sovereignty and control in those situations.

In order to have the kind of prayer life that is meaningful, you must have a childlike trust. That doesn't mean, of course, that you have to trust completely or totally. Trust is a process, and complete trust is the end of the process and probably won't happen until we "get home." However, it is desperately important that we begin the process and that we learn to lean hard, as it were, on God.

Perhaps you have heard the old story about the man who fell off the side of a mountain and grabbed a very small limb and held on for dear life. He cried out to God, asking for mercy. "O God, are you there? If you are really there, help me."

A voice came from heaven (in echo, of course): "Let go and trust me."

There was silence. Then the man hanging on to the limb cried out, "Is there anybody else up there?"

A lot of folks want to manipulate God, to bargain with him, or to find out the "rules" of prayer that they might get God to work on circumstances and get those circumstances under control. God simply won't play that game. He isn't safe, he isn't controllable, he isn't playing games, and there is "no one else up there." Sometimes in life you have to just let go.

"Lord, if I trust you, will you promise that I won't get hurt?"

No.

"Will you promise that, if I do it right, I will feel good in your presence and become a more faithful and obedient Christian?"

No.

"How about miracles and wonders?"

Maybe. Maybe not.

"Will I feel better about myself and have a better self-image?"

Sometimes. Sometimes not.

"What about my doubts and fears? Will they go away?"

Sometimes they will be worse.

"If I crawl out on that limb of trust, how do I know you won't cut it off?"

You don't.

"If I tell you what I want, have faith, and pray properly, will you give it to me?"

You're kidding, right? I'm your Father. You are the child, and you don't get to vote.

Don't you hate it?

Given my background and my need to control, for so long my prayers were empty and even silly. Do you know why? Because I thought, like everything else, if I did it right, I could control God. I found that a lot of the doubts, the fear, the confusion, and the hesitancy I felt (and still do, sometimes) in prayer have only one purpose, to wit, to disabuse me of the silly notion that God is controllable. He isn't.

If you've never stood before God and been confused—really confused—you've never stood before the un-controllable God. You've been worshiping an idol of your own making.

It was this, I think, that Sören Kierkegaard, the nineteenth-century Danish theologian and philosopher, was referring to when he talked about the "leap into absurdity." You stand at the edge of the cliff and look into the uncontrollable elements of your life, and you hear the call of God, who says, "Jump, and trust me." Many simply retreat. But some close their eyes and leap, and it is there—and sometimes only there—where they find how to trust. They find that the One who told them to leap really is trustworthy.

A Story of Answered Prayer

Highway Rescue

I was on my way to Beaverton to see my cousin to get my nails done, when I noticed that steam was coming from under the hood of my car. I quickly pulled over to the side of the freeway. I remembered that an engine can freeze up if it is allowed to boil dry. Even though I was in shorts and flip-flops, I got out of the car and opened the hood.

Just then, a man in a pickup truck pulled over in front of me. He got out and came back and asked if he could help me. I explained that my car was overheated and I needed to walk back to my church. He told me he would drive me. I thanked him but declined. He said it was silly for me to walk when he could drive me. I said, "But the only way you can go is north or south on 1-5." He became insistent, saying, "I will drive over the median and go the other way."

Why was he so insistent?

I said a quick prayer of, *God, help me.*

At that instant, I heard a splashing sound. I bent over and looked under his truck. I said, "Do you know your truck is boiling over?"

He ran, jumped into his truck, and took off. I had been saved. As I walked to the church, I thanked my Lord Jesus for hearing my prayer and answering so quickly.

Since then, I have gotten a cell phone for such occasions, but I will continue to trust in my Lord, my Savior.

—Angie F.

CAPTAINS OF VERY LITTLE

One of the things I'm learning in my own experiments with prayer is how little I actually control. We have this illusion, shattered by prayer, that we really are the captains of our souls. We are actually captains of very little. We didn't control where we were born, who our parents are, or what circumstances played in our growing up. We find that we can't control our husbands, our wives, or our children without emotionally killing them. Time and chance really are pretty frightening things, unless you learn that time and chance are just other terms for God's involvement in our lives.

We really are children "lost in a haunted wood," as poet W. H. Auden wrote,[1] and we go to great lengths to hide that fact. We pretend to have it together, to have few fears, and to be in control. But before God in prayer we realize that he is God and that very little can be controlled about him or about what he controls. Trust is the other option to denial or anger.

Closely related to childlike trust is childlike helplessness. Lincoln said during the Civil War that he got on his knees in prayer simply because there was nothing else he could do. In his or her natural state, a child is without power. A child can't loan you money or pull any strings for you. A child's fame won't rub off on you, and a child can hardly ever help you.

The apostle Paul said something amazing about power. He had gone to God and asked that God remove a particular "thorn in the flesh" from him so he would be able to serve God better. In fact, this great man of prayer went to God repeatedly about the problem. God's answer to Paul is the answer one almost always finds in prayer, to wit, "My grace is sufficient for you, for My strength is made perfect in weakness" (2 Cor. 12:9).

Children don't bring any power to the throne of God. And before him we recognize how truly powerless we are. Did you hear about the lifeguard who said to the little boy, "Son, all of that water, and you can't swim?"

"No sir," replied the boy. "There is all that air, and I can't fly either."

In prayer one recognizes that the ocean is very big and the air very wide, and that swimming and flying are very difficult. I have great problems with motivational programs that tell people how wonderful, powerful, and successful they will be if they use certain principles. God never tells us that. In fact, the most salient feeling one has when one encounters the real God is how truly helpless we are.

Playing on the words of a familiar Christian prayer, a great prayer to pray is, "Lord, the ocean is so vast and scary and lonely and confusing and dark and rough. My boat is so very small. Please have mercy on me."

As a young man, Carlo Carretto was moving up the ecclesiastical ladder of the Catholic Church with all of the power and prestige that entailed. There was no telling how high he could have gone. But at the age of forty-four he was summoned by God to the desert. He left Italy for North Africa, where he joined the Little Brothers of Jesus in a life of contemplation and prayer.

In this wonderful book *Letters from the Desert,* Carretto shares some of what he learned from God after years of living in the desert. After a significant experience with God, he wrote, "My first feeling after this was one of freedom; new, vast, real, joyful freedom. The discovery that I was nothing, that I was responsible for no one, that I was a man of no importance, gave me the joy of a boy on holiday."[2]

Carretto goes on,

> Even if I can achieve inner peace for a moment, I still have a deep sense of my inadequacy and wretchedness and I have to admit my incapacity to make my love greater. . . . Left to myself, with my own strength, I have felt the painful reality that without God's help, we cannot say even "Abba, Father." There are moments when God makes us feel the extreme limits of our powerlessness; then, and only then, do we understand our nothingness right down to the depths.
>
> For so many years, for too many years, I have fought against my powerlessness, my weakness. Often I have refused to admit it to myself, preferring to appear in public with a nice mask of self-assurance. It is pride which will not let us admit this powerlessness; pride which won't let us accept being inadequate. God has made me understand this, little by little."[3]

But childlikeness is not only helplessness and trust, but is also presumptuousness. I saw a bumper sticker the other day that read, "God loves you, but don't let it go to your head." I wanted to stop the person and say, "No, you've got it wrong! God loves you, so go ahead and let it go to your head!" There is a quality in genuine prayer that can, were it anything other than childlike, be presumptuous in the worst sense.

A lot of people are critical of me because I seem not to take religion or prayer very seriously. Not true. God is so big, so serious, so awesome, and so . . . well . . . *God* that anything that is excessively serious or pompous will be, by its very nature, silly and superficial.

The biblical book of Job, often studied to discover the reasons for suffering, in fact does not give answers to our questions. Note the things Job says to God. After reading almost every chapter, I want to say, "I don't believe I would have said that— certainly not in a thunderstorm." Throughout the book of Job—and indeed the entire Old Testament (especially the book of Psalms)—we witness a marvelous familiarity with God.

When I was a morning disc jockey in Boston, Richard Cardinal Cushing was the absolute leader of Roman Catholicism in New England. He was strong and autocratic, but he had a delightful way about him that appealed to the common man . . . and the common child. Each day right after my morning show, I would play a recording of the rosary being prayed. All the Catholic schools in Boston stopped whatever they were doing to tune in to the radio station to listen to the rosary. Things have changed so much that you aren't going to believe this, but during those years the rosary was the most listened to radio program in New England.

After I played the recorded rosary, I would pick religious music to play as fill for the rest of the half hour. Sometimes Cardinal Cushing would call me—a very young, inexperienced, and Protestant disc jockey—just to tell me how much he enjoyed the music.

At any rate, the cardinal once met a little boy at a church social function. He picked up the child and asked him his name. The boy replied that his name was Billy and then asked the cardinal his name. "My name is Richard," the cardinal replied, laughing.

Some months later Cardinal Cushing conducted a High Mass at the major cathedral in Boston. At the end of the Mass the congregation stood as the church dignitaries, dressed in colorful ecclesiastical finery, processed down the main aisle of the cathedral. The little boy who had met the cardinal months before was in the congregation and, to his mother's horror and the congregation's surprise, stood on his pew and shouted, "Richard! Richard! It's me, Billy!"

Cardinal Cushing stopped the processional of dignitaries, waved at the little boy, and motioned for him to join the procession. That day Richard and Billy walked the aisle of the cathedral hand in hand.

Presumptuous? Of course. But he was a little boy, and little boys can be excused. The relationship between the God of the universe and those who love him is indeed presumptuous. But if you are childlike, it's okay.

There was a man who was a king. He was a very short man, who was quite soft-spoken. He was asked why he did not raise his voice a little more when he gave his commands. He replied, "When a big man shouts, he is intimidating. When a little man shouts, he is silly." Just so, many of those who become pompous in their prayers or in their teaching about prayer just sound silly. It is quite presumptuous for a finite, sinful, and insignificant creature to go to God or to even think that it is possible. Only children can get away with it.

Another sign of childlikeness is an irrepressible joy. No matter how great the pain, there is joy around the corner. One of the things I noticed about the children of Iraq is that, in the midst of the horrors of war and during the quiet between the sounds of missiles and guns, they played games and laughed. As Jesus said to the religious leaders who tried to stop the joy at his triumphal entry into Jerusalem, "If these should keep silent, the stones would immediately cry out" (Luke 19:40).

Prayer is serious business, but it is not a dour and gloomy business. When we read the great contemplatives of the church—those who have traveled further down the road of prayer than most of the rest of us—we do not, for the most part, encounter the expected hair shirt and long face. One finds, rather, a winsome, unexpected, and joyful childlikeness. When Saint Teresa of Ávila prays, "Lord, you would have more friends if you treated the ones you had a little bit better," or when Billy Graham, just before preaching to hundreds of thousands at a major crusade, prays, "Lord, help me find my hat," those are not aberrations from the norm.

Prayer is serious because God is serious. And the closer one moves to his throne, the less serious a lot of other stuff becomes. The late Malcolm Muggeridge, who at the time of his conversion to Christianity was perhaps the best known personality in England, would say the most horrible things about the world and where the world was headed. Then his eyes would twinkle, and there would be such free laughter that it almost made you think he wasn't listening to what he had just said. He was listening, but he had a secret. He had come before the heavenly throne and, once there, everything else seemed quite insignificant by comparison.

My friend Chris Fabry has written *Spiritually Correct Bedtime Stories,* with wonderful stories like "The Emperor's New Bible," "Three Theological Pigs," "King Midas and the Christian Touch," and "Beauty and the Mark of the Beast." Chris writes in the introduction:

People of faith are particularly wary of too much laughing, often because we think it's childish. It is childlike to laugh from your toes. It is childlike to trust so much that you slip your hand into your father's and skip down the sidewalk. . . . Some will no doubt read too much into [these stories] or try to read between the lines. Please resist the urge. Have fun. Skip through the pages like a child. There is a Latin phrase that sums up what I want you to learn from these tales. . . . I think it's something like *Carpe Smilem*.[4]

A Story of Answered Prayer

Pennies from Heaven

We were living in Chickamauga and had picked up our horses from Virginia and brought them back home. We rented a small pasture next to our house for them, but there was no barn. We were going to have to build a barn. Well, being newlyweds and not having lots of extra money, we started calling around to the lumberyards to see how much it would cost to purchase the lumber to build a small lean-to that would get the horses through the winter. We found out it would cost around 350 dollars to build it. We didn't have that kind of disposable cash at that time, and so we just prayed for the means to build the barn.

Not long after that, I attended a conference in Nashville. One evening, my boss and a few others invited me on a road trip to one of the gambling boats a couple of hours away. I took the ten dollars I had to blow and figured it would be nice to sit and watch the water while I waited for them, since I knew that ten dollars wouldn't last very long. Sure enough, it didn't.

I spent some time watching the river and then came back in to see how my friends were doing. They took pity on me and gave me some coins to play in the slot machines. I went to one and pulled the handle a few times and won a few, which I promptly lost again. There was a man sitting near me who got up from the machine he was playing and left. It was as though an audible voice said to me, "Get up! Go over there!" So I did. I pulled the handle on that machine a few times, and lo and behold, I hit the jackpot! Coins just kept coming and coming, enough to fill up eight or nine of those big plastic cups they give you for your winnings. Well, I gave one full cup to each of my friends, since they were the ones who gave me the money to play, and I made my way over to the desk to cash in the remaining six or seven cups filled to the brim with coins.

The payout amount came up as 351 dollars! Exactly one dollar more than we needed to build the barn. I said right there on the spot, "Thank you, Lord, for providing the barn. I acknowledge this gift from you. Amen."

And that's exactly what we did with it.

—Judith S.

A Child's-eye View

There is joy in resting in One who is in charge. When was the last time you giggled and didn't care what anybody thought? When was the last time you did something "improper" and took delight in it? When was the last time you danced and shouted and sang without wondering if people would wonder if you had lost your senses? When was the last time you lay down in the grass and watched the clouds or the stars? When we are in a relationship with God, there is a childlike joy in knowing that we are accepted and cherished—no matter what. That's what it means to be childlike, and real prayer reflects that kind of joy.

Childlikeness is also disarming in its honesty. How many times have you been embarrassed by the honesty of your children? You bring the boss home for dinner, and to your horror, your son says, "Boy, are you fat!" Maybe you're visiting relatives, and your daughter says, "I didn't want to come, but Mother made me." Or at dinner at a friend's home, you blush when your child says, "This food tastes funny." Children have this way of saying what they think.

People are always asking me if it is all right to be angry with God. Do you think he doesn't know? Do you think that when you tell him you love him and are pleased with what he is doing in your life that he doesn't know the truth?

One of the most important things I have discovered about my "soft place" of prayer is that I can say whatever I need to say, and the Father will still accept me and love me. There are some things I say to God that I could never say any other place, because nobody else would understand. Religion is my business, and I sometimes hate that fact. If you are a professional "religionist," you find that people expect certain things from you—they expect that you are quite pure, good, spiritual, and godly.

I remember a friend who had walked by my study and asked me later who I was "yelling" at. "You sounded really mad," he said. I didn't have the heart to tell him that I was yelling at God. He would not have understood.

The late Anthony de Mello, the Indian Catholic priest, said a lot of things with which I would radically disagree. But I like to read him because I hear from him the joy and the honesty of someone who has been before God and knows him by something other than hearsay. De Mello's analysis of that encounter leaves a lot to be desired, but his experience is so authentic that I am sometimes overwhelmed.

De Mello illustrates a problem many of us have:

Now this is exactly what your society did to you when you were born. You were not allowed to enjoy the solid, nutritious food of life—namely, work, play, fun, laughter, the company of people, the pleasures of the senses and the mind. You were given a taste for the drug called approval, appreciation, attention. . . . So we are given the taste of various drug addictions: approval, attention, success, making it to the top, prestige, getting your name in the paper, power, being the boss. . . . Having a taste for these drugs, we become addicted and begin to dread losing them. . . . There is never a minute when consciously or unconsciously, you are not aware of or attuned to the reactions of others, marching to the beat of their drums. . . . When you are ignored or disapproved of, you experience a loneliness so unbearable that you crawl back to people and beg for the comforting drug called support and encouragement, reassurance. To live with people in this state involves a never-ending tension."5

He's right. But it isn't so with God in prayer.

Prayer is "growing down" to that time before you became addicted. It is standing before God and knowing that you are approved, accepted, and affirmed because of Christ and not because you say the right things, do the proper things, and think the correct thoughts. I have learned to write my prayers or whisper them, unless it is very early in the morning and nobody has come to the office yet. During normal working hours I'm afraid that someone will hear, and they will think that I've lost my mind.

Childlike honesty doesn't just include honesty about one's feelings. It includes telling God where it hurts. The next time you see a child fall and scrape his or her knee, watch what happens. The little boy or girl will be picked up by Mom or Dad, and in that moment there will usually be silence before the storm breaks. Do you know what is happening? The child is making sure someone is there to hear—that he is in the parent's arms—before he screams.

My friend Lea Clower says that religion is for people who want to stay out of hell, and Christianity is for people who have been there. He's right. I grow so tired of those people who "tiptoe through the tulips" with Jesus. Their testimonies are filled with victory, success, accomplishment, joy, and peace. One gets the feeling they have a special relationship with God and that God is sort of a bellhop, bringing them whatever they desire.

A number of years ago I was on the Moody Network's *Midday Connection* program with Andrea Fabry, talking about anger. A lady called and asked about anger at God. "Sometimes," she said, "I'm so angry at what has happened to me that I want to throw my Bible across the room."

"I can understand that," I said, "and if I can understand it, I suspect God can too." Then I asked her, "Are you going to leave?"

"Of course not," she said. "I'm still here. I wouldn't have called if I had decided to leave. I don't have any other place to go."

She's got it.

There are some people who seem so sanctified. They will say things like, "I never ask God why. I think, *Why not?*" Or they sometimes say, "I don't pray about me; I pray about others." Have you heard this one? "I deserve nothing and learned to rejoice in my suffering." (Paul said something like that in Philippians.)

Do you know what I want to say? I just want to say, "You need to get a life!"

People who don't ask why are crazy. People who don't tell God when it hurts are living in denial. And people who like suffering are neurotic. They sound spiritual, but they really don't understand.

If you are quiet before you scream because you want to make sure there is someone to hear, you are a prime candidate for a more fulfilling and significant prayer life. They say old age isn't for sissies. True, but *life* isn't for sissies either. You don't get from the hospital where you are born to the hospital where you die without hurting, without acquiring significant wounds, without screwing it up terribly, without falling—without pain. Childlike honesty is that kind of honesty that will scream to a parent when screaming is appropriate or necessary.

With Empty Hands

Finally, childlikeness means that you are willing to learn and grow. A child is full of questions because a child knows that he or she doesn't have answers. Jesus made a wonderful promise about the Holy Spirit to his disciples and to us. He said, "I still have many things to say to you, but you cannot bear them now. However, when He, the Spirit of truth, has come, He will guide you into all truth; for He will not speak on His own authority, but whatever He hears He will speak; and He will tell you things to come. He will glorify Me, for He will take of what is Mine and declare it to you" (John 16:12–14).

There is a lot to criticize about the Pharisees of Jesus' day. Jesus reserved his greatest anger for them. Do you know why? Because of their arrogance. He was angry because they didn't know how ignorant and sinful they were. They assumed that their knowledge was superior, that what they said came from Sinai, and that their purity was to be admired.

But when the prostitutes, the tax collectors, and the children came to Jesus, they were welcomed with open arms. Why? Because they were teachable. They brought nothing but empty hands before him. They knew that he knew that, but, more important, they knew that he loved them anyway.

One of the reasons some Mature Christians never have very satisfying prayer lives is because there is a sense in which they think they have discovered all the truth that is necessary. Children aren't like that. They aren't so sure they are right. They ask questions. They have recognized in their childlikeness that one of the great truths of the universe is that it is big enough for most of us to be wrong about most things almost all the time. To be childlike is to be teachable.

I'm a preacher, and do you know what irritates some people about me? They get irritated when I close a sermon with these words: "Fifty percent of what I just taught you is wrong. The problem is that I'm not sure which fifty percent. I guess you're going to have to check it out for yourself."

The pedagogical point? The closer one moves to God, the less one is sure of oneself, what one knows, and whether one is right . . . and the more one is sure that God is there, that he's in charge, and that he can be trusted with the things I get wrong.

The Problem with "Growing Up"

The world will tell us to grow up. But Jesus didn't tell people to grow up. He told them to grow "down." When that starts happening, then God will come.

Alfred Hitchcock was once riding in his limousine to the studio. He saw a priest leaning over and talking to a little boy. Hitchcock told his driver to stop, and then he rolled down his window and shouted at the little boy: "Little boy, don't listen to him. Don't listen to him. Run! Run as fast as you can!"

I'm not sure why Hitchcock was afraid for that little boy. I like to think that Hitchcock, being a churchman himself, was afraid the priest would try to get the little boy to grow up and act like an adult. I suspect that Hitchcock remembered the time when he had gone to God as a child and God had been there. I think that he was saying to that little boy, "Don't let him socialize you. He's trying to rob you of something very important, and that is your childhood. Hold on to it as long as you can. When you lose that, you could lose your experience of God."

C. S. Lewis understood. Evan Gibson, in his guide to Lewis's fiction, says this in referring to Lewis's children's stories:

Of course, [they] are addressed to the young reader. But Lewis did not believe that a person should leave his childhood behind like a train leaving a railway station, but that as he became older his life should be enriched like a train taking on more and more goods. In fact, he says, using the word "poetry" to mean all imaginative literature, that "only those adults who have retained, with whatever additions and enrichments, their first childish response to poetry unimpaired, can be said to have grown up at all."[6]

That's it! You can know that your prayer life is grown when it has the flavor of childlikeness. Jesus looked at his disciples— their knowing sophistication, their need for acceptance, their concern with power and control, their measured words, and their adult ways.

Then Jesus looked at the children with their dirty faces, their clumsy walk, and their broken toys in their hands, and he said: "Let *them* come."

He still says that.

FIVE

Going Deeper (I)

*He offered a prayer so deeply devout that he seemed
kneeling and praying at the bottom of the sea.*
—Herman Melville, *Moby Dick*

*Prayer is the peace of our spirit, the stillness of our thoughts,
the evenness of our recollection, the sea of our meditation,
the rest of our cares.*
—Jeremy Taylor

*Endeavor therefore to withdraw thy heart from the love
of visible things and to turn thyself to the invisible.*
—Thomas à Kempis

THERE ARE THOSE FOR whom the simple praying about which I've been speaking so far is clearly not enough. For some people there is a call—a drawing—for a deeper and much more intimate walk with God. I want to affirm that call without saying silly things about those who have not been called to that kind of prayer.

People often feel much guilt when it comes to prayer. I suspect that some of you are reading this book because of that guilt. Much of the guilt we feel about prayer, I believe, does not come from God but from those who purport to speak for him. "If you really loved God, you would want to know him better. After all he has done for you, one would think that you would care about being closer to him," they say to you. Eventually, you are saying something similar to yourself.

Of course your prayer life isn't what you would like it to be. Nothing is. We live in a fallen world, with fallen people and fallen natures.

You know those people who are always telling you, in one form or another, "You aren't living up to your potential"? In our Born Free seminar, we teach Christians to say in response to that kind of guilt-producing drivel, "Of course I'm not living up to my potential. Nobody is living up to his or her potential. If it is all right with you, I think I won't live up to my potential a little longer."

There has been enough guilt about prayer. I don't want to play that game with you. It is a game that is ultimately frustrating and counterproductive to one's prayer life.

It would be unconscionable for me to tell you that if you loved God, you would spend far more time with him, or that after all he has done for you, you would respond with more time in prayer. The truth is, if you really loved God, you might pray less and spend more time with your family. After all he has done for you, you might find that doing things for others is a perfectly appropriate way to respond to his love. It could be that spending more time in prayer would be an inappropriate response.

Besides that, how do you love more? Is there a "love faucet" you can turn off or on or which you can turn in a particular direction to get more love? We don't love God more by becoming more religious and praying more. That isn't the "faucet." Love comes—especially when we're talking about God—when we let God love us. That's it. And when we let God love us, we are drawn to him. Love that is forced isn't love.

Prayer is, of course, a necessary part of one's Christian life, but for some, there is no felt need (other than the false guilt from other believers) to go any further. Simple prayer sustains and motivates, and it is as natural as breathing. That kind of simple prayer, for most Christians, is sufficient and adequate. Most believers do not feel the need to go deeper. There is nothing wrong with that. In fact, it may be one of the most positive things in your life.

My late friend Rusty Anderson told me once, "I don't think I'm going to get much better than I am." If you knew Rusty, you would know that his statement was not a statement of pride. Rusty didn't consider himself a spiritual giant. He was saying that he had tried to be better for most of his life. Rusty truly loved God, and as with most of us, his progress in walking with Christ had been fairly slow. However, now that he had walked with Christ for a whole lot of years—with some success and some failure—he didn't think he was going to get much better.

When he told me this, I reacted the way any good American would react. I said, "Rusty, of course you are going to be better. You should be getting better and better in every way, every day."

"No," he replied, "that isn't happening. But you know something? God loves me anyway."

What a freeing statement. The truth is that only those who know this will get any better. There is an unconditional kind of relationship we develop with God that undercuts the common Christian view that the only reason we pray is to get better, pray longer, and grow in sanctification. It is this view that, more than any other, is the cause of frustration in prayer.

Better than Guilt

My wife and I have been married forty-seven years. We don't stay together because we want to "grow." We stay together because we love each other and we're committed. Anna doesn't try to make me better, and I don't try to make her better. We gave up on that after the first year of marriage. We just like being with each other. Sometimes we talk; sometimes we don't. Sometimes we share our views, and sometimes we don't. Sometimes Anna or I will point out something that needs work in the other, and sometimes we don't. But mostly we are together because we love each other, we like to be with each other, and because . . . well . . . because it's natural.

It is the same way with God. I don't want to join in with the chorus of Mature Christians who make you feel more guilty than you already feel. A relationship that is built on guilt is ultimately self-defeating, and that is as true about our relationship with God as with any person.

Guilt never motivated me in reading either. In fact, I have a rule about reading. I hardly ever read anything because it is "good for me." Some teachers almost ruined Shakespeare for me by telling me that every educated and cultured person ought to be familiar with and enjoy Shakespeare. And so I set about trying to understand Shakespeare. It never worked.

Then I met an elderly professor who loved Shakespeare because he was a bawdy, fun playwright, not because he was "good" for her. I caught her enthusiasm and to this day find myself going back and reading Shakespeare because his plays are fun. Sometimes, as a side benefit, I find important insights on human nature and not a few sermon illustrations.

It is important for a believer to have a walk with God. It is important to recognize that you can't live the Christian life without prayer. But don't let anybody, except God, define for you what your prayer life ought to be.

You may not find this or the next chapter helpful. That could be because your prayer life is reasonably sufficient. It may be that you are simply not called to go any deeper now. It may be, as it was with me, that you will go years without any need or call for more. If you are in that place, just put these two chapters aside and come back to them when you need them. There may be a period in your life when everything in you cries out for a deeper walk with God. That may be a lifelong call or only for a season. When and if that happens, it is my desire that what follows will prove helpful.

This is for those who feel called to a deeper walk with God or who, for a period of time, are called to it. The task to which you have been called is not easy, as we will see, but it has attached to it the wonderful fruit of intimacy with God, and that, dear friend, is the ultimate goal of the life of every believer. The kind of prayer I will address in this and the following chapter goes beyond the normal and the ordinary. It is a call to worship of and companionship with the Father that is more than the conventional and customary prayer of the believer. Again, not to move in this direction isn't wrong; it is simply different.

How to "Lose" Supernatural Power

I begin with some words of caution. *First, if you want to go deeper in your relationship with God because you want more power, more purity, or more admiration from your peers, forget it.* There is only one reason for a deeper prayer life, and that is to love God more deeply and to know him more fully. Too often those who begin the road of a more intimate walk with God do so with a hidden agenda.

I remember the time an acquaintance of mine associated with a major ministry called me "just to talk." Early in the conversation he said to me, "Steve, not too long ago I was talking to (he named a "famous" Christian you would know), and do you know what I told him?

I allowed that I had no idea.

"I told him," he said, "that you were one of the three great preachers in America."

Do you know what I felt? I felt "good all over." How about that? Steve Brown, one of the three great preachers in America. Even as I write this, I sort of feel good about that man's words.

Then he said to me, "By the way (always watch the "by the ways" from people who are raising money), I'm going to be in your area in the next few weeks, raising funds for (he named a ministry), and I was wondering if I could talk to some of the more affluent people in your congregation."

"Are you kidding?" I said. "Feel free to visit anybody you want, and not only that—tell them I told you to visit them."

When I hung up the phone, I was feeling really good about being one of the "three great preachers in America." That's when it hit me that I was one of the three dumbest preachers in America and that I had just been manipulated by a man with a "hidden agenda."

I didn't like it.

God doesn't either.

There is an interesting story in the nineteenth chapter of Acts where some "religionists," being impressed with Paul's supernatural power, tried to make it their own:

Now God worked unusual miracles by the hands of Paul, so that even handkerchiefs or aprons were brought from his body to the sick, and the diseases left them and the evil spirits went out of them. Then some of the itinerant Jewish exorcists took it upon themselves to call the name of the Lord Jesus over those who had evil spirits, saying, "We exorcise you by the Jesus whom Paul preaches." Also there were seven sons of Sceva, a Jewish chief priest, who did so.

And the evil spirit answered and said, "Jesus I know, and Paul I know; but who are you?" (Acts 19:11–15)

Let me give you a principle: almost anything of any importance in your walk with Christ is discovered on the way to somewhere else. In the area of supernatural power, the way to lose it is to seek it.

That is true with "becoming better" too. There is no question that growth in virtue is a result of our walk with Christ. It would be silly for me to say that obedience in this area isn't important. However, if that is the reason you want to go deeper, you may be surprised.

Madeleine L'Engle said that "the opposite of sin is faith and never virtue." She was quoting from H. A. Williams, an Anglican theologian. Let me give that quote to you:

When I attempt to make myself virtuous, the me that I can thus organize and discipline is no more than the me of which I am aware. And it is precisely the equation of my total self with this one small part of it which is the root cause of all sin. This is the fundamental mistake often made in exhortations to repentance and amendment. They attempt to confirm me in my lack of faith by getting me to organize the self I know against the self I do not know. . . . The result is that growth of self-awareness is inhibited. . . . There is sort of a devilish perversity in this organizing me not to sin by means of the very thing which ensures that I shall.

Faith, on the other hand, consists in the awareness that I am more than I know. . . . Such faith cannot be contrived. If it were contrivable, if it were something I could create in myself by following some recipe or other, then it would not be faith. It would be works—my organizing the self I know. That faith can only be the gift of God emphasizes the scandal of our human condition—the scandal of our absolute dependence on him. I have to depend completely upon what very largely I do not know and cannot control. . . . Justification by faith means that I have nothing else on which to depend except my receptivity to what I can never own or manage. And this very capacity to receive cannot be the result of effort. Faith is something given, not achieved. It's created by God's word in Christ.[1]

And so if you are trying to be a "better" Christian than others, you are going to be disappointed. Often those who have a deep and intimate relationship with God are the last people you would think would have that kind of relationship. It is said that when George Whitefield would preach (Whitefield was the "spark" that ignited the Great Awakening in America in the eighteenth century), there was an elderly crippled man back in the hotel room who traveled with him and who was praying for him. Nobody knows the man's name. He isn't ever mentioned in the history books, and those hundreds of thousands of people who were touched by the supernatural power of the ministry of George Whitefield weren't even aware of him. But if you are looking for someone, other than God, who was responsible for the Great Awakening, don't look so much to George White-field—look to the little man who prayed.

Carlo Carretto, the Italian contemplative I mentioned earlier who spent most of his ministry in the desert, said this:

"The fact that my vocation leads me to seek the lowest place means absolutely nothing. What counts is forcing myself to stay in that place every day of my life. And that is terribly difficult." Again he writes, "For so many years, for too many years, I have fought against my powerlessness, my weakness. Often I have refused to admit it to myself, preferring to appear in public with a nice mask of self-assurance. It is pride which will not let us admit this powerlessness; pride which won't let us accept being inadequate. God has made me understand this, little by little."[2]

A second word of caution: you must be called. The deeper life is a life to which one cannot, in the flesh, aspire. It is a calling to go deeper, to love more, to know more of him. You can't hustle it up or make it happen. When God calls you to himself in a deeper way, you must simply respond. It is not something a person chooses; it is something that chooses a person. Some believers are called to a ministry of prayer. Others are called to a deeper prayer life only for a season, and some are never called to it. That is not altogether different from the biblical teaching on spiritual gifts. People are wired differently, and to take that further, God wires people to himself differently.

Listen to the words of one who is called:

As the deer pants for the water brooks,
So pants my soul for You, O God.
My soul thirsts for God, for the living God.
When shall I come and appear before God?
My tears have been my food day and night. (Ps. 42:1–3)

In the years when I was feeling the call to go deeper in my walk with God (I described that experience in chapter 1), I found myself waking up at four in the morning. It wasn't guilt, it wasn't coffee, and it wasn't age. When it first happened, I would wake at four, feeling refreshed, and after trying to go back to sleep, I would get up and spend that time in prayer and meditation. I didn't know it then, but that was God's call in answer to the cry of my soul (which he put in me) to know him more deeply. Most days I'm still an early-morning person, and I look forward to those times with him more than I can say.

On January 16, 1951, Jim Elliot, the missionary whose martyrdom has inspired so many, wrote in his journal words that reflect God's call to a deeper life:

All day the sun dropped hints of spring, and at dusk, returning from the shop, I exulted in the distinct wall of purple—the Ozark foothills—close guarded by the unblinking Venus. The night spread black and blossomed brilliantly with stars. I walked out to the hill just now. It is exalting, delicious. To stand embraced by the shadows of a friendly tree with the wind tugging at your coattail and the heavens hailing your heart, to gaze and glory and to give oneself again to God, what more could a man ask? Oh, the fullness, pleasure, sheer excitement of knowing God on earth. I care not if I never raise my voice again for Him, if only I may love Him, please Him. Mayhap, in mercy, He shall give me a host of children that I may lead through the vast star fields to explore His delicacies whose fingers' ends set them to burning. But if not, if only I may see Him, smell His garments, and smile into my Lover's eyes, ah, then, not stars, nor children, shall matter—only Himself.[3]

You have probably heard the Eastern proverb to the effect that when a student is ready, a teacher will appear. That has its equivalent in terms of a call to a deeper walk with God. When it is time, the soul gets stirred, the mind is drawn, and the heart is pulled to him. It is a call for life or for a season, but it is real, and you will know it.

Third, by way of caution, it is important that one be patient. And for most of us that is quite difficult.

A friend of mine once challenged me to be still for one minute and gave me a stopwatch with which I could time my moment of silence. I went back to my office, sat in the big chair behind my desk, started the stopwatch, closed my eyes, and set about proving to my friend that being still was not all that difficult. I sat there in the silence for what seemed like at least five minutes, then opened my eyes, feeling quite good about my demonstration. Then I looked at the stopwatch and saw that I had remained silent for only twenty-three seconds.

God says, "Be still, and know that I am God" (Ps. 46:10), and that sounds so simple. For most people, it isn't simple at all. Saint Teresa of Ávila (the sixteenth-century contemplative) expresses the experience of all believers who have been called to a life of prayer. The opening section of her account of a life of prayer is devoted to the difficulties she experienced:

> It is not without reason that I will dwell so long on that which has been the most difficult portion of my life. I did not lean on my strong pillar of prayer, and so I passed nearly twenty years of my life on a stormy sea, constantly tossed with the tempest and never coming to the harbor. It was the most painful life that can be imagined, because I had no sweetness in God, and certainly no sweetness in sin . . .
>
> Very often I was more occupied with the wish to see the end of my hour for prayer. I used to actually watch the sandglass. And the sadness that I sometimes felt on entering my prayer-chapel was so great that it required

all my courage to force myself inside. In the end, our Lord came to my help. And when I had persisted in this way, I found far greater peace and joy than when I prayed with excitement and emotional rapture.[4]

If you saw the movie *Field of Dreams,* you'll recall the statement from the disembodied voice regarding the building of a baseball field in the middle of a cornfield: "If you build it, he will come." Let me promise you that if you spend the time, exercise the spiritual disciplines, and continue praying, he will come. But the truth is that he doesn't come quickly or easily— or, at least, our awareness of his coming doesn't come quickly or easily.

Do you know how to grow yams? You plant and then you wait. Then you wait some more. Then you wait some more. It is the same with the deeper walk with God. There are, I suspect, a lot of reasons for that.

For instance, our perceptions of reality are so distorted that it takes a long time to look beyond those perceptions to what is real. We think that the essence of life is to do as much, to acquire as much, to accomplish as much as possible before we die. Besides that, most contemporary Christians define themselves in terms of what they "do" rather than in terms of who they "are." It is necessary in prayer to not do anything. Success is not measured in terms of prayers answered, lives changed, or tasks accomplished. And that's hard to accept.

Most of us feel we need to be practical, and prayer, while necessary, doesn't seem all that practical. The old farmer said, "When I ask God for a chicken, I hardly ever get a chicken. But when I ask God to send me for a chicken, I almost always get a chicken." Most of us would agree with that. Prayer is often seen as that which motivates and empowers us to do something practical.

There was a time when I felt that Roman Catholics who left the real world for a life of contemplation were simply "copping out" on the need to get on about the business of serving God. I'm a lot older now and a bit wiser, and sometimes I feel that those who give their lives to a life of prayer and contemplation are probably doing more for the kingdom than all the evangelists, priests, pastors, professors, and teachers of the church combined. It is hard sometimes not to do something. But those who walk closer to God must move away from the drive to accomplish the practical for God.

A Story of Answered Prayer

Never Give Up

My father-in-law, Dick, was one of the most rebellious human beings on the planet. His enthusiasm for going against the grain was matched only by his rejection of religion and, as he would call them, "religious fanatics." My wife prayed for her father's salvation and would tell me, "God will save my father, even if it is on his deathbed!"

My father-in-law was diagnosed with pancreatic cancer and was given one week to ten days to live. He was released to go spend his last days at home. During this time, my wife gave of herself in the most unselfish ways possible. She cared for him day and night—just her and her father—in what would turn out to be the most rewarding time of her life, and mine.

On October 7, 2006, I was working about twenty minutes from Dick's home. I felt the Holy Spirit impress upon me that I should leave that second. Without even locking up, I headed toward Dick's house. When I got there, I saw my wife quietly sharing the good news of Jesus Christ with him.

I sat quietly and listened. At one point, Dick looked over at me and said, "For the last five or six days, I have been hearing voices. They have been telling me that if I accept Jesus Christ, I'm an idiot."

My wife, Donna, told Dick, in the sweetest and most caring voice I had ever heard, "You don't have to hear those voices anymore, Dad. If you accept Jesus as your personal Savior, the voices will go away."

Finally, Dick said, "I am ready," and he repeated after Donna the words, "I accept Jesus Christ as my Lord and Savior."

Then Dick asked Donna to write those words on a card, which he put in his wallet.

The last time I heard him talk, I heard him ask Donna for the wallet when Dick's boss—his religious, fanatical Christian boss—came by to visit. He showed it to his boss and said, "And it was *my* idea."

Never give up praying for a loved one.

—Ralph R.

WHO DEFINES THE PARAMETERS?

Someone tells about a man who went to a country store to find that Jimmy, the clerk who usually waited on him, was not there. After getting his goods, the man asked the manager about Jimmy. The manager told the man that Jimmy had been fired. "Who took his place?" the customer asked.

The manager replied, "Jimmy didn't leave no place."

When we die, we aren't going to leave a place either. Some of us are so self-absorbed that we simply can't imagine a world where we are not present. If prayer does nothing else, it increases the realization that we aren't that important. God really doesn't need our help. He was doing fine before we came along and will be doing fine long after we have passed from the time and space we occupy. God does as he pleases, and he can do it without our help, thank you. If that kind of thought is irritating to you (as it is to me), you have begun to understand something of the problem of a deeper prayer life.

By way of caution, it is also important that those who want a deeper life with Christ be flexible.

God's thoughts are not our thoughts, and his ways aren't our ways; we are finite, and he is infinite; we tarry but just a little while, and he is eternal. It is important that when we are called to a deeper walk with God, we recognize that God does the calling and he defines the parameters.

Thomas à Kempis wrote,

> We cannot trust much to ourselves, because grace oftentimes is wanting to us, and understanding also. There is but little light in us, and that which we have we quickly lose by our negligence. Oftentimes too we do not perceive our own inward blindness, how great it is. We often do evil, and excuse it worse. We are sometimes moved with passion, and we think it to be zeal. We reprehend small things in others, and pass over greater matters in ourselves. We quickly enough feel and weigh what we suffer at the hands of others; but we mind not what others suffer from us. . . . Let nothing be great unto thee, nothing high, nothing pleasing, nothing acceptable, but only God Himself, or that which is of God.[5]

Flexibility will, by necessity, be the mark of the finite in conversation with the Infinite. God's ways are quite circuitous. We believers who will walk closely with God might find that our judgments about other people, about ecclesiastical matters, about our importance, and about our call are quite different from God's judgments in those areas.

There is a wonderful (though corny) story about a man, Joe, who visited the church every day at noon. The pastor's study was positioned in a place where he could see Joe coming each day. After a number of months, the pastor's curiosity got the best of him. He stopped Joe on his way out of the church and said, "Joe, I've been watching you come to this church every day at noon, and to be honest, I've wondered what you were doing."

"Nothing big, Pastor," replied Joe. "I just come and stand in front of the cross and say, 'Jesus, it's Joe.'"

A few weeks later, while the pastor was on vacation, Joe was in an automobile accident and was taken to the hospital. When the pastor got back, the first thing on his agenda was to visit Joe in the hospital. As soon as the pastor entered the hospital door, he noticed that something was different—the receptionist was kinder, the nurses were a bit more thoughtful, and the doctors took time to stop and talk.

The pastor asked a nurse who was a member of his church about the difference he sensed in the hospital. She said, "You're right, Pastor. Your friend Joe is the reason. Since he has been here, things have been different."

So the pastor went to see Joe, and he asked him about what he had been doing to cause the change. "It isn't me," Joe said. "Every day at noon, Jesus comes and stands at the foot of my bed and says, 'Joe, it's Jesus.'"

When you are drawn to a deeper walk with God, it is wise not to have an agenda. Sometimes it's best to simply tell God you have come and that whatever his plan is for you, it is fine. Be flexible, hang on, and watch what he does.

There is one final caution I want to give you before we go to the next chapter, where we will look at some practical ways one draws closer to the throne: be very careful. One of the reasons most people who go to a deeper level of prayer have a confessor, spiritual director, or companion is to make sure that they don't go off the deep end and wander into spiritual territory they know nothing about. *The Christian who has been called to a deeper life should always pray and meditate within the context of historic Christianity.*

For instance, toward the end of his life, Thomas Merton made a pilgrimage to the East. He spent a significant amount of time with Buddhist monks. Now, I'm not in the business of putting down Eastern mysticism, and I have great respect for Thomas Merton. While there is much that bothers me in his writings, I have also learned much from him. However, the Christian contemplative you use as your spiritual director should be Christian. We do not simply throw out two thousand years of Christian wisdom and balance. I, of course, look at a deeper walk with God from the perspective of a Christian, and if I felt that the biblical and historical ways of approaching God were wrong, I would be something else.

Can we talk?

There is something about "religion" that will make you weird if you let it.

Most of us know the story about the writing of the famous hymn "It Is Well with My Soul." It is a beautiful story about Horatio Spafford, who had lost everything in the Chicago fire of 1871. Then an even greater tragedy happened. He sent his family ahead of him to Europe, and on the trip across the Atlantic, all four of Spafford's daughters died when the ship sank. His wife, Anna, survived and sent him a telegram that read "Saved alone."

Later, Spafford was making the same journey to Europe and stood on the deck of his ship at approximately the place where his daughters died and wrote his hymn, "It Is Well with My Soul."

It's a beautiful story that has been told many times.

Let me tell you the rest of the story: in later life, Spafford had a mental breakdown that prompted him to move to Jerusalem, thinking he was the "second Messiah." He died in Jerusalem at the age of sixty.

Why am I telling you this? Because I wanted you to be careful not to worship at anybody's altar but God's. Even the best of us has serious flaws.

But for the purposes of the point I'm making here, I told you the "rest of the story" to show you that those who are called to a deeper walk with God should never do it alone.

Throughout the history of Christianity there have been times of awakening and revival. During those times, some people have gone wild in their views and actions and have brought great harm to the church. The truth is that religion is a very powerful motivator of the human psyche. And, like all other powerful psychological forces, religion is capable of great error and harm.

Luther found this particularly troubling in his parish of Wittenberg. After being away from his people for months at Wartburg Castle, he received reports that his congregation had gone far beyond the boundaries he originally intended in his teaching of Reformation doctrine. Luther returned to Wittenberg and took charge. He preached eight sermons urging his people to moderation, love, and freedom. He worked for order and unity in his church.

Jonathan Edwards encountered a similar phenomenon. In Richard Lovelace's classic work on spiritual renewal, the author writes about what Edwards saw:

As the Great Awakening unfolded in America after Whitefield's arrival in 1739, Edwards became aware that the revival involved a spiritual struggle in which every advance of renewal would involve severe conflict with fallen human nature and the powers of darkness. Since the work of revival involves the displacement of the world, the flesh and the devil, periods of renewal are times of great spiritual agitation in which troop movements on both sides are dimly visible in the background. As the sun shining on a swamp produces mist, the rising of the countenance of God among his people may result initially in disorders and confusion.[6]

It is the nature of a deeper walk with God to get out of balance. That is why it is important that one who is called to this work be careful to maintain certain ecclesiastical, historical, and biblical boundaries. It is wise to have one person to whom you are accountable in your growth. Just as there has been a tendency toward imbalance in times of great awakening in the church, there is also a danger of imbalance as individual believers move into the new and untested land of the supernatural walk with God.

A Story of Answered Prayer

From Religion to Relationship

About thirteen years ago, while reading through the Bible, I came to Proverbs 3:5—"Lean not on your own understanding."

I really did not understand what that meant, so I asked God to explain it to me, hoping for a revelation of sorts. Instead, he decided to give me an object lesson.

I watched as my marriage failed (ending in divorce), my business rushed toward bankruptcy, and my community "empire" began to fall apart. I spent the next six months on my knees and on my face—literally—before God. I prayed more during those six months than I had in all the previous years combined.

Like Job, I have been restored. I have the most beautiful wife, along with four wonderful daughters; my business is successful, and I have been shown favor in the business, church, and social communities beyond belief. I have met with representatives, senators, secretaries of state, vice presidents, and the president.

As they say, be careful what you ask for, because you might get it. That being said, I would not trade the lesson for anything in the world. My walk with Christ is deeper because of this, and I have moved from religion to relationship.

—Jim H.

The Dragon's Tail Still Swishes

Before leaving this subject, I want to add another word of caution. I personally believe that Satan is given too much power by believers and that he only has the territory that we give him. The Bible teaches that the Holy Spirit, whom God has given to us, is far greater than Satan (see 1 John 4:4) and that Satan is a defeated foe (see Col. 2:15 and Rev. 20:10). However, that doesn't mean that supernatural evil isn't a danger. It was Luther, I believe, who said that the dragon had been slain but his tail still swishes.

As we move from the unreal world of time and space and into the real world of intimacy with God, we face new territory, and that territory can be dangerous. Just as I warned my daughters, when they were learning to drive, about drunk drivers, unobservant twits, and crazy speeders, I would warn those who move into a deeper walk with God that there are supernatural elements that ought to be noted and avoided.

For instance, there will be times of great discouragement, times when God seems to be away on vacation, times of magnified temptations, times when you will think you're being attacked by evil thoughts and ideas. Don't let those deter you. Just keep at it. It is okay to be frightened, but it is not okay to quit. It is okay to be confused, but it is not okay to quit. It is okay to have questions, but it is not okay to quit.

Between the darkness and the light, there is more darkness. If he has called you, listen to his voice and continue to walk in the direction of its sound. Don't doubt in the dark what God has taught you in the light. Don't let anything deter you. Don't give in to discouragement and fear. Just keep moving in the direction of his voice. Eventually there will be a breakthrough, and you will laugh and dance in his presence.

You will remember in *The Pilgrim's Progress* that when John Bunyan's character Christian was beginning his journey, he got talked out of the right way by Mr. Worldly Wiseman's advice. He was rescued, of course, by Evangelist. Bunyan wrote:

> Then did Christian address himself to go back; and Evangelist, after he had kissed him, gave him one smile, and bid him God speed; so he went on with haste, neither spake he to any man by the way; nor if any man asked him, would he vouchsafe them an answer. He went like one that was all the while treading on forbidden ground, and could by no means think himself safe, till again he was got into the way which he had left to follow Mr. Worldly Wiseman's counsel. So, in process of time, Christian got up to the gate. Now, over the gate there was written, "Knock, and it shall be opened unto you."[7]

So, may I play the part of Evangelist for you?
Don't give up! Don't you dare give up!

SIX

Going Deeper (2)

God invites us to come to Him and tell Him our story.
—Richard Pratt

Pray with Your Eyes Open
*We can do it [practice the Presence] for moments at
first. But from those moments the new sort of life will be
spreading through our systems because now we are letting
Him work at the right part of us.*
—C. S. Lewis, *Mere Christianity*

MY FRIEND J. I. Packer writes about prayer:

I would not want anyone to settle for praying as feebly, fitfully, and ineptly as I feel I do. Also, my heart said that trying to describe what I do in prayer would be like telling the world how I make love to my wife. Parading such intimacies would be nasty exhibitionism on my part and would pander to the unspiritual, voyeuristic interest in others' spiritual experience which is unhappily widespread today. To join the psalmist in telling what the Lord had done for my soul (Ps. 66:16) would be one thing, but to spotlight my own performance in prayer would be something else—sort of spiritual striptease, entertaining perhaps but certainly not edifying.[1]

After reading about Dr. Packer's reticence in speaking of his own times of prayer, I had about decided to junk this chapter altogether. That was when the Lord reminded me that Dr. Packer's reticence came from humility and that mine, should I be reticent, would come from pride. Dr. Packer is one of my heroes. After reading almost all his books, listening to him teach on numerous occasions, and having the pleasure of being with him on social occasions, I am convinced that he is not only an amazing theologian and scholar but more important, a godly man.

I have aspirations in that direction, and that is the danger. So be careful when you read this chapter. A part of the witness that I make is a witness of one who can serve as an example of a struggler who—failing sometimes, sinning often, frightened almost always—is still walking the road.

A number of years ago I was speaking in Pittsburgh, and a doctor told me, "All my life I've heard missionaries and ministers say they were sinners. You are the only one I ever believed." He didn't know it, but that comment set the tone of my ministry for the rest of my life. If Steve can do it—if he still believes, if he is still walking with Christ—anybody can.

It is also important that you understand how I intend my advice to be taken. Let me give you one more quote from Dr. Packer to help explain:

> Praying is not like carpentry or cooking. It is the active exercise of a personal relationship, a kind of friendship, with the living God and his Son, Jesus Christ, and the way it goes is more under divine control than under ours. Books on praying, like marriage manuals, are not to be treated with slavish superstition, as if perfection of technique is the answer to all difficulties. Their purpose, rather, is to suggest things to try. And as in

other close relationships, so in prayer: you have to find out by trial and error what is right for you, and you learn to pray by praying. Some of us talk more, others less; some are constantly vocal, others cultivate silence before God as their way of adoration; some slip into glossolalia, others make a point of not doing so; yet we may all be praying as God means us to do. The only rules are to stay within biblical guidelines, and within those guidelines, as Dom John Chapman put it, "pray as you can and don't try to pray as you can't."[2]

A physics professor told the last class he taught just before retiring, "What I've taught you for the last forty years is fifty percent wrong. The trouble is that I don't know which fifty percent." As I wrote earlier, I suspect that what is in this book might be 50 percent wrong, and I'm not sure which 50 percent either.

A number of years ago my friend Tony Campolo and I did a weekly television program (*Hashing It Out*) on the Vision Network, and now Tony is my guest a couple of times each month on our radio talk show, *Steve Brown Etc.* Tony and I don't agree on much in this world. The reason we decided to do the television show and the reason he is a guest on the talk show is that we both have a major concern with the anger and condemnation that takes place among Christians and want to show how Christians who agree on little except Jesus and the Bible can still love each other. We both are concerned that we Christians are so busy "demonizing" one another that we have forgotten to do what Jesus told us to do: love one another and bear witness to Christ.

What follows is my witness. I want to give you the flavor of what I've discovered in my own time with God. What follows reflects the efforts of one man to know God better and to love him more. But, more than that, it reflects the incredible love of God reaching out to one man who doesn't deserve it. "In this is love," the apostle John said, "not that we loved God, but that He loved us and sent His Son to be the propitiation for our sins" (1 John 4:10).

A Story of Answered Prayer

An Angel of Comfort

I once had a diabetic patient who developed a sore on his foot, so I put him in the hospital and started antibiotics. We found he had osteomyelitis. The surgeon debrided the wound, and overnight the patient's little toe turned black from gangrene. Neither the surgeon nor I had seen a toe turn black so quickly.

The patient, who was a church deacon, was furious with God. How could God do something like this to *him*? He was so angry and mad that I was worried about his attitude before going to surgery. So I began to pray for him, and I felt God's reassurance that he would be okay after the surgery. But I told God I could not seem to console the patient, that I didn't think he would listen to anyone, but that he might listen to an angel. So I asked God to send him an angel to comfort him. I went to bed and forgot the prayer.

When I made the rounds the next morning, the patient had a much better attitude. He told me that a visitor had come to his room the night before. He said the man asked him how he was doing, to which the patient replied, "Not so hot." The man said, "I know, my son." The man spoke with him for a while, and when the patient looked away for a second, the man was gone.

The patient told me, "The weird thing was that the man did not come in by the door and did not leave by the door. I think he must have been an angel."

—Sharon B.

Turning the Fire Down

Find a place and a time, get comfortable, and get to it. Simple? Yes, but very difficult. Abba Agathon, one of the desert fathers, said, "Prayer is hard work and a great struggle to one's last breath."[3] The truth is that most of us have trouble setting aside a block of time to be with God. If we can find that time, it is hard to find a "prayer closet" where the phone isn't going to ring and where people won't interrupt. And, if we manage to find the time and the place, the hard part is "turning the fire down" enough to speak and listen. However, it is doable. It is a matter of how much we want to find a place and a time and get to it.

It was Plato, I believe, who was approached by one of his students who asked for truth. Plato took him to a river and pushed him under the water until the young man was struggling to get air. Just at the moment when the student thought he would drown, Plato let him up and said, "Young man, when you want truth as you just then wanted air, you shall have it."

Can we talk?

You aren't that busy. Schedules can be adjusted. There are plenty of places where you could get away to be by yourself. The problem is the silence, the solitude, the quiet. Blaise Pascal, the French philosopher, theologian, and mathematician, talked about how the "eternal silences of the infinite spaces" frightened him. They frighten us too. We can handle the noise. We're used to noise, but silence scares the spit out of us.

I make my living talking. Whenever there is a gap in conversation, I fill it. I use words to motivate, to comfort, and sometimes to manipulate. I like to listen to words in music, words in news, and words in talk shows. But the truth is that those words often become the noise I use to cover the silence.

In other words, my comfortable place is noise, and to get quiet, turn the fire down, and be still does not sound pleasant.

In his wonderful little book *The Way of the Heart,* Henri Nouwen addresses people who are in professional ministry. But his words ring true for everyone who has ever been called to go deeper. His description of the fear of solitude mirrors my own and probably yours too.

> In solitude I get rid of my scaffolding; no friends to talk with, no telephone calls to make, no meetings to attend, no music to entertain, no books to distract, just me—naked, vulnerable, weak, sinful, deprived, broken—nothing. It is this nothingness that I have to face in my solitude, a nothingness so dreadful that everything in me wants to run to my friends, my work, and my distractions so that I can forget my nothingness and make myself believe that I am worth something. But that is not all. As soon as I decide to stay in my solitude, confusing ideas, disturbing images, wild fantasies, and weird associations jump about in my mind like monkeys in a banana tree. Anger and greed begin to show their ugly faces. I give long, hostile speeches to my enemies and dream lustful dreams in which I am wealthy, influential, and very attractive—or poor, ugly and in need of immediate consolation. Thus I try again to run from the dark abyss of my nothingness and restore my false self in all its vain glory.
>
> The task is to persevere in my solitude, to stay in my cell until all my seductive visitors get tired of pounding on my door and leave me alone.[4]

If you are reading this, I assume that you have heard God calling you to himself. I assume that you have been thinking about getting serious about prayer for a long time. I assume that you really do want to go deeper. If those things are true, you are caught. I'm sorry, but you are in a place you can't escape. It is sort of like a fish who has gone for the bait—the hook is in, and the fish keeps struggling to get free. You aren't going to get free. So you might as well get to it.

But how do we deal with the silence? How do we turn down the fire?

Another World

A number of years ago I took a monthlong trip around the world to visit missionaries. An affluent friend of mine paid for it because she said that, even if my theology was right, my passion for missions was lacking. That trip changed my life. It put fire in my heart for the world. But it also allowed the "boy" from the mountains of North Carolina to visit places where people, customs, and ways of seeing the world were so different from me and from anything I had ever experienced before.

Prayer is like that. It is going to a "different country."

I have found it helpful to realize that I am moving between two countries—two worlds, if you will. Prayer is another world, just as real and just as tangible as the one I have left. One doesn't discard the other world or act as if it doesn't exist, but that world has different ways of dressing, different customs, different rules of conduct. As I move from one world to another, I must prepare myself for the journey.

Anthony de Mello suggests that moving from one world to the other is a matter of waking up: "Spirituality means waking up. Most people, even though they don't know it, are asleep. They're born asleep, they live asleep, they marry in their sleep, they breed children in their sleep, they die in their sleep without ever waking up."[5]

One of the ways I have found helpful in moving into the "other world" is a technique called centering prayer. (You might want to read M. Basil Pennington's book on the subject, *Centering Prayer.*[6] I don't agree with the entire book, but the general thrust is quite helpful.) One problem with listening to God in prayer is the constant babble of other voices. Those other voices constantly intrude on one's prayer life, and they are quite disruptive. I'm not talking about demonic voices or anything like that. I'm speaking of the voices of our daily concerns, our pressing problems, our particular fears and pressures.

Centering prayer involves, at least for me, the imagination. I picture a river where there are lots of small boats, large ships, and flotsam floating down the river. Further, I picture myself sitting on the bank of the river, praying. Then I think of those items floating down the river as the thoughts that keep intruding. I simply allow them to continue on down the river. There is no I-must-get-rid-of-these-intrusions-or-I-will-never-hear-God's-voice reaction to the thoughts. That never works and, in fact, often makes the thoughts more insistent. I am aware of them, but I simply allow them to continue down the river and out of my thoughts.

Centering prayer also often involves the use of a biblical word or idea that can be used to call our minds away from the river and back to a focus on God. Let me explain. A word that I find filled with great power and meaning is the word *Father.* You could use the word *grace* or *mercy* or *faith* or *justified* or *holy* or a variety of other words and ideas. The important thing is that your call back to focus on God be a word or idea that brings to mind the business at hand—the silence before God. The word *Father* has become my word to call my mind back to God and the focus of the silence before him.

When I am in the silence before God, my mind fills with thoughts about the laundry I need to pick up, a staff problem at work, or bills. Instead of saying to myself, "I must not think about that; I need to focus on God," I acknowledge those thoughts as floating down the river. I notice them, but I don't focus on them; and I do that by simply saying "Father." Sometimes, as you practice this kind of centering prayer, you will use your biblical concept or word many times within a period of prayer. However, as you get in the habit of keeping your mind focused, you'll find that the use of the word or idea is not as necessary as before.

I love to read novels. Do you know why? Because for a while it is nice to live in another world, to meet different people, and to experience things that are not a part of my ordinary experience. As I do my tasks of the day, I look forward to that other world. When I'm standing in a line at an airport, alone in a hotel room, or stuck in traffic, by simply opening a book, I can enter another world that is far more exciting, interesting, and pleasant than the world of airports, hotel rooms, and traffic.

Prayer is like that. It is the realization that I have now moved into another world. It is a world where there is a different Ruler than my boss, a different set of rules from those of the social rules I usually observe, and a different landscape. So, before anything else, it is important that I begin to adjust to this new world. The best way to do that is to start to wean myself from the other world. The best way to do that is to focus on the things of God. And the best way to do that, for me, is to use Scripture (the road map, as it were, of the new world) to start thinking about spiritual things.

I find that reading a passage of Scripture, thinking about God and his faithfulness and his nature, or reading a devotional book will begin to turn the fire down. Sometimes I will slowly and thoughtfully repeat the Eastern Orthodox contemplative prayer: "Lord Jesus Christ, Son of God, have mercy on me a sinner." Then I begin to settle into the "other world" slowly as I prepare to pray.

Once you are aware of and comfortable with the other world, it is necessary to acknowledge God's presence and yours and to think about it. My friend John Montgomery, in a sermon on prayer, spent the first part of his sermon talking about the difficulty he had in preparing a sermon. After most of a week was gone, he decided to pray:

"Lord, it's John."

"I know."

"I'm having trouble with this sermon."

"I know."

"You do know, Lord, that it is getting late, and I've got this deadline coming up soon."

"I know."

"I'm uncomfortable with what I've done so far on this sermon."

"I know. Your discomfort is from me. That is so you would come to me."

Then John recounted the conversation he had with God whereby he discovered some important things about prayer by praying. At the end of the sermon, John said he said, "Lord, you know something? You are incredible and wonderful."

And then John said that God said, without a trace of arrogance, "I know."

The initial steps of prayer are simply opening the door into the other world and acknowledging God's presence, who he really is, and of course acknowledging your presence before him. Simple words or a modest statement like, "Lord, I'm here," begin to focus your mind on the other world.

I would not suggest that you forget who God is—that he is the Creator and you are the creature. But there is a wonderful childlikeness that one finds in Christian contemplatives that is free and trusting, unconfined by the "spiritual" palaver of the King James English.

Scripture says, "Let us therefore come boldly to the throne of grace, that we may obtain mercy and find grace to help in time of need" (Heb. 4:16). That gives us permission to enter the "other world," to wake up, and to do it with the assurance that we will be welcomed.

A Story of Answered Prayer

Thy Will Be Done

In 1989, my husband, Bill, had been sick for two years with liver problems. He was under excellent care. Bill held his own until August 3—our twenty-ninth wedding anniversary. Then the disease took a sudden downturn, and the only hope was a liver transplant. Liver transplants were in the experimental stage then. University Medical Center in Mississippi had a surgeon who had done three, and Bill's name was put on the list for an organ.

We called on the church for prayer.

Our church is small, but loving and caring. Other friends and family and their churches prayed. Our church set up a blood drive that gathered over forty pints. The finances (which were overwhelming) were covered.

On October 30, the transplant team called. They had a liver in New York State. It was large and a perfect fit for Bill. The prayer team was called. The answer from the Father was "Yes, yes, yes." Over these seventeen years, Bill and I have seen two daughters and a son marry. There are now fourteen grandchildren.

But let me tell you about a time when God said "No."

In 1967, we had two children, Little Bill (age six) and Michelle (age three). On a homeward trip between Arkansas and Mississippi, we had an automobile wreck in Louisiana. Michelle was killed immediately. Little Bill and I were seriously injured. My husband was supported in his tremendous grief and responsibility by the love, care, and prayers of family and the churches.

After four weeks in the hospital, I was able to go to my mother-in-law's home, though I would remain in shock (not knowing what was happening) for two more weeks.

For those six weeks, the pleading and begging of humbled hearts for the life of Little Bill was prayer at its finest. But God our Father said, "No."

Little Bill died. I came out of shock. Bill and I accepted God's will. The grace that encompassed us was the answer to prayer. Did "No" make us less prayerful? No! No! No!

Not everyone who has a confrontation with God (life) is scarred by it, but Bill and I are. We want to be. As life has brought many joys, the hope of heaven is primary.

Jesus said, "Say Thy kingdom come, Thy will be done." He didn't say, "Please explain it to me."

—Maria D.

WELCOMED

One of the questions I still have on occasion is how I will be received when I go to the Lord. I have always known that God knows me, which, of course, means that if I got what I deserved, I would be destroyed in a moment in his presence. I call this fear of facing God "cosmic claustrophobia," the realization that we are going to go before the consuming fire of God and that even if we can fool our friends and family members, he knows us. It is that understanding that God is holy, righteous, and awesome that produces the fear that we will be justly consumed.

But the message of the gospel is that God's justice has been satisfied by the sacrifice of Christ. Because of the imputed righteousness of Christ—that is, his goodness credited to our account—we can come boldly before the throne with the knowledge that we will be welcomed and accepted.

When I was in school, our principal created a specter of fear in the mind of every student in the school. In fact, whenever a teacher wanted to frighten the students, the mere threat of a trip to the principal's office was enough to bring the most recalcitrant student into line. Except me.

I remember the day I was first sent to the principal's office. I knew I was history. On the way to his office I began to write my will, leaving my bicycle to my brother and my stamp collection to my friend Billy. When I knocked on the principal's office door and he asked me to come in, I was sure that death was imminent. He told me to sit down, and then he said, referring to the teacher who had sent me to him, "Son, you don't like Miss_____ very much, do you?" I allowed that sometimes I had trouble with her. Then he laughed and told me that he didn't like her much either. From that day on we were friends, and it was the first of many visits to his office.

I never told others about him. It would have hurt his image and destroyed the necessary discipline of the school. Preachers sometimes feel that way about God—that if we tell people the truth, it will destroy discipline and hurt his plans.

I probably shouldn't be telling you this, but I must confess that I've been a preacher who didn't want to minimize God's holiness, because, if I did, I would be aiding in the transgressions, the licentiousness, and the improper freedom that "my people" would sinfully enjoy. Besides, it is so important that people understand that they worship a holy God.

I wish I could end my confession there, but there is more. I didn't want to minimize God's holiness, because it would minimize my control. Guilt can be a powerful motivator in getting people to do stuff they don't want to do.

Did you ever think that a preacher's job is really difficult? Preachers are called to get people to stop doing things they really want to do (we would never sin if sin weren't what we desired) and to do things they don't want to do (e.g., be obedient, pure, and holy). Too often our sermons on the holiness of God are no more than one of the methods whereby preachers, like me, keep their jobs and motivate their people. God becomes a sort of "cosmic police officer" whose business is to keep us from breaking the law.

The really big downside is that to pull it off, it is necessary that the preacher model the holiness of God. With me, that required a considerable effort to fashion a "mask" of holiness and obedience that I put on whenever I climbed into the pulpit and whenever I was on display.

I've given it up. It took too much out of me.

So I've decided to come clean. Let me tell you the truth about God. I didn't go to God much for the same reasons I didn't want to go to that principal—everybody told me that his consuming fire would destroy me. They told me about his judgment and wrath, and I knew that I deserved both. However, they told me that, despite this not altogether pleasant image of him, I needed to go to him because that is what Christians do. Not only did people tell me that, but I told everybody else the same thing.

But do you know something? When I finally decided to take off my mask and go to him, he wasn't like what I feared at all. He wasn't angry, and I was welcomed in the most wonderful way. In fact, wonder of wonders, I had the feeling that he wanted to spend time with me.

I have discovered that the deeper we go in faith, the more apt we are to allow our dysfunctions to determine the relationship we have with God. In almost every case I know, believers who have decided to get serious with God inevitably run into the feeling that God isn't interested in this process at all, that he is hiding, or that he is busy with other more important things.

If you don't feel welcomed, loved, and accepted by God, then you need to be still and wait. The sense that you have no business being before the throne of God is often a wall through which you must go to get to the reality of God's love. Many believers hit that wall and give up. The wall is an illusion. It isn't there—no matter what anybody tells you. That imaginary wall tests the mettle of your seriousness and is affirmed by Satan to get you to stop seeking God.

WORDS, WORDS, WORDS

Let's talk about three kinds of prayer. First, there is discursive prayer, which is cerebral and verbal. Second, there is meditative prayer. This prayer is focused and thoughtful. Finally, there is the prayer of silence. Some of the best praying I have ever done was after I had prayed. I have found that discursive prayer leads to meditative prayer and that meditative prayer leads to the prayer of silence. Let's look at each of these kinds of prayer.

Discursive prayer is the prayer of words. The most important part of discursive prayer is not a verbalization of requests, the confession of sin, or the commitment to obedience (as important as those acts of prayer are). The most important part of discursive prayer is the acknowledgment, the adoration, the worship, and the praise of the God to whom we speak.

Have you ever watched a baby who gets his or her first taste of applesauce after weeks of eating "yucky" cereal? It is a sight to behold. You can see it on the baby's face. The taste, for the first time, of the wonder and joy of applesauce. The smile and the joy seem to say, "I was created for applesauce!"

Discovering praise and adoration as the gateway to an intimate walk with God is sort of like that. We do it at first simply because that is what we ought to do, and certainly God is worthy of our worship, praise, and adoration. But the more we do it, the more we realize that human beings were created for this very thing. Praise, adoration, and worship are the keys that open the door to the house of prayer.

Richard Pratt puts it this way:

When was the last time you were fascinated with God? At one time or another, all of us have met someone we greatly admire. We admire athletes for their strength and musicians for their talents. The abilities of the sculptor amaze us. The charisma of the statesman fascinates us. Yet, we are seldom so amazed or fascinated with God. . . . Prayer is an excellent means of refreshing our appreciation for God. Simply telling God about His excellent qualities stirs our hearts to wonder. . . . Regrettably, Christians typically ignore the qualities of God in their prayers. They may say something like, "Thank You for who You are," but they never stop to talk much about just who God *is*.[7]

As you move into the "other world," think about God and his attributes. Think about what he has done for you, where he found you, and how gracious he has been to you. Think about his greatness and his power. Think about the world he created and sustains with his power. Remember what an awesome thing it is to even be in his presence.

One of our daughters had a poster of the cartoon character Ziggy in her room when she was growing up. On this poster, Ziggy is standing on top of a hill, watching a magnificent sunrise. He is jumping up and down and the caption reads: "Yea God!!!"

Take your time and be specific.

Usually, at this point in my own prayer, I start feeling uncomfortable. Once I am in the presence of holiness, the light can be blinding, and the dark places of my life cower before the light of his presence. If that happens to you, and it will, ask yourself why you are uncomfortable, and tell him about it. This is called confession and repentance. This is you knowing who you are, who God is, what you have done, and telling God about it.

And don't try to hide anything. Pray with the psalmist, "Search me, O God, and know my heart; try me, and know my anxieties; and see if there is any wicked way in me" (Ps. 139:23–24). God knows you need to get some things off your chest. Before his throne is the only place you can tell your secrets without fear of rejection, shame, or derision. It is the one place where you can be honest and know that you will be understood and accepted.

Most of us spend most of our time trying to defend our goodness and acceptability to others—trying to hide the reality of our failure and sin. We think that if only we had someone before whom we didn't have to wear a mask, it would be wonderful. God provides that place, and it is in his presence.

Take your time and be specific.

I don't know about you, but I have a tendency to verbalize my anxiety. I hardly ever suffer in silence about anything. If I'm sick, I want to be alone; but don't you dare leave until I tell you I'm sick and how much it hurts. Then just go away.

Verbalizing anxiety to friends (and don't bother with those who aren't friends—they don't care) is cathartic, and I usually feel better. Telling my Father about my restlessness is different in the sense that he ultimately caused it—and that makes me angry sometimes—and, if he wants to, he can change it.

Tell God everything. Tell him about your anger; tell him about the rejection you have felt from people you thought loved you; tell him about the abuse you have experienced; tell him about the people you wish would suffer; tell him about your fear and your shame; tell him about your needs; tell him about the fear you feel for those you care about; tell him what you think you need.

Be sure and tell him about the small things too. Pour out your heart before the throne. The deeper walk with God is often stifled by the sense that one ought not say certain things to God. That's nonsense. Whatever you think you ought not say, should not request, and must not speak, that is exactly what you ought to say, request, and speak. Do you think he will be surprised?

Words mean things. Let your words reflect the reality of who God is and what you feel and think. Don't play games with him. That's what we do, to one degree or another, with everybody else. But not with him. In this "other world" you are free to be who you are before the King who rules the land. And if you don't know who you are, be still and allow him to begin the process of showing you.

Before leaving the area of discursive prayer, let me say something about keeping a journal that chronicles your time with God. Some use the journal as a place of focus wherein they write their prayers. Others chronicle the answers to prayers that were offered, often stating the date they made a request and the date God granted the request. But perhaps more important, a journal can be a list of conversations and the words we suspect come from the Lord. Often the extraneous thoughts that come to mind are not extraneous at all. Sometimes they are the intrusions of God himself. More often than not, God will communicate by bringing to mind words of Scripture. A verse that you did not remember until that moment, a biblical image that comes uninvited to your mind, a sermon that speaks to a particular need, or maybe an offhand comment by a friend are often from the Father and can be included in one's journal.

A word of caution here. Because we are fallen and sinful creatures, we are so apt to grasp words that come from our own hearts, ideas that do not originate from the throne, or plans that conform to what we wanted in the first place. We must be very careful to check out what we believe came from God with two sources. First, we need to check out what we receive with Scripture. If, for instance, you think that God is telling you to leave your wife and marry a mistress, unless you are a biblical illiterate, you know that it didn't come from God. God is quite clear on those kinds of issues.

But second, it is very important that we have grounded Christian friends with whom we can share what we believe God has given us in our time of prayer. Sometimes, especially when what we think God is saying seems very particular and radical, it is important that we be in an accountable relationship with other Christians.

I was once asked to be the president of a rather large theological seminary. I certainly had no training in running a seminary. But the idea was so far out in left field that I thought it must be coming from God. The more I thought about it, the more I was sure that God needed my great intellectual and administrative prowess to guide that seminary. I had prayed about it and even felt that I had heard God's voice telling me to do it.

I was, at the time, speaking at a conference in another state. My friend and accountable brother, Rusty Anderson, found out where I was staying and called me. I had brought two letters to the conference and had decided that I was going to send one of them. One withdrew my name from consideration, and the other accepted the position and affirmed the continuing process. The phone rang in the hotel room. When I picked it up, Rusty's voice was on the other end of the line. He didn't even say,

"Hello" or "I'm praying for you." Rusty had a way of cutting to the chase quickly. He said (and I'm going to soften the language here for those with tender ears), "Brown, are you crazy? Who do you think you are? You can't run a seminary. God didn't call you to do stuff like that. You'll make a public fool of yourself."

Needless to say, I'm not the president of a seminary, and the folks at that seminary ought to be eternally grateful for a brother who knows the difference between the voice of God and my silly ideas.

The point is that as we grow deeper, we not discard words. Words are an important and vital aspect of the deeper walk with God.

A Story of Answered Prayer

Baby Steps

I am married to a wonderful man—my tried-and-true mate. I am proud to call Larry my husband but prouder to call him my friend. He suffers from ill health, which has very recently taken a bad and sad turn. As always, I pray for him. I submit prayers for his health, comfort, and if it is God's will and plan, his cure.

Lately, though, I have found myself to be the one ailing. I have had a serious case of "I-Can't-Do-Everything." I know my ailment has shown itself in my face, in my manner, in my words, and most sadly, in my actions. It followed me wherever I went. It hung like a dark, dark cloud. As humble as I usually am in my prayers and soulful talks with the Father, I had become resentful of carrying the load that has been given me. I was so disappointed in myself and ashamed of my behavior but unable to right myself. Larry loves me and deserves so much more.

After some serious consideration, I decided to take a new turn with my prayers. As I asked God to touch Larry with his healing hand, I also asked him to show me the path back to the strength and patience and courage he had given me. I asked him to help me reshape my heart with his love. I didn't ask for a miracle or an overnight conversion; I asked for him to work with me through baby steps.

The first baby step was to ask God to give Larry strength and an evening of diminished pain, so he could go with me to hear you [Steve Brown] speak. Check!

The second baby step was asking God to help me, over the next fourteen days, to recreate loving habits in my care for Larry. So far, day five—check, check, check, check, check, and counting.

My next baby step was asking for God's help in finding the right doctors who would have the knowledge, ability, and compassion to lead us to answers for the relief of Larry's suffering. Our internal-medicine physician provided an introduction to a new doctor who agreed to evaluate Larry. Check pending—God willing.

Most important, I asked God to help me offer up my life to his will and accept his plan. He is, always has been, and always will be in control; and by his grace, we're still here.

Baby steps. God is at work in my life in baby steps. I know it. I can feel it. God is unfolding his plan to me and through his grace showing his undaunted love—in baby steps.

Grace, grace. God's grace.

—Jane V.

Stop and Think

The next kind of prayer flows from discursive prayer and is meditative or focused prayer.

- The psalmist says, "Be angry, and do not sin. Meditate within your heart on your bed, and be still." (Ps. 4:4)

- Again: "I will meditate on Your precepts, and contemplate Your ways." (Ps. 119:15)
- Paul writes, "Brethren, whatever things are true, whatever things are noble, whatever things are just, whatever things are pure, whatever things are lovely, whatever things are of good report, if there is any virtue and if there is anything praiseworthy—meditate on these things." (Phil. 4:8)

One of the differences between Christian meditation and Eastern meditation is the object upon which one meditates. In Eastern meditative practices, the emphasis is on thinking about nothing, on being passive and emptying one's mind. Indeed, there are those "Christian" books on prayer that seem to suggest the same thing. Those might be sincere books, but they aren't Christian.

God, in an amazing demonstration of condescension, has chosen to reveal himself. And while the Scriptures are, as Calvin put it, "God's baby talk," they still reveal truth about God, about the world, about ourselves, and about reality. Because that is true, our meditation should be focused on that revelation. Christian meditation is not meditation on nothingness, it is meditation on God, his ways, his revelation, and his truth.

Here would be a good place to discuss imagination—a sanctified imagination—in the deeper life. There are those who will tell you that the use of the imagination in prayer is idolatry or that it is an inappropriate foray into the New Age or Eastern meditative practices. Don't believe that either.

Do you know what makes me angry? The whole New Age phenomenon makes me angry. What really bothers me is the reaction of Christians to the New Age. All of a sudden you have to hide your crystal sun catchers for fear of being accused of going over to the enemy camp. And I've read books by Christians who accuse faithful, honest, and godly men and women in ministry of being New Agers.

But there is no place where this New Age paranoia is more pronounced than in the area of prayer and the use of the imagination in prayer. The fact is that we cannot *not* use our imaginations in prayer. Christians are not called to have blank or passive minds in their prayers. God often comes in the context of our dreams, our imagination, and our flights of fantasy.

Let me illustrate what I mean. As I mentioned in an earlier chapter, I pray for a lot of people every morning. That can get boring. In fact, if I'm not careful, it can become an empty and meaningless ritual. I've been praying for a lot of people on my prayer list for years. Let me tell you how it got better.

There is a wonderful Trappist monastery in Conyers, Georgia. I have only been there once, but the chapel was so beautiful and so conducive to worship and meditation that I sometimes go there to pray—in my imagination. One day, instead of the altar, I pictured Jesus sitting in the chancel of the chapel and the people I pray for daily standing in the area where the congregation would be. Then, in my mind's eye, I pictured myself walking to the persons for whom I was praying, taking them by the hand, and leading them up to Jesus. Then I pictured myself moving out of the way.

It was interesting to note, after beginning that practice, the number of people who said to me: "Steve, are you still praying for me every morning?" I would allow that I was, and they would say, "Don't stop. It's working."

No, I'm not into New Age! I'm just a guy who allows his mind to create settings where prayer is more fun, more interesting, and more absorbing.

Some like to imagine themselves in a Bible text. Instead of just studying the Sermon on the Mount, the encounter of Isaiah in the temple, or Jesus walking with the men to Emmaus, picture yourself sitting in the crowd, standing in the temple, or walking on the road with the resurrected Christ.

One of my students challenged me once with the sin of idolatry. He said that it was wrong to picture God or Jesus, and not only that, but I was breaking one of the Big Ten. I asked him what he imagined when he prayed, and he said he had never thought about it. The truth, however, is that he may have been picturing a cloud or his wife. I like my way better. Besides that, isn't the incarnation of God in Christ the Trinity's idea of getting the image before the people that they might not be blown away with the angels and the smoke?

The parameters of Christian meditation are focused on God's revelation of himself in the living Word and the written Word. That meditation often uses a sanctified imagination.

Again, take your time and be specific.

LIVING IN THE SILENCE

Now we move into the area where there is apt to be the most danger. If prayer is a conversation between two persons (and it is), then it is important that you not only talk and meditate. It is important that you listen too.

During the "God is dead" movement, I was a student at Boston University. Billy Graham had said he was sure that God wasn't dead, because he had talked to him that morning. One of my professors said, "Ah, but that isn't the issue. The question is: did God talk back?" Good question.

Most orthodox Christians would say, "But of course God talks back. He does that in Scripture with the personal application of the Holy Spirit." That is true, and I certainly would not minimize the letter God has written to us in the Bible or the work of the Holy Spirit in applying God's Word to particular situations. In fact, I would suggest that Scripture is the main way God speaks to his people, and I certainly do not believe that there is any new revelation. God said it once, he said it right, he said enough, and he doesn't have to say it again.

However, if that is the only way God talks to us, it isn't very personal. It has a mechanical tone to it that simply doesn't fit the experience of Christians for the last two thousand years. Sometimes God gives direct messages to individuals.

Most Christian leaders like to make fun of those who have a message "from the Lord" for them. They usually say, "Oh yeah? Tell him to tell me too." I've said this more than once myself. And yet there are times when people have said things to me that were so accurate and so supernatural in their reference to a personal problem or issue with which I was dealing that I am not so quick to judge as I used to be.

One of the reasons I was drawn to seek a deeper walk with God was that kind of message. I prayed, "Lord, how come you don't talk to me that way? I love you too."

Buck Coombs was a dear and earthy Christian who was a member of a church that I once served. He is in heaven now, and his being there adds a major attraction to it. I loved and respected Buck a lot. He was a career Navy man and a swabbie. That meant he didn't use much religious language, and he didn't try to soften anything he said to me. I learned to trust him and the advice he gave me.

Buck became a Christian when God spoke to him verbally. The late Manford George Gutzke, one of the finest Bible teachers in America, was conducting a series of evangelistic services at the church where I was later to become the pastor. Buck attended those services and became quite agitated sitting under Dr. Gutzke's presentation of the truth. One evening he went out to his backyard, took his Bible, and held it over the garbage can. He said, "Lord, I'm not making a threat. You are God, and you hold all the cards. But I do want you to know that if I don't hear something from you, I'm going to throw this Bible into the garbage, because it isn't for me."

That was when God spoke to Buck and told him that he loved him. When I heard Buck telling the story, I found tears welling up in my eyes. However, my theological sophistication got in the way. Because of my intellectualism, I was sure that God would not bend to those kinds of methods, that God didn't speak that way, and that the Bible was sufficient. But during those early days of trying to hear God's voice, I thought of Buck and his reference to God's voice a lot. I thought of the veracity of his life and his testimony. Years later when my own walk became more intimate, I realized that God had spoken to Buck, and that it was only my arrogance that caused me to miss a possible similar experience.

Dr. Packer, from whose book I quoted earlier, tells of two occasions when God was quite specific in "speaking" to him. One was when he was the principal of a theological college that was on the verge of being closed. God gave Dr. Packer a method for a merger that saved the college. On another occasion he was led to know that a man for whom he was praying and who had cancer would be healed. "I felt," Dr. Packer said, "I was being told that the prayer was heard and I need not continue to press it. On Monday the operation revealed no trace of cancer."[8]

Does God still speak in ways other than Scripture? Not with new revelation, but yes, he does speak to particular situations and with specific ideas, impressions, and words. Usually only children and childlike adults hear him. But yes, he does speak.

The immediate questions are: How do I hear him? How do I know it is him? Will I learn to hear? The answers to those questions are: I'm not sure; you'll know; and, yes, if you want to. Let's talk about it.

God speaks in many different ways to different people. Just as I communicate to my children and grandchildren in different ways because they are different, God communicates to his people in different ways, and those ways are usually designed to fit the way a particular person is wired. I had a dentist friend who was, before his death, my closest friend. When he was young, he attended a missions conference where the game was manipulation. The preacher told the young people at the conference that if they loved God and were obedient, they would volunteer to give their lives to missions. My friend went forward and told God and the congregation that he was going to be a missionary.

It never happened. His life took turns that he never expected. He found it necessary to care for his elderly parents, he was married, and there were family and financial obligations. Before he knew it, the years had passed, and it was too late to go. He was one of the most faithful and godly Christians I have ever known, but he always felt terribly guilty about not going on the mission field. One day, amidst great sobs, he told me of the guilt that he had felt all the years of his life and how he felt he had betrayed God. I told him that the preacher at that conference was a manipulative twit. I told him that God sometimes leads us with circumstances, and that the circumstances of his life revealed that it was not God's plan for him to be a missionary. I told him that God loved him and that, if for no one else, my life was richer and my ministry more effective because he had not gone on the mission field.

But none of that helped. Let me tell you what did help.

On Sunday evenings we had a regular prayer service at the church. Instead of a benediction, all the lights in the auditorium were turned out except the light on the cross. People were then free to leave or come forward and kneel at the altar rail and stay as long as they felt was necessary. After a short prayer,

I generally went upstairs to my study and worked until I knew everyone had left. I then turned off the lights and went home.

One Sunday evening I heard the noise of someone bolting up the stairs, two steps at a time, to the second floor and the location of my study. It sounded like a herd of elephants. Then the door of my study swung open, and my friend came almost dancing in. Tears were running down his face, and he was laughing. "Steve," he said in almost a shout, "you won't believe what happened to me just now. I was telling God how sorry I was for not becoming a missionary and asking for his forgiveness. I felt a hand on my shoulder and the comforting pressure of a friend. I thought it was you. I turned around and no one was there!"

After that experience, my friend never again felt guilty about not going on the mission field. In fact, he became one of the most excited and childlike Christians I have ever known. He stayed that way until he died and went home to meet the One who had so lovingly, years before, placed his hand on my friend's shoulder.

God speaks to people in different ways. Our daughter, Jennifer, when she was a little girl, asked me one time, "Daddy, you are always talking about how God talks to you. He never talks to me. How do you hear God?"

With a rare burst of insight, I said to her, "Honey, do you know the new girl in your class and how you told me she looked so sad because she didn't have any friends?" Jennifer nodded. "Who told you that she was so sad? And who told you to be her friend?"

"Oh," Jennifer said, "so that's him."

I could go on and on. The point is this: you aren't like anyone else you know. Because that is true, God will, if you listen, speak to you in a way that you can hear. Sometimes he will speak in a circumstance, or maybe in a book you are reading, or perhaps through a friend—but he will not be silent. Scripture says, "You will seek Me and find Me, when you search for Me with all your heart" (Jer. 29:13). As Pascal said, "I would not have searched for Thee if Thou had not already found me." So even the seeking is a gift from him, and when you seek at his bidding, you will find him.

As you look back over your life, ask God to reveal those places where he spoke clearly. I can remember the time, as a young pastor, I could not drive past the house of an elderly lady who was a member of the church I served. I had such a "feeling" I needed to stop that, at the top of the street, I did a U-turn and drove back to her house. While I was there on that pastoral visit, the subject of death and her fear of death came up. I helped her work through her fear, and we prayed about the amazing and wonderful promises of the only One who died and came back to talk about it . . . and said that we would rise again too.

The next day that woman had a massive stroke and was unable to communicate, and then two days later she was dead.

I can remember in counseling sessions (and this has happened on several occasions) when I said to someone, "What you just told me is a lie. It's simply not true."

"How do you know?"

I didn't want to tell him or her that Jesus had told me. It would scare the person to death.

I can remember the time I was working late on a sermon and a man's name kept coming to my mind. In fact, I couldn't stop thinking about it. It was so strong that I couldn't work on the sermon. So I decided, even though it was rather late, to go and visit the man. When I got to his house, his wife greeted me at the door and said, "Who told you?"

"Who told me what?" I asked.

"Bill just died a few moments ago," she said with tears streaming down her face, "and I have no idea what to do."

God had "spoken" and sent me to her home to be there in a time of need.

Does God still speak? Of course he does.

The practice of discursive prayer and meditative prayer is often the sensitizing process that God uses to bring us to the place where we can hear his voice. As I said earlier, some of the best praying I have ever done was after I had prayed. Prayer is not a monologue. It is a conversation between two persons, albeit of unequal importance and power. In that conversation God will speak if you are willing to be still enough to hear. He will come if you will wait.

Let me close this chapter with the words of Dallas Willard:

My own experience, and what I have learned from others who clearly have signed their lives over to God and learned to work with His voice, leads me to believe that direction will always be made available to the mature disciple if without it serious harm may befall persons concerned for the cause of Christ. The obedient, listening heart, mature in the things of God, will in such a case find the voice plain and the message clear after the fashion of those experiences of the friends of God recorded in the Bible. This is a claim which any person can test by experience if that person is willing to meet the conditions.[9]

SEVEN

Good for Goodness' Sake

Wicked men obey from fear, good men, from love.
—Aristotle

*How will you find good? It is not a thing of choices; it is a
river that flows from the foot of the invisible throne, and
flows by the path of obedience.*
—George Eliot

*God is too great to be withstood, too just to do wrong, too
good to delight in any one's misery. We ought, therefore,
quietly to submit to His dispensations as the very best.*
—Daniel Wilson

L ET ME TELL YOU something important: obedience is far
less important to God than you fear and far more important
to God than you could possibly know. I'll explain as we go
along, but for now, relax. I've discovered some things that I
want to share with you, and it isn't going to be as bad as you
may think.

One of the reasons people don't pray is because they don't
think they are good enough, and I'm not just talking about
unbelievers either. "If I pray," they reason, "God will require
that I be good. I've tried hard to be good and can't be good
enough. Therefore I'm not going to pray much because I
already feel guilty enough."

There *is* a connection between obedience and prayer. In 1898 Abraham Kuyper, once prime minister of the Netherlands, gave a series of lectures at Princeton on the subject of Calvinism. It is amazing how relevant Kuyper's words are today. In the sixth and final lecture, he lamented the failure of material possessions, science, and political progress to affect improvement in the morals of Western civilization. Instead of getting better, he said, things were far worse. Our own legitimate concerns about the direction of ethical standards, political integrity, and moral behavior could do with a healthy dose of Kuyper:

> Our personal life as men and citizens subsists not in the comforts that surround us, nor in the body, which serves us as a link with the outward world, but in the spirit that internally actuates us; and in this inner consciousness we are becoming more and more painfully aware how the hypertrophy of our external life results in a serious atrophy of the spiritual. Empirical science is more brilliant in her attainments than ever, universal knowledge spreads in constantly widening circles, and civilization . . . is almost dazzled by her too rapid conquests. But even the intellect does not constitute the mind. Personality is seated more deeply in the hidden recess of our inner being, where character is formed, whence the flame of enthusiasm is kindled, where the moral foundations are laid, where love's blossoms bud, whence spring consecration and heroism and where in the sense of the infinite, our time-bound existence reaches out unto the very gates of eternity.[1]

While there is a vital connection between prayer and obedience, the connection is far different than most of us suppose.

Henri Nouwen once visited with Mother Teresa in Calcutta. He asked her how to live out his vocation as a priest. Her answer was, I believe, the key to why God used her in such a marvelous way. She said to Nouwen, "Spend one hour a day in adoration of your Lord and never do anything you know is wrong, and you will be all right."[2] Don't let the simplicity of that advice fool you. The advice she gave was profound.

Let's talk about it.

I mentioned in an earlier chapter that almost everything of any importance is found on the way to something else. C. S. Lewis talks about the danger of the "inner ring." He says that most of us would do almost anything to be a part of an inner circle, to be accepted by the members of it. He describes with devastating accuracy how people will cast off friends who love them, compromise their integrity, lie, and steal to be a part of the inner ring. Then Lewis asks a rhetorical question: "In the whole of your life as you now remember it, has the desire to be on the right side of that invisible line ever prompted you to any act or word on which, in the cold small hours of a wakeful night, you can look back with satisfaction? If so, your case is more fortunate than most."[3]

Lewis's remedy is wonderful. He says that one must forget about the inner ring and acceptance by those who are a part of it. He says that the quest for the inner ring will break your heart unless you break the quest. One, he says, should simply get on about the business of living, of doing the right thing, and of doing what one does well. Then, almost without knowing it, you will find yourself accepted in the only inner ring that is important. "If in your spare time you consort simply with the people you like, you will again find that you have come unawares to a real inside: that you are indeed snug and safe at the center of something which, seen from without, would look exactly like an inner ring. But the difference is that its secrecy is accidental, and its exclusiveness a by-product, and no one was led thither by the lure of the esoteric."[4]

The point is this: almost everything of any importance is found on the way to somewhere else. If you want to be accepted, seek it and you will never find it. If you want to be spiritual, work hard at it, and your lack of spirituality will rival that of a pagan. If you want humility and work at it, your pride will become your most outstanding trait.

Nowhere is this major life principle more apparent than in the connection between prayer and goodness. God didn't design prayer so that you would get better, even though you will. God didn't design prayer so you would be holy, even though that does happen. God didn't design prayer to make you more like Jesus, even though that is its by-product. God designed prayer—and get this straight before we go any further—because he likes you and wants to spend time with you. How about that, sports fans? God loves us so much that he went to a lot of trouble just to spend time with us.

Brennan Manning relates a wonderful scene in Paddy Chayefsky's play *Gideon*. Gideon is out in the desert and is ticked at God. He feels deserted and rejected by God. Then God comes and absolutely overwhelms Gideon.

"God, oh God," Gideon cries out, "all night long I've thought of nuttin' but You, nuttin' but You, I'm caught up in the raptures of love. God, I want to take You into my tent, wrap You up, and keep You all to myself. God, hey God, tell me that You love me."

God replies, "I love you, Gideon."

"Yeah, tell me again, God."

"I love you, Gideon."

Then Gideon asks God why He loves him and God

scratches His head and answers: "I really don't know. Sometimes, My Gideon, passion is unreasonable."[5]

God's passion really is unreasonable. I've never understood it. As someone has said, "If I were God, I would kick the world to pieces. Aren't you glad that I'm not God?" He doesn't need us. He was doing fine before we came along, but for some reason known only to himself, he wanted to be close to us. That is what the world is all about. God created the world so we could know him.

Let me go down a doctrinal side street so that we are clear on this point. The relevant doctrines are called justification and imputation. Justification is the biblical doctrine that teaches that, because of Christ's vicarious death on the cross on our behalf, we have been made just or justified. Scripture puts it this way: "For when we were still without strength, in due time Christ died for the ungodly. . . . But God demonstrates His own love toward us, in that while we were still sinners, Christ died for us" (Rom. 5:6, 8).

But the good news doesn't stop there. Not only are we justified by the sacrifice of Christ—our sins are taken away—but we are given something of priceless value to replace the sin: the righteousness of Christ. Again, listen to the Bible: "'It [i.e., faith] was accounted to [Abraham] for righteousness.' Now it was not written for his sake alone that it was imputed to him, but also for us. It [righteousness] shall be imputed to us who believe in Him who raised up Jesus our Lord from the dead" (Rom. 4:22–24). That means that the goodness, the purity, the obedience, and the perfection of Christ were imputed to us, or given to our account.

One time someone came to Martin Luther and asked him, "What about works of penance?"

In Luther's own earthy and wonderful way, this was his answer: "What is it about your own miserable works and doing that you think you could please God more than the sacrifice of his own Son?" Luther continued: "Either sin is with you, lying on your shoulders, or it is lying on Christ, the Lamb of God. Now if it is lying on your back, you are lost; but if it is resting on Christ, you are free, and you will be saved. Now choose what you want. According to law and justice, your sins should no doubt remain on you; but grace has cast them upon Christ, the Lamb. If God were minded to reason with us on other terms, we would be done for."[6]

You see, Luther understood that we can't be more righteous than Christ and that *he* is our righteousness when we stand before the throne of God in prayer. This is why Luther said to the perfectionist, Philip Melanchthon, his colleague at Wittenberg, "Melanchthon, why don't you go out and sin a little so you would have something for which to repent?"

Perhaps the most important thing we can know when we pray is that the goal of prayer is not righteousness—the goal of prayer is prayer. Prayer is the ordained place where the God of the universe spends time with people he likes. God doesn't have to fix you, because you have already been fixed by the blood of Christ and by the righteousness that has been imputed to your account.

It was Saint Teresa, I think, who prayed, "Lord cause me to love you even if there is no heaven and to fear you even if there is no hell." She was pointing to a central reality of prayer. Prayer is delightful and valuable in itself, not in its practical results.

Do you know why most Christians don't get any better? They don't get better because they're obsessive about being better. We think that the whole reason for religion is to make us good. We become obsessive with our purity, our goodness, and our obedience. And then, in our obsession with the wrong thing, we don't even see the horrible monster of pride that created the obsession.

The only people who get better are people who know that, if they don't get any better, God will still love them.

Got it?

Good.

Now we can talk.

God is a holy God, and he desires holiness from his people. *Antinomianism* (a word coined by Martin Luther to label those who believe that the law is no longer relevant to the Christian) is a heresy. God, as far as I know, has not changed his mind about what believers are to be obedient to. You will find nothing in this book that minimizes the law of God. In fact, it is very important that all believers remember what is required and that we never compromise or change those requirements; further, we are to present God's law as the standard whereby God judges the world. Remember that believers have already been judged on the cross, and the Bible says that there is "therefore now no condemnation" (Rom. 8:1) for those who have accepted that judgment. Anything less than a clear presentation of God's law is heresy.

But a whole lot more needs to be said than that. Philip Yancey, in an article in *Christianity Today*, points to the problem we all have: the standard of God's law is always before us. I've listened to enough confessions to know that human beings (myself included) fall so far short of what God requires that we ought to be—and are, in fact—ashamed.

In his article, Yancey compares Leo Tolstoy and Fyodor Dostoevsky. Tolstoy's life is marked by guilt and pain. He, for instance, took everything in the Sermon on the Mount literally and made all sorts of pledges and efforts to live up to the teaching of Jesus there. When you read the Sermon on the Mount in Matthew 5–7, you know how impossible Christ's commands really are. Jesus says that if we are angry, we have committed murder; if we ever lust, it is the same thing as adultery; if evil attacks, we are not to resist. Jesus says that we are to be perfect as God is perfect.

Tolstoy made the thrust of his life an effort to live by the teachings of Jesus in the Sermon on the Mount and, of course, failed miserably. His life was marked by guilt, pain, and an acute sense of failure, which are reflected in his novels and especially in his religious writings. Though harsh, narrow, unbending, and judgmental toward others, Tolstoy was more harsh, narrow, unbending, and judgmental toward himself.

On the other hand, Yancey points out, Dostoevsky, whose sin was great, understood God's grace. The joys of forgiveness, redemption, and love are reflected in almost everything he wrote. Yancey points out that the purpose of the law is to keep before God's people the goal for which we, by grace, are striving. The law must never be compromised. However, the law has a greater purpose than being our goal; the law is a measure to show us how much we need God's grace.

In referring to the Sermon on the Mount, Yancey writes:

The worst tragedy would be to turn the Sermon on the Mount into another form of legalism; it should rather put an end to all legalism. Legalism like the Pharisees' will always fail, not because it is too strict, but because it isn't strict enough. Thunderously, inarguably, the Sermon on the Mount decrees that before God we all stand on level ground: murderers and temperthrowers, adulterers and lusters, thieves and covetous. We are all desperate, and that is, in fact, the only state appropriate to a human being who wants to know God. Having fallen from the absolute ideal, as Tolstoy did, we have nowhere to land but with Dostoevsky, in the safety net of absolute grace.[7]

And so the life of the believer on his or her knees is an understanding that grace is the defining factor in prayer. We don't go to God in order to be good; we go to him because he has called and wants us to spend time with him. In his presence we have the awareness that we have failed to meet his standards, but we also have the awareness that he loves us anyway. And that brings me to something that is very important to remember when you pray, and that is the unconditional love with which he loves us.

A Story of Answered Prayer

Not a Peep

When I was around twenty-two years old, I worked for a prison in Texas. I was offered a position in the "back" of the prison, in the inmate-classification department. It was scary! You had to go back into the prison through lots of locked doors. You had to be around prisoners who were not always friendly and oftentimes were downright frightening. The worst part was that every day when I walked back to my office, I had to walk on a sidewalk that had windows to the cellblocks on either side of it. The prisoners would yell the most vile, horrible things to any woman who walked that way. It really demoralized me to the point where I wanted to quit.

One day on my lunch break, I went out to my car and just prayed that God would intervene and that those inmates would quit yelling those vile, awful things at me. I prayed that when they looked at me, they would see Jesus and not me, and they would never think to yell such awful things to him. When I returned from lunch and set foot on that sidewalk, amazingly, not a peep was heard from the inmates. It was that way for the rest of the time I worked that job. They never yelled at me again! It was like they saw Jesus and had respect.

—Stacy S.

Constrained by Love

The side effect of prayer is a changed life. No, that isn't right. The side effect of prayer is a *changing* life. When Paul said that "the love of Christ compels us" (2 Cor. 5:14), he was referring to something that all those who have truly prayed have experienced, and that is the incredible love and unconditional acceptance of God. When I am obedient, it's not because I work at and say to myself, *I'm going to be obedient if it kills me.* If I did that, it probably would. I'm obedient because, as much as any man you ever met, I want to please the One who loves me that unconditionally.

Psychological and sociological studies have confirmed over and over that some children who have been abused become abusers. In other words (and this is highly oversimplified), when authority figures are harsh, abusive, evil, and angry, they produce harsh, abusive, evil, and angry children and followers. God is not a child abuser. His grace and mercy toward us make us gracious and merciful people. That's why when you encounter Christians who are negative, narrow, and critical, you can rest assured that they haven't been spending much time with God.

We grow to resemble what we love. Have you ever noticed how people who have lived with one another often start looking alike? The next time you are with a couple who have been married for a long time, notice how much they resemble each other. Because we do grow to be like what we love, believers who are in prayer before the throne become more and more godly and Christlike.

Let me tell you something that might surprise you. I've preached some of my best sermons after I have sinned the worst. Now, that isn't the defining principle of homiletics (i.e., sin more and preach better), but it is, I believe, a statement from God about why I am his. It isn't because the relationship is earned, but it's because it is a gift.

I can remember coming out of the pulpit amazed with the power of a sermon following my sin. I think I heard him say, "Child, I just wanted you to see that it isn't your goodness or your purity. It's mine. Don't become presumptuous about what I just taught you, but don't forget it either."

Someone has said that when you first meet God, he gives you a mirror wherein you see yourself as you really are with all of your sin, your anger, and your hatred. But you are also given a picture of Jesus, and God says, pointing to the picture of Jesus, "Child, I'm going to work in your life, and one of these days you are going to look just like that." Scripture says, "We know that when He is revealed, we shall be like Him." (1 John 3:2).

I used to believe the "lies" people had told me about God, to wit, that he was angry and that his anger was directed at my sin and disobedience. Do you know what that caused in me? It caused a rebellion that you wouldn't believe.

God said, "Thou shalt not," and something in my heart stood up and shouted, "I shalt." The more I believed what they told me about God and the more I tried to be better, the more I, as Spurgeon said, "kicked against the goads."

Then I discovered how much God loved me. I found out that my refusal to obey because of my "authority" problem didn't change God's love for me one iota. I found out that, as I said above, the only people who get any better are those who know that, if they don't get any better, God will still love them.

That's how I became such a pure, holy, and obedient spiritual giant!

Just kidding. But every place of growth in my life, every point of obedience, and every place of righteousness didn't come because I was afraid of a God who would not love me if I didn't grow, be obedient, and become righteous. The places of growth came because those things weren't even the issue.

A Story of Answered Prayer

Miracle Baby

I was fresh from Bible College, and my wife and I were at our first church in New Bedford, Massachusetts. She was pregnant and had a diseased gallbladder. It was way too early for the doctors to take the baby, but the pain was constant, and my wife, Sharon, was jaundiced. The stress of the disease might kill the baby, and if they operated, they were sure the trauma would kill the baby. But my wife was fast coming into jeopardy as well, and as of Saturday, they decided to operate on Monday.

I prayed, "Lord, we give this baby over to your keeping. He belongs to you. Preserve his little life, and we will attempt to raise him for your glory and to serve you all his days."

I called other churches in the city, some of which stopped services to pray for my wife and the baby.

On Monday morning, the doctor came in, expecting to do surgery. He started poking around and said, "Either you're being very brave, or it doesn't hurt."

Sharon said, "It doesn't hurt."

The severe jaundice had vanished. She was able to carry the baby to term without any more attacks.

After delivery, when the gallbladder was removed, it was found to be very diseased. The doctor said, "There is no way that your symptoms could have abated like that!"

But we knew it was an answer to the saints' prayers and our giving God that little life.

By the way, that little baby, Jeremy, is now a tremendously gifted pastor and church builder, anointed as God's servant.

—Wayne B.

Love Produces Love

Let's look at what happens as the believer encounters the love of God and increasingly understands how amazing that love is.

First, love by its nature produces love. The principle is this: you can't love until you have been loved, and then you can only love to the degree to which you have been loved. Just as you can tell how guilt ridden a person is by noting how guilty you feel in his or her presence, you can tell how much a person is loved and accepted by seeing how much you feel loved and accepted in his or her presence.

There is a section in my prayer list that my friends call my Hit List. Generally, when I start praying for the people in that section of the prayer list, it is with great reluctance and sometimes anger. In other words, I don't do it because I want to but because I'm told by God that I have to. A lady once said to Phillips Brooks, "I want you to know that I have been praying for your death and that I have been quite successful in this kind of prayer on three previous occasions." I don't generally pray for the death of those who are on my Hit List, but sometimes I would like to.

There are two salient points to which I would like to bear witness in regard to my Hit List. First, something begins to happen, and what started with obedience becomes a delight. That doesn't happen quickly or without a couple of backward steps, but it does happen. Generally by meditating on the cross of Christ, the Father says to me, "Child, if I felt about you the way you feel about this person, where would you be?" And then, second, no one is on my Hit List who was there a year ago. They didn't die, I did. In other words, something happened as I was loved that enabled me to love the unlovely or at least those I thought were unlovely.

Love Produces Honesty

Have you ever met people before whom you feel you must always defend yourself? By their very demeanor, they give you a feeling that you have spinach hanging from your front tooth. The more I'm around people like that, the more I find myself trying to defend my goodness, my worth, my perfection, and my views. But whenever I go to the Father, I don't have to defend myself anymore.

That doesn't mean, by the way, that the Father doesn't bring me out of denial about who I am and what I've done. Let me give you an important principle: love allows confession without demanding correction. Correction takes place within the context of a process, and the process is lifelong, finally culminating in my being like Christ. If immediate correction were demanded as soon as confession was given, I would never confess. But that isn't God's way. When love is unconditional, confession is possible.

If I tell you my secrets, will you accept me? Probably not. If I examine my life before your eyes, and I find things about which I am ashamed, will you promise not to reject me? You aren't sure. If I take off my mask and let you see the scars and the disfigurement, will you promise not to turn away? I know, you can't make any promises. What if I get angry at you because you know me; will you still be my friend? You don't think so.

So I'll have to go to the Lord, because you see, he always accepts me, he never rejects me or turns away from me, and he has promised always to be my friend. In that context of prayer, I can begin the painful process of self-examination, because you see, love allows confession without demanding correction.

Love Makes Me Different

My friend sacred-recording artist Buddy Greene, often travels with our Key Life ministry team as we do Born Free seminars. Sometimes when he is leading the participants in singing, he will stop and say, "Now, I want you to turn to the person on your right and say, 'God loves you just the way you are.'" Then Buddy says, "Before you sit down, turn to the person on your right and say, 'God loves you too much to let you stay that way.'" People laugh. Those who have been walking with Christ know that it's true.

God changes people, but he doesn't do it quickly, and he doesn't do it by beating them over the head with his law. He is far wiser and gentler than that. And he never dumps the whole load on us at once. We probably couldn't stand it if he did. But that doesn't mean he doesn't work in the circumstances of our lives to bring us to obedience.

And never forget this: God doesn't bring us to obedience to make us miserable. Just the opposite. His way really is the best way. Believe me, I know. I've done it my way, and I've done it his way, and his way allows me to sleep at night. When Jesus said he had not come to destroy the law (see Matt. 5:17), he said it because God's way is the best way to live. Jesus didn't destroy the law; he fulfilled it by increasingly giving us the power to live it and joyful forgiveness when we don't.

Love Sets Me Free

Archimandrite Sophrony, the great Russian contemplative of the early part of the last century, left a life of acclaim and affluence to follow Christ. He went from the life of a painter exhibiting in the great Paris salons to spending the rest of his life as a monk at Mount Athos. Listen to what he says:

> Prayer affords an experience of spiritual liberty of which most people are ignorant. The first sign of emancipation is a disinclination to impose one's will on others. The second—an inner release from the hold of others on oneself. Mastery over the wish to dominate is an extremely important stage which is closely followed by dislike of constraining our brother. . . . Those who are possessed by the lust for power cloud the image of God in themselves. The light of true life departs, leaving a tormenting void, a distressing tedium. Life is bereft of meaning.[8]

There is great freedom in not having to be right or good. Most religionists have a need to be right. At the ministry, we receive thousands of letters each month. Because I spend some time each week on the daily broadcast, answering questions, I get a bunch of letters from people who violently disagree with some of the answers I have given. Not only that, they feel the need to convince me that they are right and I am wrong. Those letters often consist of page after page of argument as to why what I said was heresy, stupidity, or outright ignorance.

I used to spend a considerable portion of my time trying to answer the objections expressed in those letters. I found, however, that if I answered a ten-page letter with five pages, I would always get a response of twenty pages. It was a losing battle until a friend of mine told me how to answer the letters. Now, more often than not, my answer is: "Dear_____, You may be right, but you are probably wrong. Sincerely, Steve Brown." It drives them crazy! You see, it is very important that they be right.

Whenever you see someone who has to be right, you are looking at someone who is spending more time reading about God than praying to him. They have assumed that we are in a relationship with propositions instead of a Person. When we go before the God of the universe, one of the things we experience is the overwhelming conviction that the world is so big, our knowledge is so limited, and God is so . . . well . . . God, that we could all be wrong.

But there is more than that. Prayer before a God who loves unconditionally frees the believer from the need to appear to be right. There is a direct correlation between real prayer and real freedom from the tyranny of others' opinions and our own arrogance.

A Story of Answered Prayer

Rescue in White

It was August and hot, as you can well imagine. I thought my little Honda motorcycle was finally running, after being in the garage for quite some time. I asked my husband to follow me, just in case it broke down.

About a mile and a half from the house, sure enough, it sputtered to a stop. I had my full-face helmet, leather jacket, and jeans on, and I was not happy about the idea of having to push the motorcycle up and down all those little foothills near Lookout Mountain to get home. My husband gallantly offered to push it for me, but my stubborn self just wouldn't let him suffer for my failure.

It was Sunday about noon (no, I didn't go to church that day!). I was so mad at myself, and I just prayed to God, *Lord, I know you have so many other important things to attend to, but if you would just see your way to sending someone to come and get me and my motorcycle so I don't have to push it all the way home in this heat, I would surely appreciate it.* At that point, I envisioned a white *thing* coming to pick me up to take me *wherever I wanted to go.* Those were the words I imagined.

Well, about ten minutes later, a white pickup truck with a little old lady in the passenger seat pulled up next to me. It was pulling a white motorcycle trailer, and she said to me, "Honey, do you need some help?"

I said, "Yes! I prayed for you ten minutes ago!" She said she had passed me on her way home from church about ten minutes before. Since her brother had motorcycles, she drove over to his house to "fetch" him to come take me "wherever I wanted to go!"

Now, how immediate an answer to prayer can you get?

—Judith S.

Love Creates Purity

We're going to talk about purity, but the danger of talking about purity is that if God creates purity through prayer and we don't get much purer, our proclivity is to fake it. We pretend that we have something we don't, and even while pretending, we deny the reality that we are phonies.

Not only that, but when we start talking about the purity that comes from prayer, we are in great danger of defining our walk with God in terms of that purity and then going right back to the prison from which we have been liberated.

And teacher/preachers like me are in danger of returning once again to our weapons of manipulation and judgment, as we misuse the truth that God makes us better.

Don't do that, and I won't either!

Don't allow this final lesson—that needs to be taught because it is true—to rob you of all the blessings of love I've shared to this point. If you allow that to happen, do you know what God will do? He'll allow you to get worse.

Self-righteousness is so very dangerous and sometimes leads to public drunkenness where you confess your deepest and darkest secrets to your worst enemies. Well, maybe not that. But God does have the proclivity to "pluck the feathers" of "peacock Christians."

Okay, I was constrained to tell you that before we talked about purity.

Do you remember what I said about God's law? Well, it seems that the closer I get to him, the more I understand his love and acceptance, the more I want to please him. His law is the expression of his perfect will for his people.

Listen to what Jerry Bridges says:

> But human morality and submission to God's law are entirely different in principle, though they may appear to be similar in outward appearance. Human morality arises out of culture and family training and is based on what is proper and expected in the society we live in. . . . Submission to God's law arises out of a love for God and a grateful response to His grace and is based on a delight in His law as revealed in Scripture. . . . Sanctification (i.e., getting better) begun in our hearts by the Holy Spirit changes our attitude. Instead of being hostile to God's law, we begin to delight in it. . . . This radical and dramatic change in our attitude toward God's commands is a gift of His grace, brought about solely by the mighty working of His Holy Spirit within us.[9]

Not being changed by prayer is sort of like standing in the middle of a spring rain without getting wet. It's hard to stand in the center of God's acceptance and love without getting it all over you. And that is the secret to being good for goodness' sake.

Earlier I said that obedience is far less important to God than you fear and far more important to God than you could possibly know. That's true. God doesn't need your obedience. He cares far more for you than what you do or don't do. Within the context of prayer, however, one grows to love and copy the object of love. He knows you, and he knows what you need. He will never let you go or turn his back on you.

There is a strange pathology among people who are serious about God, and it doesn't come from him. This particular view is that if it is good, fun, and enjoyable, it must be a sin. Don't you believe it. God is making you better because his desire is that you fulfill the purpose for which you were born: to love him and enjoy him forever.

He will never let you go. However, he is our Father and this Father really does know best.

EIGHT

Invitation to the Dance

Gladness of the heart is the life of a man,
and the joyfulness of a man prolongeth his days.
—Apocrypha: Ecclesiasticus 30:22

It is comely fashion to be glad,—
Joy is the grace we say to God.
—Jean Ingelow: *Dominion*

If you have no joy in your religion,
there's a leak in your Christianity somewhere.
—Billy Sunday

MIKE GLODO, MY FRIEND and colleague at Reformed Seminary where we both teach, said something to me recently that I've been thinking about ever since. He said, "Individuals and institutions live by their metaphors. The church has always used the metaphors of war or athletic contests or struggle. Those are good metaphors, but what if in evangelism we used the metaphor of a dance? What if we invited people to a dance? What a difference it would make to those we invite to him."

For a while, I want to put aside all the theology and the analysis and talk to you about a very important side of prayer. We have made fleeting reference to it up to this point, but here I want to focus on something that is very important. I want to talk to you about the dance to which those who pray are invited.

I believe our prayers are often stifled because we take our prayers too seriously. In other words, we sometimes are so weighted down with our sin, so pressured with our lives, so overwhelmed with our needs, and so forced into cultural molds of how to pray that we forget that the basic thrust of prayer is celebration. It is a child coming to spend time with a Father who loves the child—dotes on the child, if you will—and who is pleased with the time spent together.

You will remember that when the Israelites sent spies into the Promised Land, the majority group came back with a negative report about the possibility of making any headway against those who occupied the land. However, there was also a minority report, and one of the two members of the minority was Joshua. Joshua said this: "The land we passed through to spy out is an exceedingly good land. If the LORD *delights* in us, then He will bring us into this land and give it to us, 'a land which flows with milk and honey'" (Num. 14:7–8).

The refusal of God's people to recognize that God really did "delight" in them cost them forty years in the wilderness. Something like that has happened with many who have seen prayer as a very serious, intense, dismal, arduous, and demanding experience.

Now don't get me wrong. There is a serious side of prayer. But there is a major element of prayer that most of us miss, and that element is laughter—a free, joyous, wholesome, hardy laughter. That laughter can only come from those who have realized that God isn't mad at them, that he is their Father, and that nothing will ever change that.

When the Puritan minister "slipped" in his prayer and prayed, "Lord, let me tell Thee a joke," he didn't offend God or anyone else who knows the joy and freedom of prayer. God, I'm sure, had heard the joke but enjoyed hearing it the second time anyway. If you find that offensive, we need to talk.

Listen to the verses we never memorized in Sunday school:

- He also brought me out into a broad place; He delivered me because He *delighted* in me. (Ps. 18:19)
- Trust in the LORD, and do good; dwell in the land, and feed on His faithfulness. *Delight* yourself also in the LORD, and He shall give you the desires of your heart. (Ps. 37:3–4)
- You shall no longer be termed Forsaken, nor shall your land any more be termed Desolate; but you shall be called Hephzibah [literal meaning: "My delight is in her"], and your land Beulah [literal meaning: "Married"]; for the LORD *delights* in you. (Isa. 62:4)

My friend Reggie Kidd, a professor of New Testament at Reformed Theological Seminary, says:

Western philosophy, including Western aesthetics, is a history of a tired pendulum swinging back and forth between rationalism and romanticism. . . .

The fact is: our faith is more rational than the most elaborate paradigm of the atheistic foundationalist, more romantic than the wildest dreams of the unbelieving postmodernist. Our faith is a dogma that makes you dance—David's wife Michal didn't get the dance side of the equation and experienced the barrenness of childlessness (see 2 Samuel 6:23). Michal may not have had physical children, but her spiritual children survive to this day, still mocking the dancers, and still as joylessly barren themselves. Our faith is a romance between persons; to be sure, a romance predicated on the recitation of certain saving facts, but a romance nonetheless; it's an assent that is completed not just in obedience, but in applause as well. It wasn't, after all, some big-haired, flashy-teethed, arm-flailing, southern gospel cheerleader who invented the concept of "giving the Lord a big hand." . . . It was the psalmist.[1]

When God invites his people to prayer, he invites them to the dance—a celebration of the relationship and who created it, a celebration of who he is and what he has created, a celebration of life and meaning and forgiveness and heaven. When the Father invites us to prayer, he issues an invitation to a joyous party.

Prayer, when it is taken too seriously, ceases to be prayer. Rather, it becomes a formal exercise in obeying rules, in being proper, and in doing the religious things that are necessary in order for "prayer" to happen. God went to a lot of trouble to make sure that prayer was something different from that.

Not too long ago I attended a board meeting of a wonderful ministry with which I'm associated. After the formal board meeting, it is the practice of the board to pray specifically for the needs of the staff members. In this ministry, we have a fairly large number of staff members.

The staff member tells the board where he or she has needs and how he or she would like us to pray for them. Generally, one of the board members is assigned to pray for the staff person.

At this particular board meeting for some reason, the floor was opened for board members to pray "as they were led." That sounded like a good idea until it became apparent that several board members wanted to pray for each of the staff members. By eleven o'clock, we were only halfway through the prayer time for the staff members, and I was falling asleep. By the time the clock was moving to midnight, I discovered that I was getting quite hostile. And then, after midnight, I had just about decided to become a Buddhist.

When I got back to the hotel room, I decided that I needed to repent of my "un-Christian" attitude. I said, "Lord, I'm so sorry. I don't think I'm ever going to get any better."

I think he said to me (and if he didn't, it would be like him), "Child, get up. I understand. In fact, I left the meeting before ten."

Sometimes it is possible to take prayer too seriously. And, not only that, the Holy Spirit says, in Hebrew of course, "chill out!"

In what follows I want to use six biblical images that call to mind the celebratory aspect of prayer: a loved child, a freed slave, a recovered patient, a welcomed prodigal, a victorious soldier, and a party guest.

A Story of Answered Prayer

God's Puppy

I was worrying about what to get my father-in-law, Earl, for his birthday. My husband and the family didn't offer any suggestions. My motto is that if it is enough to worry about, then it is enough to pray about it. So I asked God to tell me what to get Earl for his birthday.

It seemed that God said I should get him a dog. A dog?

I asked my husband and his sister, and they said that Dad would love a dog but that Mom would have a cow!

Well, I didn't want my mother-in-law to birth any calves, so I opted for some silly something. Then I asked my mother-in-law, "What would you have done if I had gotten Earl a dog for his birthday?"

"Why, we would have loved it," she said.

I told my husband, Dennis, that God had some reason for Earl to get a dog and that we needed to get him a dog for Christmas. As Christmas drew near, I began to worry about where to find this dog. Do I go to the pet stores, the animal shelter, the newspaper ads? Where do I find this dog? Oops . . . I am worrying . . . time to start praying.

A few days later, a patient came in and said, "Hey, doc, do you want a pup?"

I laughed and said, "Yes, I do." I knew that that was the dog God had picked out. Now I am thinking that this is probably a mutt or a stray or something. But it was a six-month-old Yorkshire terrier with papers, and the patient just gave him to me.

On Christmas Eve, I gave the dog to my father-in-law. Only God could have pulled that one off. That dog is my in-laws' baby! We call him God's Puppy. (That puppy helped my mother-in-law deal with her depression over placing her mother in a nursing home more than anything or anyone could have.)

—Sharon B.

A Loved Child

Recently I was flying home from New York to Orlando, and I had a rather harrowing experience because of the great number of thunderstorms in the area. My seat was next to a young mother whose small son sat in her lap during the whole trip. I was quite frightened but managed to hide my fear from the other people on the plane who were quite frightened and managing to hide their fear from me. The most interesting thing about the whole trip was the little boy. He wasn't frightened at all. He and his mother had a wonderful time. They played together, laughed at the "bumps," and during the most turbulent time of the storm, slept in one another's arms. That's the way prayer ought to be. As I watched the mother and child in the storm, I thought of the prayer of the psalmist:

> LORD, my heart is not haughty,
> Nor my eyes lofty.
> Neither do I concern myself with great matters,
> Nor with things too profound for me.
>
> Surely I have calmed and quieted my soul,
> Like a weaned child with his mother;
> Like a weaned child is my soul within me.
>
> O Israel, hope in the LORD
> From this time forth and forever. (Ps. 131)

Sometimes we are so busy trying to do it right that we forget that rules are never the primary reality of the love of a parent for a child. The little boy on the airplane didn't go through a checklist of things that needed to be done in order to go to sleep in his mother's arms in the middle of the storm. He didn't ask forgiveness for all the bad things he had done the day before, nor did he tell his mother how wonderful she was. He was with his mother, and he just went to sleep.

People are always asking me how to stay awake in their prayers. They will say something like, "I simply can't stay awake. I start off well, but then I find myself drifting, and before I know it, I'm asleep. When I wake up, I feel so guilty." Why? Guilty for sleeping in your Father's arms? Is there something wrong with that? Something that is impious, something that violates the rules? If you fall asleep in your Father's arms, you probably needed to sleep more than you needed to talk. If he needs to talk, he'll wake you up.

A Freed Slave

Paul wrote to the Galatians, "Stand fast therefore in the liberty by which Christ has made us free, and do not be entangled again with a yoke of bondage" (Gal. 5:1). Those words reference the way we were (in bondage) and what we have become (freed slaves).

We believers sometimes forget that we have been set free. Freedom scares us, and more important, it scares those religious leaders who are into control. Jesus said, "If the Son makes you free, you shall be free indeed" (John 8:36). We want to change that, to create some parameters, and to ameliorate the "dangers" of the freedom Jesus gives. When we do that, we miss the joys of being free from the bondage of our slavery to rules and manipulation.

The freedom given us by God has some tremendous implications for our times of prayer. It means, for instance, that while God is God, he doesn't crack the whip and load on the guilt in order to keep us in line. A lot of people don't pray because of the guilt they feel about what they have done, and then they don't pray because of the guilt they feel about not having prayed. If you have never prayed, you are still free . . . so now you can pray.

Being free enables us to go to God without the need to act like proper slaves. When the writer of Hebrews says that we have been given the privilege of coming "boldly" into God's presence, he is making reference to the fact that we come as a son or a daughter—not a slave.

Being free means that, in prayer, we don't have to work for "slave's wages." We are going to talk later about the power of prayer, but for now we need to remember that the bounty of the King is often reserved, not for his slaves, but for his children.

Being free means that we don't have to worry about every word and every thought that is uttered in the presence of God. My family and I once took in a German shepherd, Calvin, who had been beaten horribly by his previous owner. The dog was okay with my wife and daughters but was always frightened of me. Evidently, he had been abused by a male owner. When I would come into the house, Calvin would run and hide. If I raised my voice about anything, Calvin felt that it was directed at him and would cower.

I did everything I knew to win Calvin's friendship. I never disciplined him, I never struck him, and I always gave him treats. It took months to gain his trust. It was a gradual process. I would be reading the paper in the evening, and I would feel a nudge at my elbow. I would turn around, and Calvin would flee to the other side of the room. I would compliment him on his courage and go back to reading the paper, and before long I would feel another nudge at my elbow. I'd turn, and once again Calvin would flee . . . but this time not so far. Over an extended period of time he came closer, until finally I was able to pet him or scratch behind his ear without his fear being the predominant trait in the relationship.

There are people who pray like that: "God, if I say what I think, will you strike me down with a lightning bolt? If I relax a bit, will you be angry? If I'm not perfect, will you kick me out? If I say the wrong thing, can I still be your slave?" God says, "Stop it! You aren't a slave. Quit acting like one."

A Story of Answered Prayer

Directions from Above

It was our first time in Turkey. My husband, Knute, and I were about to test the truth that God is always with us. We had just landed in Istanbul, and we were all alone.

We were tired and, after a couple of tries, we couldn't find a place to stay for the night. We finally walked into a hotel that was able to get us a reservation at another hotel—Hotel Istanbul—but we had to walk there.

Given directions, we began walking, but I became leery of the scenery. The farther we walked, the more uncomfortable I became. I was scared . . . really scared. Nervously, we took out our map to see where we were.

Everyone had taken notice of us, and one Turkish man approached us and asked if he could help. We didn't want to create an incident or show our true inward trepidation, so Knute asked him if he knew where the hotel was.

He said, "Oh, sure. I can take you there. But first, have you eaten? Come and eat with me, and then I will show you the hotel."

My husband said that we weren't hungry. I became more anxious as those around us appeared more hostile. If we ran, it would only create a reason for them to chase us or accuse us of whatever they wanted, and we knew no one.

"Come with me," he was more forceful this time.

I was now more terrified than ever because he had his arm out pointing down a back alley.

Knute lied, "We have friends waiting for us, and if we don't arrive soon, they will come looking for us."

God, help us, silently but desperately I pleaded with Jesus, *Please help us.*

The man became more insistent and pulled on our arms.

Suddenly, a very tall and rather large man appeared beside us and asked what the problem was. We both looked up to him, he was so tall. My husband quickly told him we were looking for Hotel Istanbul.

"It is this way," is all he said. He took off walking so fast and taking such large steps, that we had to run to keep up with him. We didn't look back as he took us back the way we had come, and while we stood on the street corner, he stood behind us and pointed toward the left. "Do you see that travel agency up one block? Turn right. The hotel is down half a block on the left."

We turned to thank him, but he was gone. We looked in stores, doors, and alleys where he could have disappeared, but he was nowhere to be found. We were standing on the corner and could see in all four directions, yet as quickly as it took us to turn around, he had gone.

He had said he was half Turk and half Australian, but where did he come from and where did he go? We don't know, but we thanked God for answering our cry for help in such a unique way in such a unique place.

—Angie F.

A Recovered Patient

Third, the Bible speaks of us as recovered patients. Jesus called himself the Physician and, in giving his own self-definition, he quoted from the prophet Isaiah: "The Spirit of the Lord is upon Me, because He has anointed Me to preach the gospel to the poor; He has sent Me to heal the brokenhearted, to proclaim liberty to the captives and recovery of sight to the blind, to set at liberty those who are oppressed; to proclaim the acceptable year of the Lord" (Luke 4:18–19).

I have a friend who had a terrible scar on his hand. Some Christians prayed about the scar, and over a period of time, the scar disappeared. His witness was not very sophisticated, but it had a reality that was refreshing. He would say to anybody who would listen, "You want to see what my Father did for me?" And then he would show them his hand.

Real prayer, when it is properly understood, is a place of emotional and sometimes physical healing. God's unconditional love allows for honesty, acceptance, and resolution.

A WELCOMED PRODIGAL

You remember Jesus' story. A man had two sons, and the younger son asked for his inheritance before his daddy had assumed room temperature. The father granted the request. Then the son went to another country and, while the money lasted, had a wild time. However, when the money was gone, he had no place to go. He lived on wages from a menial job, hardly enough to put food on his table. Then he decided that he would go ask his father for a job. *Surely,* he thought, *as demeaning as it would be, my father could always use a good hired hand, and I would certainly do better than I'm doing now. I'll ask him to forgive my horrible actions and rebellious attitude, and then I'll ask him for a job.*

Jesus said that the father saw his son coming down the road and ran to him, interrupting the young man's confession and apology. Jesus said, "But the father said to his servants, 'Bring out the best robe and put it on him, and put a ring on his hand and sandals on his feet. And bring the fatted calf here and kill it, and let us eat and be merry; for this my son was dead and is alive again; he was lost and is found'" (Luke 15:22–24).

That story has wonderful implications for those who have left and are afraid to come home. I suspect that there are as many believers who have rebelled as there are people who never believed. I meet them all the time. Someone told them that God was going to destroy them, that he was angry, that he would never use them again, that he would never forgive them. And they believed it! You can see them hovering just outside the warmth of the fire, standing in the street looking at the old home place, and sometimes turning away so that those inside will not see the tears. They are often hungry, lonely, afraid, guilty, and sure that they can never go home again.

I have a friend who has two boys and a girl. One of his sons left home a number of years ago, and my friend doesn't even know where he is. One time I asked him which of his children he loved the most. "No father can answer a question like that," he said. "I love all my children." Then, thinking for a moment, he referred to his lost son, and I noticed that he was working at holding back the tears as he said, "But I do love Jimmy more than I can say."

When Lincoln was asked what he was going to do about the South after the Civil War, he said, "It will be as if they never left." God says that too. The joyous announcement that the Bible makes to those of you who are just outside the warmth of the fire, who are standing in the street, and who are about to turn away and run again is this: "Come on home! He'll love you! It will be as if you never left."

A Victorious Soldier

When the apostle John saw the end of all things, he wrote, "He said to me, 'It is done! I am the Alpha and the Omega, the Beginning and the End. I will give of the fountain of the water of life freely to him who thirsts. He who overcomes shall inherit all things, and I will be his God and he shall be My son'" (Rev. 21:6–7). Paul spoke of the ultimate end of all things: "God also has highly exalted Him and given Him the name which is above every name, that at the name of Jesus every knee should bow, of those in heaven, and of those on earth, and of those under the earth, and that every tongue should confess that Jesus Christ is Lord, to the glory of God the Father" (Phil. 2:9–11).

There is a wonderful story about Elisha when the king of Syria sent horses and chariots and a great army to Dothan to get the prophet. Elisha's servant was frightened when he saw the great army of Syria, and he said to Elisha, "Now, we are in trouble . . . real trouble." Then Elisha said something to his servant that every prayer warrior knows. He said, "Don't worry. Our army is greater than their army." The servant looked around and said, "What have you been smoking? It's just you and me." (Well, maybe that isn't exactly what he said, but it was something like that.)

The text reads: "Elisha prayed, and said, 'LORD, I pray, open his eyes that he may see.' Then the LORD opened the eyes of the young man, and he saw. And behold, the mountain was full of horses and chariots of fire all around Elisha" (2 Kings 6:17).

One of the problems with our prayers is that we think of ourselves as losers praying to a loser God. After all, how many legions does God have? The other side controls the media, the political institutions, and the money. But, we reason, it is better to be a loser in a righteous cause than to be a winner in an unrighteous cause. It is no wonder that our prayers are so somber and pitiful.

The truth is that the Bible says we are winners in a righteous cause, and that is even better than being losers in a righteous cause. The Bible teaches that the battle has already been fought, and our side won.

I have two friends who drive Mercedes (albeit, used ones). One time when we were all serving on a committee together, I noted their fancy cars in the parking lot of the hotel where we were meeting. I decided to kid my friends about the cars they drove. I said, "I can't believe you guys! And you call yourselves men of God! With all of the starving people in the world, you guys are driving Mercedes!"

One of them, without even looking up, said, "We work for a first-class God. Who do you work for? Buddha?"

We sometimes do forget who we work for, don't we? We sometimes forget about the "chariots of fire" and the defeated foe. That's the reason we are so intense and sour. But we don't have to be so uptight. It is already over; the outcome is decided; the smoke has cleared and we are still standing. Our prayers need to reflect the victory, not the cries of those who have no hope except the hope of failure.

Have you ever listened to soldiers talk about former battles where they were victorious? Heaven will be heaven because it will be the place where old, battle-scarred soldiers share the war stories. But we don't have to wait until then. You can celebrate now because you know how the story will end and how the contest will be scored. It is the message of Revelation—God wins!

Losers pray prayers of fear and grief. Victorious soldiers hardly ever do.

A Story of Answered Prayer

A Delivery Angel

My husband and I have been married for almost twenty-six years. In 1983, we had the first of our nine children. Up until the last pregnancy, all were very uneventful and textbook. In 1999, we found ourselves expecting for the eighth time . . . and we were having twins, due in September.

By April, I began having contractions, and by the end of May, the doctor put me on complete bed rest. We needed to keep them in there as long as possible. We had prayed for twins since our first pregnancy.

On July 12, I went to the hospital because I couldn't feel any movement. However, everything was fine, and they sent me home.

On July 14, I woke up feeling really strange. I couldn't describe it. I am probably the most laid-back person in the world, but that day I was so restless and nervous. I took a shower for about an hour and a half. The whole time, I just cried out to Jesus! I just kept saying over and over, "Please, make my babies be safe!"

A few hours later, I began to contract. I was only at thirty-three weeks. The doctor told me to come on in—even though he thought it was nothing. We got to the hospital and had been there an hour and a half when things started happening! The placenta of one of the babies separated from the uterine wall. Suddenly, he was without oxygen, and I was bleeding out. They took me to the operating room. My doctor wasn't even there. The doctors who were there had come in only because they had an early gynecological procedure the next morning. Talk about the providential care of God!

Anyway, my poor husband was left out in the hall because they didn't know if there would be life or death. He counted the doctors and nurses going in and out. He counted four male doctors and two female nurses.

They did an emergency C-section, and both Park and Zach were eventually thriving. They were only in the hospital for seventeen days.

After it was all over, my husband went around thanking nurses, doctors, and the anesthesiologist. But he could never find the fourth doctor! They said there had only been two doctors and the anesthesiologist—not a fourth man present. We are convinced we experienced our fourth man in the fire—like in the story of Shadrach, Meshach, and Abednego in the fiery furnace!

Park and Zach are now eight years old and in the third grade. They are so wonderful and have completed our family in such an awesome way. Just the other night, Zach came into my bedroom and asked me to help him become a Christian. I got the privilege of leading my "lost" baby to Christ. Isn't God good and faithful!

—Tam N.

A Party Guest

Finally, the Bible says that we are guests at a party. There is, of course, the marriage supper of the Lamb (see Rev. 19:17) to which Jesus referred at the final supper with his disciples on earth (see Luke 22:16). But there is also the present relationship we have with Christ. When Jesus and his disciples were criticized for their joy, Jesus said, "Can the friends of the bridegroom mourn as long as the bridegroom is with them?" (Matt. 9:15). Did you ever realize that the first miracle Jesus performed in his earthly ministry was turning water to wine in order to salvage a party? (see John 2:1–10).

The father's welcome for the prodigal son did not come with the requirement that the boy get on his knees, don a hair shirt, and for the rest of his life wear the *P* brand of a prodigal. In fact, the breathtaking response of the father is almost too good to be true. He had a party!

Now, let's do some biblical exegesis of that story from Luke 15. A careful reading of the text will show that the story isn't really about the young man who went away to the far country. That boy is just a literary technique that Jesus used to say something to the good, righteous, and proper religious folks who listened to the story. The parable is really about the other brother who stayed home, did everything right, never rebelled, and worked hard. That boy had an attitude problem not dissimilar to those who pray according to the rules and who assume that because of their goodness and their obedience they have earned the right to make demands on the Father.

Listen, if you will, to the words of the obedient son who stayed home. Jesus said that when the son heard the music and dancing, he refused to come to the party. He said, "Lo, these many years I have been serving you; I never transgressed your commandment at any time; and yet you never gave me a young goat, that I might make merry with my friends. But as soon as this son of yours came, who has devoured your livelihood with harlots, you killed the fatted calf for him" (Luke 15:29–30).

It still goes on, you know? "Mature" Christians beat you over the head with their righteousness, stifle your joyous prayers, and speak of propriety and prayer.

She had come out of the Jesus Movement. That meant she had first come out of the drug culture and had found something far better than drugs. There was a wonderful freshness about her as she stood before the congregation and prayed. But nobody told her about the language of prayer, about the seriousness of the enterprise, about the "fear" of God. She wanted to sing and dance and laugh before the God who had found her, and she just couldn't understand why everyone didn't feel that way. So her prayer, by the measurement of the Mature Christians, was not a very good prayer. She thought about God and what he had done, and she started laughing. It didn't last long, though. They got her and gave her their disease. They forced her into their mold, and God wept as she prayed longer prayers with far less meaning.

Don't let them do it! If you get too serious, you will miss the joy, the celebration, and the abandonment.

I was speaking for a church recently where the service was being televised. After the service a man handed me a note and said, "Don't read it now. Read it later and pray about it." Let me give you the exact quote from the note (and I'm not making this up):

Dear Sir,

You rightly said that you are a sinner too. When you started praying, you casually leaned with your right elbow onto the side of the pulpit. Later, while still praying, you casually folded your arms. By the time you finished your prayer, your left hand was in the pocket of your trousers. Yes, when a new preacher comes, some of us might look at him a little bit longer. Perhaps I should have closed my eyes while you prayed; but in all honesty, when we pray and when we talk to the mighty and glorious King of kings and Lord of lords, shouldn't we give Him the honor He deserves and pray in humility, especially when hundreds of people are watching in the congregation and thousands on television?

A Brother in Christ

When I first read that note, I was angry. Nobody likes criticism. I wanted to give him a piece of my mind. But the man had already left the church, and I couldn't find anyone who knew him. That was probably best, because my mind would not have been the "mind of Christ," and I would have said things then that would have hurt the man.

But time has passed, and I have prayed for him often. Although I doubt it, there is a possibility he is reading this book. If not, there may be others like him who are reading it. Let me say to him and to them:

You missed it! You've been so busy doing it right that you never noticed that God was trying to get your attention . . . to tell you that he loved you. Your prayers have been a religious exercise, and while God was pleased with your efforts, he was distressed with your pain. He said that it didn't come from him. He told me to tell you to listen; he wanted to tell you a joke.

In John Bunyan's *The Pilgrim's Progress,* Christiana hears Mercy laugh in her sleep and asks her why. Mercy says that she had a dream, and in the dream she was dirty, dressed in rags, bemoaning her hardness of heart. Then an angel came to her and asked her what was wrong, and she told him.

Mercy then describes what happened next:

> Now when he had heard me make my complaint, he said, "Peace be to thee." He also wiped mine eyes with his Handkerchief, and clad me in Silver and Gold; he put a Chain about my Neck, and Earrings in mine Ears, and a beautiful Crown upon my Head. Then he took me by the Hand, and said, "Mercy, come after me." So he went up, and I followed, til we came at a Golden Gate. Then he knocked; and when they within had opened, the man went in, and I followed him up to a Throne, upon which one sat, and he said to me, "Welcome, Daughter." The place looked bright and twinkling like the stars, or rather like the Sun, and I thought that I saw your Husband there. So I awoke from my Dream. But did I laugh?[2]

I'm not a charismatic who speaks in tongues, but I understand. We Presbyterians aren't sure that dancing is appropriate anywhere, much less before the throne of the God of the universe. I certainly don't shout very much because I always think prayer is supposed to be done quietly, "decently, and in order." But listen: sometimes I have trouble keeping my feet from dancing, and my voice from shouting when I think about him and his love.

NINE

It's a Family Kind of Thing

Great souls by instinct to each other turn,
Demand alliance, and in friendship burn.
—Joseph Addison, English essayist and poet

Prayers travel more strongly when said in unison.
—Petronius

In prayer one should always unite oneself
with the community.
—The Talmud

AMERICANS ARE RADICAL INDIVIDUALISTS. I am too. One day a second-grade teacher asked her class, "Can anyone tell me something that is here now that wasn't here twenty years ago?"

A little girl in the front row raised her hand and said, "Me!"

Part of the greatness of America is the value the culture places on the individual. Individualism is a good thing, and I don't want anyone to think that anything I'm about to say minimizes the value I place on the value Americans place on individualism. Just so you know, I sometimes visit Newport Beach, and whenever I'm there, I stop in the street and bow three times in front of the home where John Wayne lived. But you know what?

Our individualism is going to kill us.

Our cultural proclivities of "looking out for number one," of measuring all values by personal values, and of thinking *if it feels good do it* do not bode well for our nation. Nathan Hale, the Revolutionary patriot who was hanged while spying behind British lines and who said on the scaffold just before his death, "I only regret that I have but one life to lose for my country," would be considered by many today to be a fool. Our cry would be, "I have one life, it is mine, and I will spend it on myself."

Charles Sykes has expressed the temper of our time this way:

> Something extraordinary is happening in American society. Crisscrossed by invisible trip wires of emotional, racial, sexual, and psychological grievance American life is increasingly characterized by the plaintive insistence, I am a victim.[1]

While I'm concerned about the increasing and selfish individualism of America, I'm far more concerned when I see it in the family of God. And for our purposes here, I am concerned when I see it in myself and in our prayers. The "It's you and me, God, against the world" kind of prayer will destroy genuine prayer, and it is important that we spend some time talking about the community implications of prayer. While individual prayer is important, if the "prayer closet" is the sole definition of our efforts, we are going to miss something very important and powerful about prayer. Prayer really is a family kind of thing.

I love to read and learn from the desert fathers; John of the Cross and Teresa of Ávila have much to teach us; Brother Lawrence inspires me to worship while doing things I thought were trivial. But in all of them and their ways of praying there is something vital missing: an us factor. Contemplative prayer, as pleasant as it is, must have a connection to the family, or it will produce cranky hermits who make Scrooge look benevolent. Not only that, prayer is robbed of its power when its focus is directed only toward an individual and his or her God.

Once there was a contemplative who struggled to spend time alone with God. Finally finding the time, she was on her knees in prayer when there was a knock on the door. She tried to ignore it, but the knock grew louder. Finally, asking God's leave, she went to the door only to discover that no one was there. When she returned to her prayers, she asked forgiveness for having left. God replied, "Had you not answered the door, I would not have remained."

Almost always prayers have repercussions beyond the individual. The one who prays will often become the answer to the prayer. The Christian who prays for solutions to urban problems will often find that he or she is sent to work in the city. Prayers for racial reconciliation are often answered more by people reaching across racial lines than by a supernatural change in the racists' views and actions. Serious prayer for missions will often produce from those who pray more missionaries than money. Prayer that ends with the individual is never "real" prayer. Prayer is a family kind of thing.

It is no accident that when the disciples asked Jesus how to pray, he taught them a corporate prayer replete with plural pronouns. It is also no accident that when Jesus followed that corporate prayer with commentary, the one thing he emphasized was a proper relationship with others (Matt. 6:9–15). Jesus constantly emphasized the connection between believers and the power that flowed from relationships. If we miss the truths Jesus wanted us to know about corporate prayer, we will be "the sound of one hand clapping."

In this chapter I want to give you some biblical truths about prayer and its connection to the family of God, but first I want to give you a major, organizing biblical principle. It is this: when God calls one, he always calls a bunch.

Our individualistic, American viewpoint misses how often the Bible talks about covenants—covenants that are generally made between God and a people as opposed to a person. Paul says that the family covenant, even if it is made with only one person in the family, is such that the whole family is "sanctified" and the children are called "holy" (1 Cor. 7:14). God did not call Abraham only to a personal relationship. He called an entire nation to that relationship (see Gen. 12:1–3). When the Philippian jailer was called to Christ, Paul and Silas told him that all he had to do was believe and he and his entire household would be saved (see Acts 16:31). Over and over again the biblical promises that believers apply to themselves are not individual promises at all. They are covenant promises given to a people, a family, or a nation.

The point is this: when we came to belief, we came into a family. It is a family so connected that the Bible says the only thing to which it can be compared is the human body (see 1 Cor. 12:12–27). Within that body, my tears ought to create the taste of salt in your mouth. When my heart is broken, you will bleed. When you are afraid, my hand will shake. When I'm lonely, you will feel the loss. When you are in trouble, there will be perspiration on my upper lip. We really are one in a supernatural and very real way.

In that kind of context, individual prayer alone is not only wrong, it is impossible.

I know. I know. It doesn't feel that way much of the time. There is nothing worse than a church fight. Overnight, very nice, kind, loving Christians become serial killers. Not only that, but many churches would rather have a program than a prayer, and softball generally draws more folks than a prayer meeting.

Paul Reese, the late missionary statesman, tells a story about a Christian church in Korea where, at a church congregational meeting, there was strong division. The division led to a church fight that was so bad the police had to be called. One of the policemen, a Buddhist, was heard above the noise of the fight, shouting, "Why don't you people act like Christians?" Well, we don't sometimes, and that is the reason our prayers can be so empty, formal, and staid.

The late Francis Schaeffer, whose books have touched thousands of people, said this about corporate prayer:

> Prayer now becomes something more than merely an abstract religious, devotional act. It is a place where the Church is the Church, and where Christ is in the midst in a special, definite, and real way. Organization is not wrong; let us say this with force. Organization is clearly commanded in the Word of God, and it is needed in a fallen world. But it becomes wrong if it stands in the way of the conscious relationship of the Church to Christ. Simplicity of organization is therefore to be preferred, though at the same time it is all too easy to get one's eyes fixed on simplicity of organization and forget the reason for simplicity, which is that Christ may truly be the Head of the Church.[2]

I'm an "old cynical preacher" and have been working in the church for a very long time. And, frankly, that hasn't always been a great experience. Every time an unbeliever points to some flaw in the church as an excuse for why he won't have anything to do with it, I want to say (and have, often), "You don't know anything. You think the church is screwed up? You have no idea how really screwed up it is! I could tell you stories of hypocrisy, selfishness, and condemnation that would keep you up at night . . . and some of those stories are about me."

Augustine said (in a variety of ways) that the church was a prostitute but, nevertheless, his mother. If you've been in the church and a part of the covenant people of God for very long, you know exactly what he's talking about. The church is an "ugly" bride . . . but she is his bride. And prayer has to do with the Bride of Christ. In fact, prayer, without its corporate and family implications, is often shallow and ineffective.

The old cliché said, "The family that prays together, stays together." There is truth to that, and it is true of Christians praying together too. When Christians pray together, not only do they stay together, but their prayers have power and are vibrant; they make a difference in the lives of those who pray.

Now let's examine the principle that when God calls a man or woman, he calls a bunch, and see how that works out in the specifics of prayer.

A Story of Answered Prayer

A Friend in Need

I was awakened one night at exactly 11:55 p.m. Not knowing exactly why I woke up so suddenly and clearly, I asked the Lord why. Suddenly a picture of a friend came to my mind. I instinctively started praying for him, asking God to be with him—whatever his situation.

About a week later I was shopping, when I saw my friend walking down an aisle. We started talking. He told me that he was going through a divorce and was having a difficult time. He started to tell me about a life-and-death situation he was in before I stopped him. I said, "When was this?" He answered, and then I told him about God's waking me up at exactly 11:55 that same night, how I had prayed, and what I prayed before going back to sleep.

My friend told me he had driven up to a high cliff in the mountains that night. He had planned on jumping off the cliff, committing suicide. He said he went to the edge of the cliff and looked at his watch. It was exactly 11:55. At that moment he said, "God forgive me, but I have to end the pain." At that very same moment, he had the feeling of huge arms wrapping around him, keeping him from jumping. At midnight, he fell to his knees and asked God to forgive him. He turned back to his car, tore up the suicide note, and went home.

—Ron J.

How God Spreads Out the Gifts

First, one of the clear teachings of the Bible is that God gifts people in different ways. Paul talks about the gifts of the spirit in Romans 12, 1 Corinthians 12, and Ephesians 4. The Bible teaches that every believer has a gift, and that gift is to be used for the entire body of Christ. When the people of God are together, then they are complete. Now, to extrapolate from that, let me tell you at least one of the reasons God spreads out the gifts. He does it so that the heavy load of what the church does in the world will be shared among Christians.

When I first became a pastor, the immediate thing that impressed me about the job was that it couldn't be done. I was expected to be an administrator, a secretary, a Bible teacher, a motivational speaker, a youth director, a janitor, a psychologist, and a chaplain . . . and I just couldn't do it. I felt like a mosquito in a nudist colony—I had so much ground to cover, I didn't know where to begin. In fact, it was worse than that. I knew what to do, but I didn't know how to do it. I could fake it, of course, and I did that for a long time, until I realized that I wasn't called to fake it. God had gifted different people in the congregation so that, when we were working together, all that needed to be done was done.

Prayer works exactly the same way. Praying isn't easy business. It will cost you time and tears. Just as God gave gifts so that Christians would share the load, he has called Christians to come together and share the load of prayer.

One of the most difficult things about being a pastor was the loneliness of prayer. To this day I bear secrets that I can never tell anyone. People would tell me about their sin, their pain, their dysfunctions, their abuse, and their backgrounds, and they would ask me to pray. Because I could tell no one, I ended up being the only one who prayed for those particular needs. How often I would have liked to have had some others helping with the load of prayer.

Perhaps you are carrying too much in your own life. Only you and God know the secrets. God didn't want you to be the only one. You need a friend with whom to pray. You need to spread the load out. The Bible says that we are to "bear one another's burdens" (Gal. 6:2), and you can't do that if you don't share one another's burdens. Burdens are shared because the prayer load simply is too heavy for one person. That may be the reason God allows the load to be heavy, that we might reach out to others who will share the burden.

God's Corporate Address

But second, when God calls a bunch, he resides in their midst. First Corinthians 3:16 is often used inappropriately to get Christian friends or family members to quit smoking, to exercise, and to eat more spinach: "Do you not know that you are the temple of God and that the Spirit of God dwells in you?"

Let me tell you why that verse is used inappropriately in

getting people to take care of their bodies. Paul is not talking about the human body, but the body of Christ. The "you" in the text is plural. It should read (if you are from the South where English is used properly), "Y'all are the temple of God and the Spirit of God dwells in y'all."

Now let me show you one more thing about that verse. The word translated into English as "temple" doesn't mean the entire temple. There was another Greek word Paul could have used to say that. The word Paul used is the word for the most holy and sacred place in the temple, the Holy of Holies or the Most Holy Place. If you are familiar with the Old Testament, you know that the Holy of Holies was only visited once a year on the Day of Atonement and then only by the high priest. You also know that the ark of the covenant was there and that the ark was the resident place of God himself.

Now you begin to see the amazing and wonderful statement Paul is making in 1 Corinthians 3:16. He is saying that God's resident place is in the midst of his people. He is saying that the people of God (corporately) are now the Holy of Holies, the place where God chooses to make his residence. Once we understand what Paul is saying, the ancient words of invocation from the prophet Habakkuk take on new meaning: "The LORD is in His holy temple. Let all the earth keep silence before Him" (Hab. 2:20).

Along this line, listen to the astonishing words of Jesus: "Where two or three are gathered together in My name, I am there in the midst of them" (Matt. 18:20). In other words, there is something very special that happens when God's people come together to pray.

Practically, all of this means that the reason the church will never die isn't because the church is that wonderful or the people of God good or pure. It is because the church is the resident place for the God of the universe. And even more important, when the people of God come together to worship, the ushers need to count One more. It means that worship is not a performance for the congregation, it is a performance for the God who is in residence. It means that corporate prayer does not mean individuals coming together to pray individual prayers but rather a group of people who because they are together are themselves the place where God resides.

A Story of Answered Prayer

A Child Goes Home

I was a physical-therapy student and was working in the burn ward at my hospital to gain expertise for my thesis on wound care. One of my patients was quite elderly and had deep burns over half of her skin surface. Her burns had become infected to the point that her lower leg had to be amputated. Long-standing arthritis was particularly painful. The wall opposite the foot of her bed was covered with get-well cards—most of them with Bible verses.

One beautiful morning, as I was walking to work, I talked with the Lord about this patient. I prayed, "Lord, I think she is your child. If she truly is, won't you end her suffering and take her home to be with you? If she is not, let her live, touch her heart, and give me the words to lead her to you."

I arrived at the hospital and was "scrubbing in" when the nurse came and told me, "Don't bother, she just passed away."

Every time I think God isn't listening or doesn't care, I remember that day. I hope to meet this sister in heaven.

—Susan S.

Two Are Better than One

Third, when God calls a bunch, he sometimes doesn't respond except to the bunch. Listen to what God said to Solomon: "If My people who are called by My name will humble themselves, and pray and seek My face, and turn from their wicked ways, then I will hear from heaven, and will forgive their sin and heal their land" (2 Chron. 7:14). That verse reflects the great power of God moving at the request of the people of God. Of course, God hears and answers when one person prays, but there is a phenomenal effect when a bunch pray.

Listen again to the words of Jesus: "Assuredly, I say to you, whatever you bind on earth will be bound in heaven, and whatever you loose on earth will be loosed in heaven. Again I say to you that if two of you agree on earth concerning anything that they ask, it will be done for them by My Father in heaven. For where two or three are gathered together in My name, I am there in the midst of them" (Matt. 18:18–20).

I'm one of the few Calvinists who, when I was a pastor, conducted regular healing services. I had been praying about the words of James to the effect that if anyone was sick, they should call the elders and the elders would anoint them with oil and pray and the sick would be made well (see James 5:13–15). The elders of the church I was serving at the time often anointed with oil and prayed for the sick, but only in private. The plan that I presented to the elders was that we do the anointing and the praying in public worship.

It has been said that Presbyterians have to be careful how they do something the first time, because they are going to be doing it that way for the next two hundred years. So it took some convincing to persuade the elders that the plan was of God.

Before we instituted the services, I taught for a number of weeks about what the Bible says about God's people praying for the sick. I explained to the congregation that things would be done "decently and in order." (I did say, referring to a dear lady who was paraplegic, "If Patti gets out of that wheelchair, however; I *will* speak in tongues.")

The healing services took place at Holy Communion. People came forward to receive the elements of Communion, and those who desired prayer from the elders would remain. The elders would, in teams, go to those people, anoint them with oil, and pray for them. I asked those who were not being prayed for to quietly remain in their seats and pray for those who were being anointed by the elders.

The response to these services was astounding. In the first service the auditorium was packed, and we ran out of anointing oil. The service was, of course, Presbyterian, but you could hear people quietly weeping in their pews as they prayed for their brothers and sisters. The experience of God's presence in those services was so real that at any moment I fully expected to hear the rustle of angels' wings. We saw God's amazing answers to prayer. A little girl scheduled for surgery was examined just before the surgery, and the problem had disappeared. A man who had suffered with arthritis for almost twenty years was completely healed. (His wife told me, "He is usually the skeptic, but I keep asking him, 'Are you sure it's gone? Are you sure?'") We saw people recover from health problems, spiritual struggles, and relational difficulties that had existed for years.

But here is the important thing for the purposes of this chapter. All of the people who were prayed for in those services had been prayed for before, but when the family of God prayed together, there was an amazing and wonderful visitation of God. God was teaching us something important. He was teaching us to pray together; he was teaching us that he bends down low and listens to the sound of his people praying together.

Coming Clean with One Another

Fourth, when a group of believers prays, it becomes a place of accountability. Scripture says, "Confess your trespasses to one another, and pray for one another, that you may be healed" (James 5:16). Paul wrote to the church at Galatia, "Brethren, if a man is overtaken in any trespass, you who are spiritual restore such a one in a spirit of gentleness, considering yourself lest you also be tempted. Bear one another's burdens, and so fulfill the law of Christ. For if anyone thinks himself to be something, when he is nothing, he deceives himself" (Gal. 6:1–3).

We are so prone to denial that the only way we can remain honest is to pray together. I have found that the one place where I can be totally honest is in prayer. I can lie to everyone else, but when I am before the throne, he simply doesn't allow it. That kind of honesty carries over in corporate prayer.

I have a friend who was the pastor of a church where there had been very destructive division and hostility. He had tried preaching, politicking, and pleading, but nothing seemed to help. One time my friend, while on vacation, invited the leader of a Christian organization to preach as his substitute. When my friend returned from vacation, he called the man who had substituted for him and asked how it had gone. The man said, "I don't know if I have ever experienced such hostility in a congregation. I asked a number of the people to pray with me about it, and they refused. When people refuse to pray together, you've got a very serious problem."

Why do you suppose those Christians who were so angry refused to pray? Let me tell you. They knew that once they stood before the throne of God together, they would have to be honest and change, and they didn't want to change. Their reaction to prayer was not dissimilar to the man on his deathbed who told his wife, "After I'm gone, call your brother and tell him that I forgive him. But make sure I'm dead before you call him."

Corporate prayer is one of God's ways of bringing Christians together and keeping them honest with one another. I can pretend to you that I am good, pure, wonderful, kind, loving, spiritual, honorable, committed, and obedient. But don't ask me to pray with you. When we pray together, I have to take my mask off, and I've grown quite comfortable wearing it.

I believe that Promise Keepers is one of the healthiest movements in America. This is an organization where men covenant together to hold one another accountable to be men of integrity. One of the best things about the whole movement and the thing that keeps it from being just more religious drivel is prayer. If they ever stop praying together, Promise Keepers will become just another empty movement where people lie to the world and to one another. As long as they are praying together, however, God will keep them honest.

THE INTERCESSORY CONNECTION

Fifth, God works within a bunch so as to ensure that the connection produces power. Intercessory prayer is the stuff that brings believers together, because when I pray for you, I pray better than when I pray for myself. When you pray for me, you pray better than when you pray for yourself. In fact, God has designed his family in such a way as to bring great blessing to both the intercessor and the "intercessee."

There is an interesting statement in the book of Job. Almost everyone knows the basic story. Job was a good man to whom very bad things happened. He lost everything he loved, all his possessions were taken away, and he suffered horrible physical ailments. Most of the book consists of a philosophical and theological discussion between Job and his friends as to the nature of suffering, the conclusion of the matter being that there is no conclusion of the matter. The answers for the problem are beyond our understanding.

Then God enters the picture in person. Through a series of questions without answers posed to Job, God reveals his greatness and his power. Job's response to the revelation of God is the only proper response of a man or woman before a sovereign God: he decided not to talk so much. He repented of his arrogance and his sin, and God, as everyone knows, created a happy ending to the story by restoring Job's fortunes.

What most people don't notice is a little verse in the last chapter of the book of Job: "The LORD restored Job's losses *when he prayed for his friends.* Indeed the LORD gave Job twice as much as he had before" (Job 42:10). Do you see the connection between intercessory prayer and health and blessing? There has always been that connection. God fixed things that way. We need one another for lots of reasons, and one of the most important is that God listens to his people when they pray for his people.

There is a wonderful story about the difference between heaven and hell. Both places have a lavish banquet table laden with the most sumptuous food for the residents. The problem is that the only eating utensils are ten-foot-long spoons, and the residents are required to eat with the utensils. In hell people starve because they simply can't get the food from the end of the utensil to their mouths. However, in heaven everyone is happy because they are feeding one another. Prayer within the context of the family is like that. We minister to one another with intercessory prayer.

A Story of Answered Prayer

The Master Technician

I used to work as a talk-show host and chief engineer of several northeastern stations. One of my favorite subjects was blasting Christianity. If there wasn't a scandal, I would still cook up derogatory things to say and ridicule those who defended the Word.

At one of my stations, I had an ongoing, intermittent technical problem, which I could only troubleshoot with a component substitution. It was Saturday night when I decided to tackle this problem, and after several hours, at 3:00 a.m., I decided to quit and try again another time. Only problem was that after the last part substitution, I couldn't get the transmitter back on! I tried everything, even waking up my friends and a representative of the transmitter's manufacturer. So here we were, it was rapidly getting close to sign-on time and I had no transmitter—and certainly a manager who would blow his stack! I was at the end of my rope.

At that time, I was not a Christian, but I believe God answers the prayers of a non-Christian if it serves God's purpose. What I knew about God could have been put on a molecule, but I did remember that the best way to pray was to go into a private place. So that's what I did. I took the schematic and spread it out on the men's-room toilet seat and pleaded my case with the Master Technician!

When I finished praying, I left the men's room, and as I rounded the corner into the transmitter room, I turned my head away from my path of travel and focused on a telephone panel behind the transmitter. And there it was! On top of the panel was the part I had removed but failed to put back in! When I saw it, a tingle went through me from head to toe (and no, there was no lighting in the area!). Replacing that part (a capacitor) took five minutes, and we were back on the air!

I should have dropped to my knees on the spot, but no, I chose to wallow in the stench of secularism for a number of years. Finally, I reached the point of needing to deal with what I termed "The Jesus issue" and in 1998 responded to the Invitation.

—Jim T.

CELEBRATION TIME!

Finally, when God calls a bunch to pray, he provides a special joy in the process. It's hard to have a party by yourself. You may like the company for a while, but it turns old on you . . . quickly. Laughter in private eventually sounds hollow, and dancing with oneself will grow wearisome if you do it very long. Prayer is a celebration. Prayer is a party where everybody knows the joke.

Contrary to what you have been told, the heart of the Christian faith is celebration and joy. At the beginning of Luke an angel said to Zacharias, the father of John the Baptist and the "announcer" of Jesus, "Do not be afraid, Zacharias, for your prayer is heard; and your wife Elizabeth will bear you a son, and you shall call his name John. And you will have joy and gladness, and many will rejoice at his birth" (Luke 1:13–14). The angel announced to the shepherds, "Do not be afraid, for behold, I bring you good tidings of great joy which will be to all people. For there is born to you this day in the city of David a Savior, who is Christ the Lord" (Luke 2:10–11).

It is no accident that the message of the New Testament is called the gospel, which means "good news." The corporate worship of God's people is a time when the family gets together to shout and sing the praises of the One who brought them to himself and to one another. The Bible says that "the joy of the LORD is your strength" (Neh. 8:10). Paul expresses the experience of every Christian who has known the beauty of the bunch when he writes, "I thank my God upon every remembrance of you, always in every prayer of mine making request for you all with joy, for your fellowship in the gospel from the first day until now" (Phil. 1:3–5).

Richard Foster points out that Jesus' announcement of the kingdom is rich in the imagery of Jubilee (see Lev. 25), a sabbath year of great joy for God's people.

> The social implications of such a concept are profound. Equally penetrating is the realization that as a result we are called into a perpetual Jubilee of the Spirit. Such a radical, divinely enabled freedom from possessions and a restructuring of social arrangements cannot help but bring celebration. When the poor receive the good news, when the captives are released, when the blind receive their sight, when the oppressed are liberated, who could withhold the shout of Jubilee?
>
> In the Old Testament all of the social stipulations of the year of Jubilee—canceling all debts, releasing slaves, no planting of crops, returning property to the original owner—were a celebration for the gracious provision of God. God could be trusted to provide what is needed. . . . Freedom from anxiety and care forms the basis for celebration. Because we know He cares for us we can cast all our care upon Him. God has turned our mourning into dancing.[3]

I spend a considerable portion of my time traveling and speaking at church functions. I used to think that one could measure the spirituality of those places by the obedience to Scripture manifested in the people or by the seriousness with which they took their religion. There was a time when I felt that my job was to affirm people in the gravity of their enterprise.

I'm a lot older now and a bit wiser, and now I know the truth. If there is no laughter, Jesus has gone somewhere else. If there is no joy and freedom, it is not a church: it is simply a crowd of melancholy people basking in a religious neurosis. If there is no celebration, there is no real worship.

I've found that it is easy to fake most of the things that are Christian. If you aren't a believer and want to be a part of the church, let me tell you how to do it. First, memorize some religious words, and learn how to use them. Second, get a big black Bible and carry it whenever you come to a church meeting. Next, volunteer for everything. And finally, be nice and smile a lot. (Frankly, I have no idea why you would want to do that. Maybe it's the handsome men and beautiful women. Now that I think about it, that would be a good reason.)

Almost everything about being a Christian can be faked. But there is one thing I've found that can't be faked, and that's laughter—free, childlike, infectious laughter.

Going to church used to be such drudgery to me until I found out that drudgery was a sign that I had not gone to church. Real church is worship, praise, and adoration manifested in celebration and very often laughter. If that isn't happening, it simply isn't the real thing.

Of course, our corporate worship is serious because it is about God. If it were only about us, it would be silly. It does, of course, contain the elements of self-examination, confession, and lament. But, dear friend, it doesn't stop there, and if it does, it isn't real worship. The ultimate definition of worship is celebration. It is a time when the people of God remember who they are, whose they are, what he has done, who he is, and where they are going. Then they shout and laugh and sing and pray because of that memory.

I don't attend worship because I ought to or because that is what a Christian does or because I must maintain my reputation in the Christian community. I attend worship because I live in a very sad world, and sometimes the pathos is overwhelming. I love to be with the people of God in worship because there isn't enough booze or drugs in the world to erase the memory of my sin and my pain. And I can't live without relief. I worship because I'm more than the aggregation of my work and my things and my efforts. I worship because God has called me to celebrate. I worship because worship is, if you will, a touch of home before I get there.

I have a missionary friend who serves in one of the poorest and most oppressed countries in the world. I talked to her when she was home on furlough and asked her if she was going back. She smiled and said, "But of course."

"Why do you want to go back to such a horrible place?" I asked.

"I'm going back because I have a calling. I have been called to plant flowers in hell."

That's worship. It is God's people planting flowers in hell and then enjoying the fragrance.

TEN

Signs and Wonders

We carry checks on the bank of heaven
and never cash them at the window of prayer.
—Vance Havner

And now let us pray for good luck.
—Anonymous

Prayer is not conquering God's reluctance,
but taking hold of God's willingness.
—Phillips Brooks, late rector, Trinity Church, Boston

LET'S POSE AN INAPPROPRIATE question: how can I get positive answers to my prayers? In other words, how can I get God to do what I want him to do?

The question is inappropriate because that isn't what prayer is all about. It is inappropriate because God is not a bellhop or a magician. It is also inappropriate because a what's-in-it-for-me? question misses the point that the world isn't about you; it's about God.

A number of years ago a young preacher garnered a fair amount of publicity with a sermon he preached. The title of the sermon was: "What does God say when we say, 'What's in it for me?'"

There was a good deal of interest in the sermon as the preacher got up, smiled at the congregation, and sat down.

(The young man saved a lot of time on sermon preparation that week!) In other words, God doesn't even respond when we ask that kind of question.

Nevertheless, we still ask the question, don't we? Those of you who never ask that question should not read anymore of this chapter. Just go on to the next chapter and the rest of us will join you later. Go ahead. We'll catch up to you soon.

What Does It Mean for Me?

Now that the honest ones are left, let's talk.

One of the things I've noticed about God is that he does a lot of things that are inappropriate—or at least inappropriate according to the standards of the religious folks. It is quite "spiritual" to say that God's glory is the purpose of our living, that ego-centered prayers are selfish and beneath the mature believer, and that the purpose of prayer is not what you can get from God. It sounds good to say that prayer doesn't change things—it just changes you.

However, most people who say things like that have never experienced the desperation of a child who is dying, a business that is failing, or a life that has come unglued. When the doctor tells you that you have cancer, the officer tells you that your daughter is on drugs, or your husband tells you he doesn't love you anymore, mature Christianity doesn't mean squat. In those kinds of situations we all become frightened children crying out to our Father to make it better.

I often tell my students, who can be quite critical of charismatic and Pentecostal folks (those brothers and sisters are quite emotional and demonstrative in their faith, and that is rather unseemly for Calvinists), "If you are really sick, who do you want to pray for you—a Pentecostal or a Calvinist?"

There is a nervous laugher. Do you know why? It is because,

if you're in real trouble, you don't want good theology, you want powerful prayers by people who believe in prayer even if they have never read a systematic-theology book.

Before we begin, let me say something that is important. God is not a monster. "As a father pities his children, so the LORD pities those who fear Him. For He knows our frame; He remembers that we are dust" (Ps. 103:13–14). God knows that, as children, we will ask inappropriate questions, utter inappropriate words, and pray inappropriate prayers.

One time a rich young man came to Jesus and asked how to get to heaven. Among other things, Jesus told him that he must sell all of his possessions. The young man went away despondent because he had a lot of stuff. However, the interesting thing about the incident from the perspective of this chapter in Luke is that Peter made an observation to Jesus to the effect that the disciples had—contrary to the rich young man who had just left—left everything and followed Jesus. The clear implication to that observation was a question: "What's in it for us?"

Jesus didn't reprimand Peter for the question. He didn't tell him he was selfish or superficial. He didn't tell Peter he should be following Jesus for Jesus' sake and not for what he could get out of it. What did Jesus do? He answered Peter's question. He told Peter what was in it for him: "Assuredly, I say to you, there is no one who has left house or parents or brothers or wife or children, for the sake of the kingdom of God, who shall not receive many times more in this present time, and in the age to come eternal life" (Luke 18:29–30).

So while it may be inappropriate to ask questions about how to have a more effective prayer life, how to get positive answers to our prayers, and how to have spiritual power—let's ask anyway.

Listen to some of the amazing statements of Jesus:

- Ask, and it will be given to you; seek, and you will find; knock, and it will be opened to you. For everyone who asks receives, and he who seeks finds, and to him who knocks it will be opened. (Matt. 7:7–8)
- Have faith in God. For assuredly, I say to you, whoever says to this mountain, "Be removed and be cast into the sea," and does not doubt in his heart, but believes that those things he says will be done, he will have whatever he says. Therefore I say to you, whatever things you ask when you pray, believe that you receive them, and you will have them. (Mark 11:22–24)
- Whatever you ask in My name, that I will do, that the Father may be glorified in the Son. If you ask anything in My name, I will do it. (John 14:13–14)
- If you abide in Me, and My words abide in you, you will ask what you desire, and it shall be done for you. (John 15:7)
- You now have sorrow; but I will see you again and your heart will rejoice, and your joy no one will take from you [referring to the time after his resurrection]. And in that day you will ask Me nothing. Most assuredly, I say to you, whatever you ask the Father in My name He will give you. Until now you have asked nothing in My name. Ask, and you will receive, that your joy may be full. (John 16:22–24)

Now I may be missing something here, but it seems to me, at minimum, those are pretty astounding promises. Jesus clearly says that there is great power in prayer, far more power than most of us have ever experienced.

I referred in the last chapter to the healing services at the church where I was the pastor. Do you know the most difficult thing about those services? It was convincing the people in the congregation (and myself) that God really did answer prayer— sometimes even with a yes. It was my own fault. For so long I had taught about the dangers of presumption in prosperity theology that when we started suggesting that God might not always say no, it took some convincing. In my overreaction to those who assume that God will jump to our command, I found I had created a stoic congregation of Christians who decided there was no use in asking anyway.

We serve a supernatural God who "owns the cattle on a thousand hills," controls all the forces of the world, and can act on our behalf in any situation. He is attentive to the prayers of believers, and he still, despite what you may have believed, intervenes supernaturally in the lives of his people.

If you have read many books on prayer, you already know some of the conditions that ought to be present in order to appropriate God's supernatural power through prayer. I don't need to repeat in detail something that has been repeated so much in so many other books. Besides that, there is a great danger that in giving too much emphasis to "the list," I could give you the impression that there is a road map to power— that in obeying the rules, pressing the right buttons, and meeting the right conditions you could then wave a wand and cause miracles to happen.

Nothing could be further from the truth.

None of the conditions may be present, and God may still decide to say yes to prayer. Conversely, all of the conditions may be present, and our prayers may seem to get no higher than the ceiling. We love to put God in a little box and talk about things he will or won't do.

You may remember a number of years ago when a famous Christian got into trouble after he said that God didn't listen to the prayers of unbelievers. I know what he was saying, and there is something to it—in the sense that, if your children really need something from me, I'll try to help; but if my own children need something, I'll move heaven and earth to help.

However, it is dangerous to put God into our little boxes and to then tell the world what he will and won't do. He might just do something to disabuse us of our arrogance.

God does as he pleases, and he hardly ever checks with us about anything. When we say that God doesn't listen to the unbeliever's prayers, for instance, or that he no longer gives the gift of tongues, and that faith must be present in order for there to be power, God, with his wonderful sense of humor, just might turn things on their heads. He may take a pagan without faith, convert him or her to Christ, give him or her the gift of tongues, and then perform a miracle through that person before he or she even knows what faith is.

Then God will say, "So there."

So fulfilling the conditions that ought to be present in seeing God's supernatural intervention in your life situation may or may not produce a mountain-moving prayer life. Our relationship is with a Person and not with a principle. God doesn't act according to our rules. If he did, he wouldn't be God.

A Story of Answered Prayer

Let Go of the Buckets

I must say I am very blessed and understand that there are situations I can help with and those that I must leave alone and with God. When I got the news that my son had been shot, I got on a plane and was on my way to California. I asked God for his life, and God, in my prayer, gave me the thought from the Gospel of Matthew that my son would live.

He did.

Years later, another son drowned, and through my grief, I continued to pray for God's strength, guidance, and peace.

I'm from a farming family. When I was young, one of my jobs was to milk the cows. I was always telling my dad that the buckets were too heavy.

When my son died, I told God that the buckets of grief were too heavy. He came to me so quietly one morning and said, *Are you ready to let go of the buckets?*

I said "yes," and instantly I felt his peace come to me. I knew it was his answer to my prayers.

—Loyann S.

The Ten Suggestions for Prayer

"Okay," you say, "I understand, but, just so I don't have to do the research, would you give me the list?" I'll do that because I like you, but, after giving you the list, I want to say some things that are more important than the list. Hereupon follows: the *Ten Commandments for Effective, Powerful Prayer.*

Well . . . maybe that's a bit strong. How about some suggestions?

First, in order to see great power in prayer, you must have faith. If you note the reference in Mark 11 where Jesus talks about prayer, you will note Jesus' heavy emphasis on faith and belief. You probably wouldn't be reading a book like this if you already had mountain-moving faith, but the good news is that you don't have to generate faith on your own. You can't hustle up faith, anyway; it is a gift from God. If you are going to pray for something, pray first for faith. That is what the disciples did (see Luke 17:5), and it was what the father of the boy possessed by a demon did (see Mark 9:24). They were wise.

Second, faith doesn't come quickly, it is a process. Most believers ask for a mountain to be moved when their faith is geared better for molehills. Pray that God would make you a bit kinder than you have been, that you would be more faithful in little things, that you would be a better mom or dad—not perfect, just better. Then watch as God answers those prayers. The faith you receive from the answer will enable you to move to some bigger requests.

Third, effective prayer is always within the parameters of God's will. Listen to the witness of the apostle John: "This is the confidence that we have in Him, that if we ask anything *according to His will,* He hears us. And if we know that He hears us, whatever we ask, we know that we have the petitions that we have asked of him" (1 John 5:14–15). If you pray for your enemy's death, is God going to grant your request? Of course not. If you pray for a date with your favorite person or for a new house, is God going to grant that request? Maybe. If you pray for a closer walk with him, for the filling of his Spirit, or for more love toward those who persecute you, is God going to grant those requests? Absolutely! How do I know? Because those requests are clearly revealed in the Bible to be according to the will of God.

Fourth, effective prayers are specific. James said that we don't have because we don't ask (see James 4:2). The farmer who prayed in a storm, "Lord, come and help us. And, Lord, come yourself, this ain't no time for boys," knew about specific prayer. Tell God what it is that you need, what you desire, or what concerns you. It is important that we be specific and detailed in our requests.

Fifth, remember that God is God, and that he knows better than you do concerning what is needed. "I have tried to thank God," said a man looking back at his life, "that not all my prayers have been answered."

Sixth, know about the power of praise. There is something

about praising God, even when bad things happen, that will open the gates of heaven. If Romans 8:28 is true—"We know that all things work together for good to those who love God, to those who are the called according to His purpose"—then no matter how bad it gets, praise is appropriate. Not only that, but praise is often the missing ingredient in ineffective prayers.

Seventh, be obedient (or, at least, want to be obedient) to what God tells you to do. I have a friend who is the mother of a teenager, and she said to me once, "I don't tell him what to do anymore, because I know that he won't do it." A desire for obedience is a sign of your response to God's love, and, without that, there is hardly any use in asking.

Eighth, keep on praying. Jesus spoke of the power of persevering prayer in Luke 18:1–8 when he spoke of a widow who, like a dog with a bone, wouldn't give up asking a judge for justice. Finally, the judge granted her request. Jesus said, "Ask, and it will be given to you; seek, and you will find; knock, and it will be opened to you. For everyone who asks receives, and he who seeks finds, and to him who knocks it will be opened" (Matt. 7:7–8). It is interesting to note that the way the Greek reads in this scripture suggests perseverance and frequency. In other words, "Ask, and keep on asking; seek, and keep on seeking; knock, and keep on knocking."

Ninth, don't make demands; only make requests. That was Job's problem—he forgot that God was God. After God revealed himself to Job, Job said (in Hebrew, of course), "Oops!" His exact words were, "I know that You can do everything, and that no purpose of Yours can be withheld from You. You asked, 'Who is this who hides counsel without knowledge?' Therefore I have uttered what I did not understand, things too wonderful for me, which I did not know. Listen, please, and let me speak; You said, 'I will question you, and you shall answer Me.' I have heard of You by the hearing of the ear, but now my eye sees

You. Therefore I abhor myself, and repent in dust and ashes"
(Job 42:2–6).

Finally, God will take your prayers as seriously as you take them.
If your prayers are not important to you, they probably won't
be that important to God. "You never mentioned it to me," is
the comment of the husband whose wife felt that he ought to
know things without being told. This may be the comment of
God about those areas about which we didn't pray.

That's the list. It's a good list, and in one form or another, it
has been a trustworthy guide for believers from the beginning.
I've always known about the list, and for most of my Christian
life I have worked, with varying degrees of success, to fulfill its
conditions. I would not be so presumptuous as to minimize
that list at all. However, let me bring my witness to the table
and tell you some things that the Father is teaching me about
prayer.

A Story of Answered Prayer

God's Play Book of Eternity

I am the son of a preacher. When I was seventeen, my mother, the
typical pastor's wife and always gracious, died at the age of thirty-
nine. Why did she die? That question was asked more than once; in
fact, my dad and I asked God that question a lot for many years.

On the eighteenth anniversary of Mom's death, my dad went to
the cemetery and then to a 7-Eleven store for a cold soda. He was
approached by a total stranger asking if his name was Jerry. He said
that he was but he could not place where he might have met her
before. She apologized and gave her name and said she was Mom's
nurse the last week of her life.

She explained that she never thought she would ever have a

chance to share with Dad what happened that week. You see, Mom led this nurse to a saving faith in Jesus just three days before her death. On top of that, this nurse went back to school and trained for medical missionary work and was just returning from spending the previous fifteen years in the Philippines as a medical missionary. She was on her way to a friend's house from the airport when she stopped for a drink at the same 7-Eleven my dad was in, right around the corner from the cemetery.

At that moment in time, God was kind enough to open his play book of eternity and show us firsthand that "All things do work together for good."

—Tim M.

God Always Gives Himself

Consider these scriptures:

- Jesus said, "I will pray the Father, and He will give you another Helper, that He may abide with you forever—the Spirit of truth, whom the world cannot receive, because it neither sees Him nor knows Him; but you know Him, for He dwells with you and will be in you. I will not leave you orphans; I will come to you." (John 14:16–18)
- Again: "These things I have spoken to you while being present with you. But the Helper, the Holy Spirit, whom the Father will send in My name, He will teach you all things, and bring to your remembrance all things that I said to you. Peace I leave with you, My peace I give to you; not as the world gives do I give to you. Let not your heart be troubled, neither let it be afraid." (John 14:25–27)
- Once more: "Now I go away to Him who sent Me,

and none of you asks Me, 'Where are You going?'
But because I have said these things to you, sorrow
has filled your heart. Nevertheless I tell you the truth.
It is to your advantage that I go away; for if I do not
go away, the Helper will not come to you; but if I
depart, I will send Him to you." (John 16:5–7)

Harold DeWolf, who was the systematics professor at Boston University School of Theology when I was a student there,
would sometimes lecture on the doctrine of the Holy Spirit.
He would tell the students about the time his infant son died in
his wife's arms and how, over a period of months, he watched his
wife literally die of a broken heart. In those lectures he would
talk about the power of God's presence during those days and
how, looking back, he simply would not have survived without
the comfort, sustenance, and power of God's Spirit.

In the next chapter we are going to examine questions
about unanswered prayer, and then we will explore some questions surrounding events such as the death of Dr. DeWolf's son
and wife. But that isn't the issue here. While I'm sure Harold
pleaded with God to change those horrible circumstances, God
didn't change them. But God did answer the prayer in a supernatural way. God gave *himself* to Dr. DeWolf. He always does.

Does that sound like a cop-out to you? It isn't. It is the
greatest of all signs and wonders. It is the message of the incarnation when God said to the world, "I know about the pain
and the anguish. If I tried to explain it all to you, you probably
still wouldn't understand. But I have come. I'm here." That
incarnational reality for the world is a pattern of the incarnational reality that is personal and real. God may not answer the
prayers we pray the way we want him to answer them, but he
does come.

There is an old Jewish prayer that speaks to that reality:

Thou art great, and we are small.
Thou art sovereign, and we are weak.
Thou art infinite, and we are finite.
Thou art eternal, and we tarry but just a little while.

But with all Thy greatness and all Thy power,
Thou dost bend down low,
And listen to the sound of our tears
As they strike the ground.

But there is more, isn't there? God not only listens to the sound of our tears as they strike the ground; he comes to work with us, and his tears mingle with ours.

When my brother, Ron, died, I felt I could almost die. He was my best friend, and I loved him very much. During the time of mourning, I was the rock of the family. It was my role. My brother had been a lawyer, the district attorney in our hometown. Our father used to say, "I have two sons. One is a lawyer and the other is a preacher. There is no problem I can have that one of my sons can't get me out of." Because I was the elder brother and the preacher, I didn't have the luxury of personal grief until the immediate needs—our mother's grief, the arrangements for the funeral, the ministry to my brother's sons and wife—were met.

The events surrounding my brother's death were bitter-sweet. He received a twenty-one-gun salute from the Marine Corps where he had served with distinction. The streets of the city were closed for the funeral procession, and the police officers saluted as the hearse drove by. The dignitaries were there, and there were many tributes to my brother's life and work. But during the whole time, it was important that I be strong.

A number of weeks after Ron's death, I flew back to the mountains where he and I had lived as children, and I went to the cemetery to have my own private time of grief. It was raining. It was a cold and miserable day, and when I got there, I couldn't find his grave. No stone had been placed on his grave, and everything looked so different from the way it had looked the day of the funeral. I remember standing there and weeping. "God," I cried, "I can't stand this. This has been the most terrible time of my life. My brother's dead, and now I can't even find his grave."

That was when I had the most overwhelming sense of peace. God came. He really did. It was the difference between night and day. He said, "I'm here, and you are in the wrong place. You are looking for the living among the dead." That doesn't mean that the grief wasn't real. I would have given my life if I could have brought Ron back. I will never understand why one so young and vital was taken. Maybe someday I'll get some answers to those questions. But it really was okay. God had come. He had given himself. I could trust him with the pain.

That's what the incarnation of God in Christ is about. The writer of Hebrews said, "We do not have a High Priest who cannot sympathize with our weaknesses, but was in all points tempted as we are, yet without sin. Let us therefore come boldly to the throne of grace, that we may obtain mercy and find grace to help in time of need" (Heb. 4:15–16).

That means that when we pray in our pain, our temptation, and our loss, we will always hear in response: "I know, child! Don't you hate it?"

I answered a letter recently from a man who has gone through a horrible time. He has pleaded with God to change the circumstances, and it hasn't happened. When I saw his letter, I winced because I knew I would be called upon to explain God's ways to him once again, and I wasn't that sure of God's ways myself. But when I read his letter, I was pleasantly surprised. This is what he wrote, "Things aren't a whole lot better, but this morning I experienced something wonderful. In all of my life I have never known such acceptance, understanding, care without condition, total absence of manipulation, confidence, and trust."

That's it, and it's an incredible sign and wonder.

THE PRAYER OF RELINQUISHMENT

Probably the most important prayer you can ever pray is the prayer of relinquishment. The best example of that kind of prayer is, of course, the prayer Jesus prayed before going to the cross. Jesus said to his disciples that his soul was "exceedingly sorrowful, even to death." This was what he prayed: "O My Father, if it is possible, let this cup pass from Me; nevertheless, not as I will, but as You will" (Matt. 26:38–39).

When my late friend Catherine Marshall went with her husband, Peter, to Washington, where he had been called to serve as the pastor of a major church in that city, the joy of the move was greatly diminished by a lung infection that left her bedridden. She did everything that any Christian would do to get better. She got the best medical attention. She asked people to pray, and they did. She decided that perhaps God was chastening her, and she wrote and asked forgiveness of everyone she had ever sinned against, including a grammar-school teacher in whose class she had cheated. She pleaded with God to make her well. Nothing happened; if anything, she got worse.

Finally she gave up. She prayed what she called the prayer of relinquishment. She told God that she had done everything she knew to do, that she hated being in bed when her husband and family needed her, and that she wanted to be healed. But she also gave up her "rights" to be healed. She said in effect, "Father, if you want me to stay in this bed the rest of my life, I accept your will in the matter. I relinquish the whole situation to you." At that moment Catherine Marshall started getting well and was soon fully recovered.

Does that mean that if you relinquish your rights to get a positive response from God, you will then get a positive response from God? Of course not. Relinquishment is just that: relinquishment.

There is, I believe, something to be said about God's checking our willingness. I have an acquaintance who was going to a speaking engagement and was late for the plane. Just as she was going out the door, her little boy asked her to help him with his homework. She almost told him that she was too busy. But she decided that being a mother was more important than being a speaker, and she put her suitcase down and got down on the floor to help her boy with his homework. He laughed and said, "That's okay, Mom. I just wanted to see if you would do it. You had better hurry or you'll miss your plane." Sometimes God checks to see how willing we are to relinquish.

The life experience of the believer is an increasing realization that God really does know best, that he controls our lives better than we do, and that given the choice between doing it his way and our way, there is no choice. Relinquishment is the understanding that it is stupid to make demands of God. He might submit to those demands, and we would be in serious trouble.

I have a friend who has a ministry of praying for the sick. His prayer is always: "Father, we come to you knowing that you are the great Physician, and we don't question your love or your power. However, we also come to you knowing that we are to glorify you in all that we do. If you are better glorified in this sickness, we accept that and praise you for it. If you are glorified in healing, we will rejoice and give you all the credit for it." It is amazing how often the prayers of my friend have resulted in restoration and healing. The secret is relinquishment.

When God is glorified, that is a sign and wonder.

A Story of Answered Prayer

Cattle Money

I felt the calling to go into medicine. My mother would freak when I mentioned it to anyone. I came from a poor family from the mountains of North Carolina, and my father had a devastating stroke when I was only five years old. She thought I was "dreaming too big." Eventually, I walked up to my mom and told her that God wanted me to be a doctor and that he wouldn't let me see any peace until I did what he had chosen. She told me that they couldn't help me. I told her that God had resources that we didn't have and, if he calls you to do something, he will provide.

And that is just what he did. I thought I would test God, so I applied to only one medical school.

I got accepted the first time I applied to that one school. I said, "Lord, I don't have any money, and my family won't cosign a loan." Before the end of the day, without my having to ask, four people volunteered to cosign my school loans. When I ran out of money, I received checks and scholarships from people without asking.

My last semester of medical school, I took my last five thousand dollars to pay the tuition. I had nothing left for my books, rent, gas, groceries, utilities, etc. I sat down and calculated that I would probably need about two thousand dollars to cover those expenses. So I said, "Lord, you own the cattle on a thousand hills. You said that you would provide according to your riches through Christ Jesus. I would not have tried to do this if you hadn't told me to. Lord, it is time to sell a cow."

Well, in less than two weeks I received a check in the mail for twenty-five hundred dollars, which was just enough to cover my expenses to the end of school.

I always call money like that my "cattle money."

—Sharon B.

The Difference between Petition and Praise

There are some things for which you don't have to pray. The Bible tells us that, because we are his, certain blessings are always ours, and we don't have to plead for them. For instance, don't plead with God for forgiveness, for his love, for his acceptance, or for his presence. In all those areas, all we have to do is thank him. I have often thought that the invocation part of a church worship service was senseless. When I was a pastor, I was praying for God's presence during the service and was overwhelmed with the silly nature of that invocation. I stopped and thought about the request I was making of God and said to the congregation: "This is silly. We don't have to ask for God to be in our midst. He already is!" From then on we thanked him for being there; we didn't issue an invitation for him to come.

It is an old story, but it makes a point. There was a man in a flood who watched the water rise in his house and pleaded with God for deliverance. By the time he was on his roof, he was getting frightened, but he continued to trust God. A rescue boat came by and offered help, but he refused, telling them that he was trusting God. Later, a helicopter came, and the pilot offered to take him out of danger. Again, he refused because, he said, he was trusting God. Eventually he drowned. When he arrived in heaven, he asked God why he had not saved him. God replied, "I tried. I sent you a boat and a helicopter."

Just so, there are some items of petition that ought to be items of praise. Read the Bible, find out what is already yours, and then thank him. Don't plead with him.

But this idea of the difference between prayer and praise goes further than the gifts that are already ours as delineated in the Bible. Sometimes God will call you to pray for someone or some need and will assure you in the call that your prayer has already been answered positively. J. I. Packer's comment (to which I referred in an earlier chapter) about being called to pray for his friend with cancer and knowing, even as he prayed, that his friend would be healed is an example of this kind of prayer.

Once, a friend of mine had been going through some physical problems, and I was praying for him. He was going in the next week to get some results of the tests that had been administered by his physician. As I was praying for him, I had the overwhelming sensation that the tests would be negative. I "knew" that the doctor was going to tell him that he would be fine. Not only that, I felt impressed to tell him what I knew. Later that day I said to my friend, "I know how silly this sounds, but next week when you go to the doctor for the results of your tests, you are going to find that they are negative. When you find they are negative, remember that I told you so."

I felt so presumptuous in what I had said to him and told God how I felt. He said that we weren't going to make a habit of it, but that he was teaching me something important. Watch for those places where the answer is given in the actual call to prayer. On numerous occasions I have had friends call me when I was going through a difficult time about which they knew nothing and say, "Steve, are you okay? This morning I had such an overwhelming sense that I should pray for you." When you are called to pray . . . pray. In that prayer, God is giving you an item of petition that has, built into it, an item of praise.

That's a sign and wonder.

WHEN YOU ARE THE ANSWER

Sometimes the answer to your prayer is found in what God tells you to do. In the third chapter of Exodus, God tells Moses, "'I have surely seen the oppression of My people who are in Egypt, and have heard their cry because of their taskmasters, for I know their sorrows. So I have come down to deliver them out of the hand of the Egyptians. . . . Come now, therefore, and *I will send you*'" (Ex. 3:7–8, 10).

Do be open to becoming the answer of God to the need expressed in your prayer. When God supernaturally sends and empowers you, that is a sign and wonder.

THE POWER OF WEAKNESS

God's ways really aren't our ways. We talk about authority, and Jesus talks about serving. We want to have political power so that we can make things right; he makes us of no account that we might see him make things right. We want to be strong that we can help, and he makes us weak that we might be powerful. We take pride in our accomplishments that we might praise him with our efforts; he allows major failure that people might see him. We bask in our purity that we might bear witness to his dominion; he allows us to sin and shows us the sin that we might bear witness to his grace. We really do think that helplessness is a liability. It may be if you are a soldier, a policeman, or a teacher, but in spiritual matters just the opposite is true.

When you read the Gospels, you find that Jesus never refused help to the helpless, that he never refused forgiveness to the sinners, that he never turned away from the unfit. The people Jesus didn't seem to care about—no, the people who really "ticked" him off—were the secure, the strong, the pure, and the self-righteous.

Howard Hendricks tells about an elderly pastor who told him, just before the old man died, "You can't glorify Christ and Howard Hendricks at the same time." That is important. God is in the business of taking nobodies and using them in powerful and supernatural ways.

So if you are in a hopeless situation or you are praying for someone in a hopeless situation, is that bad? No, that's good. It's God's opportunity. It is rarely in the hands of a religious media giant or a well-known saint that God performs miracles. It usually happens through the prayers of a child . . . or something quite like one.

Then it is truly a sign and a wonder.

ELEVEN

The Pain of Unanswered Prayer

When the gods wish to punish us, they answer our prayers.
—Oscar Wilde

Now, boys, remember one thing: Do not make long prayers;
always remember that the Lord knows something.
—Joseph H. Choate

Good when He gives, supremely good,
Nor less when He denies,
E'en crosses from His sovereign hand
Are blessings in disguise.
—James Harvey

A FATHER OVERHEARD HIS SMALL daughter saying over and over, "Tokyo, Tokyo, Tokyo." He asked her what she was doing, and she replied that she was praying.

"What kind of prayer is that?" he asked.

"I had a test in school today," she replied, "and I was praying that God would make Tokyo the capital of France."

The question before the house is this: why does God answer some prayers and not others? C. S. Lewis put the matter quite simply:

As regards the difficulty [of unanswered prayer], I'm not asking why our petitions are so often refused. Anyone

can see in general that this must be so. In our ignorance
we ask what is not good for us or for others, or not
even intrinsically possible. Or again, to grant one man's
prayer involves refusing another's. There is much here
which is hard for our will to accept but nothing that is
hard for our intellect to understand. The real problem
is different; not why refusal is so frequent, but why the
opposite result is so lavishly promised.[1]

We, of course, know why God doesn't make Tokyo the
capital of France. But what about prayers for a dying child,
a faltering marriage, a divided church, or a straying daughter
or son? Those kinds of prayers are reasonable and urgent. The
granting of those requests would not seem to take anything
from anyone else. A good and loving God would grant those
kinds of requests. Why doesn't he?

There are, of course, the quick and glib answers to those
questions: God always knows what is best, and what is best
might not be what we desire; God sees the whole picture
and knows the beginning from the end, and he is working to
bring forth good; we need to grow more than we need to have
answers to our prayers; we aren't exercising the right principles
of prayer; God is chastening us for our good. I suspect that
some of those answers may be true. I'm just not sure.

The Bible is strangely silent on why God doesn't answer our
prayers. It faces the fact that prayer isn't answered. The Bible
talks about sin and its negative effects on prayer. There are lots
of recorded prayers in the Bible. But, mostly, the Bible doesn't
tell us why God doesn't answer our prayers. What we can glean
from the Bible on the subject is almost always indirect and not
all that clear. The one book that brings up the questions is the
book of Job, and it doesn't give any answers.

So, don't expect clear, easy, and simple answers in this chapter. I don't know any. Believe me, if I did, I would give them to you.

In this world things don't always make sense, consistency is hard to come by, and everything doesn't fit into a nice theological box. I grow tired of those who seem to have God in their back pocket. God isn't in anybody's back pocket, and we must beware of those who pontificate. They either don't know what they are talking about or they are fools. God's response to Job who had been discussing with his friends his existential and theological dilemma was very much to the point: "Who is this who darkens counsel by words without knowledge? Now prepare yourself like a man; I will question you, and you shall answer Me" (Job 38:2–3).

As I write this, our daughter Jennifer is visiting. She is the mother of three daughters (my grandchildren are better than yours), is married to a fine doctor, loves Christ with all her heart, and is the social organizer for the world. To this day, every time I look at her, I remember the first day of her life. She had a blood count that was climbing and a maudlin leg that wasn't getting nourishment. There was a good chance that her leg might not grow.

When the doctor told me about the problems, I was devastated. I'm not a good person, but my socially redeeming value is that I love my family, and Jennifer, only a day old, was loved by both of her fathers—the One in heaven and the one on earth. I remember listening as the doctor told me about the possibility of taking Jennifer to Boston Children's Hospital for a complete blood transfusion. He spoke of what was then a fairly high mortality rate for that kind of procedure. He told me he had called in a specialist who had examined her leg, and the specialist didn't know what to say or what would help.

That night I was with some Christians who knew how to pray. I will never forget the simple prayer those dear Christians prayed: "Lord, we pray for Jennifer. In the name of Christ we ask that you would intervene and heal her. We will give you all the glory."

The next morning Anna, my wife, who was still in the hospital, called very early. She didn't say "hello" or "good morning." She said, "Honey, did anybody pray last night?" I told her about those who had prayed. She said, "The doctor came in early this morning and said, 'This is miraculous. The blood count is normal, and I'm no longer worried about the leg.'"

That was an amazing answer to prayer. You may have some alternate explanations, and you may talk about coincidence . . . but don't talk to me. I don't have ears to hear that kind of nonsense. God acted in a definite, supernatural, and loving way. That is my personal witness, and it is true. John the apostle gave his witness to Christ and it was hard to ignore: "That which was from the beginning, which we have heard, which we have seen with our eyes, which we have looked upon, and our hands have handled . . . we declare to you" (1 John 1:1, 3). My witness is sort of like that. I've been there. Not only in the case of our daughter, but on hundreds of occasions I have seen God answer prayer in dramatic ways. I've seen God act. I know the reality of answered prayer.

Now you may think that an answer like the healing of our daughter would still all the questions. Not even close! In fact, the whole, wonderful action of God has created more questions than you would believe. Why, for instance, if God acted in that kind of definite way, do I still sometimes have doubts about him and his love? How in the name of all that is holy have I managed to be unfaithful to him after he has treated me and my family with such kindness? Where in the world do I get off being anything but a faithful, obedient, and loving servant? There are some answers to those questions, and those answers are not very comforting. They have to do with my own sin and rebellion—my tendency to want to be autonomous. That is why Christ had to die for me.

There are, however, other questions that aren't so easily answered, and those are the questions of this chapter. Over the years I have buried a great number of babies, have dried the tears of the parents, and have spoken the ancient words of comfort and solace. Why did my baby live and their baby die? They know God better, follow God more closely, and love God more deeply than I do. Why didn't God save their baby instead of mine? What was it about the prayers for Jennifer of those believers that caused God to hear them and answer their prayers? What is it about the prayers of so many others who love Christ just as much that are not answered in that kind of dramatic way?

And then the questions form a wider circle: Why didn't God answer the prayers of the Jews in the Holocaust? Was God deaf to the Christians who were killed in the massacre in Rwanda? Did the suffering people in Bosnia and Iraq pray? Why didn't God answer? Then there are the questions that come from observing the people I love. Why can't my friend get a job after all the prayers we have offered on his behalf? Why did that Christian marriage fail when the whole church was praying? Why did this one die? Why doesn't that one quit drinking? After all, we prayed. We prayed hard.

I don't know. I simply don't know. But there are some things that I do know, and I want to share them with you in what follows. Again, no simple answers, just some thoughts from a man who has dealt with the unanswered prayers of many people and has a bunch of unanswered prayers of his own. For what it's worth, I want to tell you why I'm still a Christian after examining a whole lot of data that would suggest that I'm a fool.

A Story of Answered Prayer

At the Very Heart

I'm a Lutheran pastor in New Jersey and prayer is at the very heart of all we do. We have seen the Lord do some remarkable things—like the incident I'm about to describe.

A member of our church named Ashley (who was fourteen at the time) suffered severe head trauma when she fell from the roof of a moving vehicle. She was rushed to a trauma unit in a local hospital, and her parents were told that her head injuries were extensive and that she might not survive.

The next few days were touch-and-go for Ashley. She was purposely kept in a comatose state. Her brain swelled from the injury, so a hole was drilled in her skull and a tube was inserted to release excess fluid. Doctors began to think that she could survive, but because of the brain trauma she had experienced, they believed she would be severely debilitated and would probably never walk or talk again.

Members of our congregation, including several of our prayer teams, prayed fervently for Ashley's recovery. We also organized a prayer service for her and invited the whole community to attend, including students from our local high school.

On that chilly November evening, our church was filled to overflowing and anyone who wished was given an opportunity to voice their hopes and concerns in prayer. After a great outpouring of compassion for Ashley and her family, we concluded the service by singing "Awesome God." As we did, we truly sensed His awesome presence among us. We did not know what the future would hold for Ashley, but we were certain of one thing—the Lord was truly present with her and her family. Many of us left worship with a sense of peace that was quite unlike anything that we had ever experienced before. Deep in our souls, we knew that no matter what happened next, somehow it was going to be okay.

Ashley made a recovery that even the doctors termed miraculous. She was able to talk perfectly just a few days later, and her ability to think clearly was intact. In a very short time, she had full use of her limbs and was walking without difficulty. She resumed her normal activities at school, home, and church, and even went skiing several times!

Ashley is now a student at Rutgers University.

We give·great credit to Ashley for her determination and to the hospital staff for their expertise and skill; but most of all, we give the credit to our awesome God and the power of prayer.

—Jack S.

When God Says No

Throughout this book I've related a number of incidents of answered prayer. The question isn't why some prayers aren't answered. The real question is why any prayers are answered at all. Art DeMoss, perhaps the most effective one-on-one evangelist I have ever known, would always respond to the query about how he was doing with these words: "Better than I deserve." The truth is that we are all doing better than we deserve.

I grow tired of people who look down on those whose prayers are unanswered and assume the reason is because of the sin of those who prayed. The truth is that if God handed out positive responses to our prayers in proportion to the inherent evil in our hearts and actions, no prayers would ever be answered. If the doctrine of radical and pervasive human depravity is true—and I believe it is demonstrably true—then, by rights, every prayer you ever prayed would have fallen on the deaf ears of a holy and righteous God.

The story Jesus told of the Pharisee and the tax collector is instructive. You will remember that the Pharisee stood before

God and was thankful for his personal goodness. He was especially thankful that he was not like the tax collector. There is nothing in the story Jesus told to suggest that the Pharisee was not as good as he said he was. I suspect he did all the things about which he bragged to God: He had not committed extortion, he was not unjust, he had never committed adultery, and he had certainly never taken money from poor people through taxes. He did fast often, and he gave a lot of money to good causes.

You will remember that the tax collector (the most vile of human beings, with the possible exception of a swine keeper, imaginable to a Jew) didn't talk about his goodness. He didn't have any about which to talk. Jesus said he stood "afar off" and dared not even look to heaven. His prayer was simple, "God, be merciful to me a sinner!"

Jesus made this amazing assessment of the prayer lives of the two men: "I tell you, this man [the tax collector] went down to his house justified rather than the other; for everyone who exalts himself will be humbled, and he who humbles himself will be exalted" (Luke 18:14).

Jesus makes at least three salient points in that story. First, Jesus pointed out that external acts of goodness, even proper ones, are no reason for God to act positively on the prayers that are offered; those external acts of goodness often mask the sinful pride and arrogance of those who do them. Second, Jesus showed us that God listens to bad people who know they are bad. And third, Jesus was showing us that there is no correlation between external acts of goodness and God's positive response to our prayers.

The main point, however, is that God heard and answered the prayer of the bad man. If he didn't, he would never hear my prayers, and he would never hear yours. The question is not why doesn't God answer?—the question is why does he answer at all? When God doesn't answer our prayers the way we want him to, the proper response of a wise Christian is praise because he answers any of our prayers at all.

Getting the Picture Clear

Let me give you a principle: the nature of one's actions can only be determined by the disposition of one's motivations. In other words, it is not enough to know what a person does—it is also important to know why a person does what he or she does. For example, a man with a knife in his hand going after a strapped-down and helpless victim takes on a different meaning when that man is a surgeon performing a surgical procedure that will save a life.

It is desperately important that we know what God is like before we question what he does. If God is a monster, a cosmic child abuser, or a vindictive sadist, our unanswered prayers mean something quite different from the unanswered prayers by a God who is kind and loving. That is, by the way, the central issue. The Bible teaches that God isn't just loving, but that he *is* love (see 1 John 4:8). The Bible doesn't stop there either; it says that God is not only love but that he is sovereign too (see Rom. 11:34–36).

Rabbi Kushner's very good book *When Bad Things Happen to Good People*[2] deals with the problem of pain and suffering (and indirectly with the problem of unanswered prayer) by saying that God is loving but *not* sovereign. His book is an example of a compassionate and loving treatment of the subject by a man who has paid his dues and is struggling with the issue. The problem is that if either one of those biblical revelations of God's nature (that is, his love or his sovereignty) isn't certain, prayer doesn't matter. If God is just as upset, helpless, and powerless as we are, then we are in serious trouble. If nobody is in charge of this mess or if the One who is doesn't care, we have a problem bigger than unanswered prayer.

Belief is a volitional act. When Job said, "Though He slay me, yet will I trust Him" (Job 13:15), he made a volitional choice. It is the same one we all make in the face of prayers that are not answered. At that point, we can choose to look at the unanswered prayer and say, "There isn't anything to it," or we can look at the answered prayers we have experienced and the revelation of God's love and sovereignty and say, "My Father, I don't understand you, but I trust you."

C. S. Lewis—by now you have discerned that C. S. Lewis is my hero, so if you know any dirt on him, just keep it to yourself—has written on this subject with great eloquence. Late in his life, he fell in love with and married an American woman. She died of cancer, and he was forced to go through a very difficult and painful time. During that time he wrote a small book titled *A Grief Observed*, which was first published under a pseudonym. Listen to what he says:

> The terrible thing is that a perfectly good God is in this matter hardly less formidable than a Cosmic Sadist. The more we believe that God hurts only to heal, the less we can believe that there is any use in begging for tenderness. A cruel man might be bribed—might grow tired of his vile sport—might have a temporary fit of mercy, as alcoholics have fits of sobriety. But suppose that what you are up against is a surgeon whose intentions are wholly good. The kinder and more conscientious he is, the more inexorable he will go on cutting. If he yielded to your entreaties, if he stopped before the operation was complete, all the pain up to that point would have been useless. But is it credible that such extremities of torture should be necessary for

us? Well, take your choice. The tortures occur. If they are unnecessary, then there is no God or a bad one. If there is a good God, then these tortures are necessary. For no even moderately good Being could possibly inflict or permit them if they weren't.[3]

Either way, we're in for it.

When you face the grim reality of unanswered prayer—or at least, prayer that seems unanswered—remember who God is and remember the principle: the nature of God's actions can only be determined by the disposition of God's motivations.

A number of years ago, I attended a Monday-evening worship service at a church in our community. They have seven full services and one of them is on a Monday evening. Because I often travel and speak on weekends, this church's worship service on Monday is ideal for me.

On this particular occasion, I came to the church rather early. Only a few people were in the auditorium. I noticed a lady who was crying three or four rows in front of me. She looked so sad—disheveled and in great sorrow. I didn't feel that it was appropriate to intrude so I bowed my head and prayed for her.

Shortly, the auditorium began filling up, and the woman passed from my mind as we began to worship. During that early worship time, the congregation sang the wonderful praise song with the words, "God is good. He is good all the time."

I remembered the lady for whom I had prayed and sort of leaned over to see if I could see her. I noticed she wasn't singing the song. Her head was bowed, and she seemed so far from the lyrics of the song. But the second time the congregation sang the chorus, I noticed that her lips were moving. When we got to the third repetition of the chorus, I leaned over and looked at her, and very slowly she raised her hands in the air, looked up with tears streaming down her face, and sang loudly with the congregation: "God is good. He is good all the time!!"

Charles Spurgeon is often quoted as saying, "If you can't trace God's hand, trust his heart." That is so good. The nature of God's actions can only be determined by the disposition of God's motivations.

A Story of Answered Prayer

A Day in the Park

I have been a Christian for a long time, but not a "practicing" Christian until about 2002.

I was in an abusive marriage for many years and had three beautiful daughters. After the divorce, the girls and I were put out on the street. With the help of my wonderful father, who loved me and the girls, we began to get our lives in order.

But then I began getting into stupid relationships going nowhere and doing all the wrong things. That's when I encountered an angel in the local park who told me if I would just begin trusting God, he would do the rest. I fell on my knees that very week and gave it all to God.

I'm now married to a wonderful man I met in a restaurant, and my daughters are grown.

I wanted to tell you the story of a really lost little girl who has finally found her way through the grace of God.

—Amy S.

HONESTY IN THE FEARS

Here's an interesting question in our musings about why prayers seem to go unanswered: did God lie to us about life in general and prayer in particular? It is one thing to be upset with a person who makes a promise about doing something good and then fails to fulfill it and another thing to be upset with a person who has not made the promise in the first place. In the last chapter I gave you a number of biblical references to Jesus' promises regarding prayer. It is very important to recognize that those promises do not constitute the entirety of what Jesus said about prayer or about the reality of pain and suffering.

Jesus also said, "Blessed are you when they revile and persecute you" (Matt. 5:11). "For nation will rise against nation, and kingdom against kingdom. And there will be earthquakes in various places, and there will be famines and troubles. These are the beginnings of sorrows. But watch out for yourselves, for they will deliver you up to councils, and you will be beaten in the synagogues. You will be brought before rulers and kings for My sake, for a testimony to them" (Mark 13:8–9). "They will put you out of the synagogues; yes, the time is coming that whoever kills you will think that he offers God service" (John 16:2). "In the world you will have tribulation" (John 16:33). Not only did Jesus say those things, he himself faced the pain of unanswered prayer when he asked the Father to remove the necessity of the Cross.

There are great dangers in believing or teaching that God will always do good things for you if you will only ask him, and if he doesn't, it is because you didn't have enough faith, exercise the proper principles of faith, or try hard enough. The truth is that the Bible never says anything even close to that.

I remember her tears.

She was a teacher in a community college and had invited me there to speak to her religion class on Paul's theology. When I got there, I found out that God had a far more important agenda than Pauline theology. The previous night some well-meaning Christians had told her that her child with juvenile diabetes had already been healed. They had prayed, and they had faith. They told this mother/professor that if she would prove her faith by removing the regular insulin injections from her child, God would honor that by affirming the healing. Her tears mirrored her dilemma: if she stopped the insulin injections, her child could die. If she didn't, her lack of faith would be the cause for her child's continuing diabetes and eventual death.

I'm glad I was there. She needed someone who knew what the Bible really said on the subject. She needed someone to tell her that, while those Christians who told her that may have been well meaning, they were ignorant. In my own experience that story could be repeated countless times. More times than I can remember, I have had to pick up the pieces of the believer who didn't "exercise the right principles of faith" and who, because the problem got no better, was rejected by those who promulgated that kind of spurious teaching.

Listen to what the Bible says: "These all died in faith, not having received the promises" (Heb. 11:13). Now that is an honest statement of reality. Tell your friends who say the Bible is unrealistic to put that in their pipes and smoke it. The Bible faces the reality of prayers that don't get answered, of needs that aren't met, and pain that is not healed.

The much-quoted prayer of the unknown soldier is relevant:

> *I asked for strength that I might achieve;*
> *I was given weakness that I might obey.*
>
> *I asked for health that I might do great things;*
> *I was given infirmity that I might do better things.*

I asked for riches that I might be happy;
I was given poverty that I might be wise.

I asked for power that I might have the praise of men;
I was given weakness that I might feel the need of God.

I asked for all things that I might enjoy life;
I was given life that I might enjoy all things.

I received nothing I asked for
But everything I hoped for;
My prayer was answered.
I am greatly blessed.

The next time your urgent prayers aren't answered in the way you would like them to be answered, ask yourself three questions: (1) has God loved me? (2) has he demonstrated that love? and (3) has he ever lied to me? The proper answers to those questions won't make the pain go away, but they will remind you that he is there, that he knows what he is doing, and that, even if you don't understand, he does. It will remind you to never doubt in the dark what he has taught you in the light.

CATCHING GLIMPSES OF PROVIDENCE

Everything I have said so far in this chapter presupposes something that we ought not to presuppose—that the only answer to a prayer is yes. It's been said so often that I hate to say it again, but I will: God always answers prayer, though not always in the way we would like. Sometimes he says yes, sometimes he says no, and sometimes he says wait.

We are an instant-gratification kind of people. What we

want, we want right now—and sooner if at all possible. God is hardly in a hurry about anything. It has been said that God is very slow, but he is never late.

I can't tell you the tears, the pain, the worry, and the fear that my father's alcoholism engendered. Nevertheless, my father was the kindest man I have ever known, and he, more than any other, taught me unconditional love. I can understand why those who had horrible and abusive fathers wince when the heavenly Father is mentioned. But that has never been true for me. When Jesus referred to the Father and his goodness, I always thought of my earthly father and figured that if God was as kind, as gentle, and as unconditional in his love as my earthly father, I was going to be fine.

However, alcoholism is a horrible thing, and our family paid a high price for it. My mother, one of the most godly and earthy women I have ever known (she read Charles Spurgeon in the morning and the Bible in the evening; in between, she taught me how to cuss), prayed for my father for thirty years. My brother and I, when we were old enough to understand, joined our prayers to hers.

I can remember the time we thought our prayers had finally been answered. A colleague of my father, whom he respected and who was a recovering alcoholic himself, asked Dad to go with him to an Alcoholics Anonymous meeting. For the first time in his life my father admitted he was helpless in dealing with his alcoholism and consented to do something about it. Do you know what happened? The night before the meeting the man who had invited my father was killed in an automobile accident.

You have no idea how many prayers were said or how often asking God to grant my father sobriety. I often saw my mother pleading with God for this one thing. But it never happened . . . until three months before my father's death.

There isn't room here to tell you the whole story, but in the short version, my father's witness at the time of his death touched many people. He is in heaven now because a godly doctor said to him, "Mr. Brown, you have three months to live. First, we are going to have a prayer, and then I want to talk to you about something more important than what I just told you." My father is sober now. And he's safe because he's "home." He's home because God's timing was better than our family's timing.

Am I suggesting that if God says no or wait to your prayers that eventually you will get that for which you pray? Of course not. The truth is that we may never know until we get to heaven why some of our prayers weren't answered. "We walk by faith, not by sight" (2 Cor. 5:7). That is the reality of having unanswered questions and unanswered prayers. However, sometimes God will allow you to look back and see his hand in the slow and certain answers to your prayers. When he does that, be glad.

A Story of Answered Prayer

Surprise Scholarship

I grew up in a family of moderate means. Some forty-four years ago, God overwhelmed me with his love on the cross, and I decided to head in the direction of seminary. My family helped with college but had no funds for me to go to seminary. So all through college I prayed fervently for the finances to make it through seminary.

But by the time I was a senior in college, the money I had earned in high school and college and summer jobs was about gone.

That's when my parents decided to move. I was upset and angry because I was going to be the first student from Alaska to attend one of our seminaries!

My folks moved and, through a miracle, were able to buy a house in an area where there was a waiting list of 100–150 homes to be built. Right away, they got a constructed house and ended up joining the closest church in our denomination.

And that congregation gave scholarships to students going into full-time church work. They paid for 90 percent of my seminary education—even for the last year after my folks had moved to another part of the country and had joined another congregation!

—Glenn Z.

When We Get Home

Someone has said that there are two magnitudes that most of us forget: the shortness of time and the vastness of eternity. Those magnitudes are not without relevance when we consider the subject of unanswered prayer. It can be a cop-out if we make those magnitudes too glib and utter them too quickly. Those who say too quickly that they don't fear death are often those who have never dealt with the certainty of their own death.

That being said, don't forget about heaven.

There is a delightful story about a missionary who came to New York Harbor after a lifetime of work in missions. He was on the same ship with the man who was eventually to become the president of the United States, Teddy Roosevelt. Roosevelt was, at that time, the police commissioner of New York and was quite popular.

When the ship came into harbor, there was a crowd waving banners and a brass band playing. The missionary wished the crowd had come to cheer him and that the band was playing for him. But of course he quickly discovered that they were there for Roosevelt. He watched as Roosevelt was lifted onto the shoulders of the adoring crowd, and to the sound of band music, the crowd made their way into the city.

The missionary walked down the gangplank of the ship to the dock. He was by himself. He was lonely, hurt, and dispirited. He prayed, *Lord, all these years I have served you in difficult places. When Roosevelt comes home, he is greeted by a cheering crowd and a band. When I come home, there is no one to greet me, no band, no joy, no shouting.*

Child, he heard a voice reply, *you aren't home yet!*

I don't want to minimize the pain of unanswered prayer. I have been there, and it hurts. I don't want to give you clichés about heaven when you are having trouble dealing with the wounds of right now. But while the pain is doing its work and the wounds are beginning to heal, remember that you aren't home yet. Remember the ancient words of the apostle:

> I heard a loud voice from heaven saying, "Behold, the tabernacle of God is with men, and He will dwell with them, and they shall be His people. . . . And God will wipe away every tear from their eyes; there shall be no more death, nor sorrow, nor crying. There shall be no more pain, for the former things have passed away."
>
> Then He who sat on the throne said, "Behold, I make all things new." (Rev. 21:3–5)

On Not Orchestrating Heaven

The purpose of prayer is prayer, not what you can get God to do for you. In other words, God's desire, indeed, the reason you were created, is to be in a relationship with him. That relationship is the most important of your life. When the relationship becomes an exercise in seeing how we can manipulate God for our own purposes, the relationship is violated.

When I was a young Christian, I spent considerable time in prayer asking God for the salvation of my friends, for the protection of my family, for guidance in my life and ministry, for health, for resources to feed my family, for forgiveness, for my father's sobriety, for the right husbands for our daughters, and on and on. It was after I had been walking with him for a long time that I heard him saying, *Child, I know all of that. I know all your needs. I won't ever fail you. Now let's spend some time together.*

I have a dear friend who is quite wealthy. She has been a benefactress for countless universities and educational institutions. She has made a difference in numerous ministries with the benevolent use of her wealth.

We have been friends for over twenty-five years. One time I said to my friend: "I wish you were homeless, penniless, and without any kind of resource." She was surprised at my words until I told her that one of the major problems of her life was in not being able to have a relationship with someone without wondering why that person wanted the relationship. "You never know," I told her, "why someone is being nice to you, whether it's because of who you are and the money you have. You have to always wonder what they're after. If you had nothing, I could tell you I loved you, and you would believe me."

God doesn't have that problem. He knows why we come to him. Not only does he know, he understands. Don't feel guilty because you have needs and the only resource you have is God. Bible teacher Ron Dunn said, "People are always saying, 'Jesus is all I need.' You will never know Jesus is all you need until Jesus is all you've got. When Jesus is all you've got, then you will know that Jesus is all you need." Don't feel guilty because the main reason you go to God is that you are afraid and have great needs. I suspect that he even created things that way so we would go to him.

If our pain were not so deep, our needs so great, and our resources so little, we might never go to him. If we never went to him, we would never find out how much he loves us and what a delightful thing this relationship really is.

TWELVE

I'm Glad You Asked

If you would be a real seeker after truth,
it is necessary that at least once in your life you doubt,
as far as possible, all things.
—Descartes

No person really becomes a fool
until he or she stops asking questions.
—Anonymous

When somebody says, "That's a good question," you can
be sure it's a lot better than the answer you're going to get.
—E. C. McKenzie

T HE *KEY LIFE* RADIO program is a daily program heard
on a number of stations in the United States and Canada,
and I'm the program's Bible teacher. We receive thousands of
letters each month, and many of those letters contain questions.
Because there were so many questions, we decided to devote a
portion of the broadcast each week to the questions people ask.
What follows is a compilation of some of those questions as
they relate to the subject of prayer.

In case you have never heard the broadcast, let me say to
you here what I say on the broadcast: "The only dumb ques-

tion is the question you don't ask, so we are glad to get your questions. We take you and your questions seriously. Before I answer these questions, it is important that you know that I don't speak from Sinai, and I don't have a hotline to God. Please remember that I have been wrong on numerous occasions and probably will be wrong again. Also remember that I have changed my mind fairly often—not about the Bible's being true and God's being faithful but about my understanding of the Bible and God. I will be honest; I will try to be accurate; I will endeavor to be biblical; and I will do my best. But you must remember that I'm not your mother. You have a mind, and you have a Bible; so if I were you, I would check every answer that I give."

Let's get to the questions.

I have been a Christian most of my life, but recently God seems to have gone away on vacation and my prayers are just empty words. How do I get back to where I was?

First, it is important to remember that you don't need to "get back" to where you were. You need to go forward. The problem with most of us is that we don't remember things the way they really were. Our minds select the good and forget the bad. Nostalgia is fun, but it is hardly ever accurate or productive. For instance, I'm not much for going back to the first-century church when Christians were faithful and the church was pure. The truth is that they weren't always faithful, and the first-century church was not always pure. They fought and questioned and sinned just as we do. Thank God that he gave us the Bible to remind us of the way it really was.

Our spiritual life is sort of like that in that we remember

when we first knew him and measure all that is going on right now by the initial excitement we felt then. We remember the times when God was so real and our commitment so deep. The truth is that we have forgotten the struggles, the times of dryness, and the doubts.

Second, recognize God's hand in your prayer life right now, even during this dry period. Thomas à Kempis said that God sometimes withdraws the sense of his presence such that, when he restores it, we might know its "sweetness."

Tell God how you feel. Tell him that you want to know him more deeply. Get out of your prayer rut by praying at different times and in different ways. And then wait. He will come.

When he comes, don't assume that you will never go through a dry and empty time again; and when you do go through those periods, don't assume that you will never sense his presence again. He gives us feelings as we need them. He is sovereign. You can trust him.

Whether or not you feel that God is there, he is. Whether or not you have doubts about the truth you learned, it's still true. And whether or not you pray with joy, it's still prayer, and God is still listening.

If God already knows what I'm going to pray, why even bother?

He likes to hear the sound of your voice.

Not only that, but he has created the relationship that you have with him so that he will often wait to act until you bring the concern before him. Our daughter Robin is quite independent. When she was growing up, her attitude was often, "Please, Dad, I would rather do it myself."

Sometimes I would know her needs and would be perfectly willing to meet those needs. But I also knew that, for her sake, she needed to ask. When she did ask, I remember thinking, *I was just waiting for you to ask.*

Finally, remember that we need to express our concerns, our fears, our desires, and our requests in a place where we know we will be accepted and where our expressions of needs won't be denounced. That place is before the throne of God. God is our Father, and he likes us to come to him. He likes us to tell him where it hurts. Often, I believe, he waits for that very thing.

If God is sovereign and everything is already ordained, why pray?

Did you ever think of God as outside of time? We think of things as moving along on a time continuum. In other words, we measure the passing of time by hours, days, months, and years. We mark the passing of time with events like our birth, our years in school, our first job, our marriage, the birth of children, and our death.

In the Bible, God is called the "eternal now." That means that he doesn't look at things on the time line. He looks at all things as if on a plain. All things—past, present, and future—are eternally present with God right now. That has amazing implications for questions like how Jesus, if he was God, prayed to God. It also has amazing implications for how one explains the apparent contradictions in the Bible between "the dead in Christ" rising at the sound of the last trumpet and the thief who would be with Christ "today" in paradise. God is using time words to express a nontime reality. Calvin calls the Bible

God's "baby talk." In other words, God expresses truth, but in a way that we can understand and comprehend.

But in reference to your question, you need to remember that your prayers, the prayers of Abraham and Moses, the prayers of your great-great-grandparents, and the prayers of your great-great-grandchildren are all present with God right now. In other words, before there was the timeline in which you now live, God took into account the prayers you are praying right now. Those prayers were a part of the creation of the events about which you now pray.

Does God ever change his mind because of my persevering prayers?

No. But it looks that way sometimes.

Those passages in the Bible that seem to suggest that God changed his mind or that he might change his mind in response to the actions of his people are accurate from our perspective. But, in truth, God isn't surprised by anything we do, he doesn't have alternate plans, and he knows what he is doing. The persevering prayer to which he calls us is for our benefit, not so that he can change his mind.

If what you just said is true, does anything we ever do (including praying) really matter?

Yes. We are responsible human beings, and our prayers and our actions really do matter. My friend J. I. Packer calls this an antinomy. An *antinomy* is two truths you know are true but seem to contradict each other. It is true that our prayers make a difference, and it is true that God knows beforehand what will happen. That means we don't understand.

That shouldn't bother us. The essence of Christian, intellectual maturity is a high tolerance for ambiguity. Anything we can understand, we can control. If we could understand God, we could control him. If we could control him, he wouldn't be God. I think I mentioned it before, but it's worth saying again: If you have never stood before God and been totally confused, then you have never stood before the real God. He is infinite, and we are finite; he is big and, we are little; he is sovereign, and we just "muddle in the muddle." Confused? Of course we are confused. If we weren't, we would be worshiping an idol. And that's a no-no.

What does it mean to pray "in the name of Jesus"?

Jesus has given us a lot of wonderful gifts. One of the best is that, when we go to God in prayer, we can use his name.

I sometimes tell my students who are looking for positions in the church that they can use my name. "There are some places," I often say, "where my name will help you and other places where it could hurt you. So bring up my name in conversation, and if they smile, tell them that you know me and that I like you. If they wince, tell them that you know me and you think I'm weird."

Whenever we bring up the name of Jesus, the Father always smiles.

Of course, there are other implications in praying the name of Jesus. In the Bible the name is the essence of that which is named. Jesus, in effect, has given us the privilege of using his power and his authority when we pray. There is power in his name.

When we pray in the name of Jesus, we are affirming that we are coming to the Father based on Jesus Christ and all that he has done for us—not what we have done or who we are.

What do you think about the "faith movement"? Is it biblical?

The faith movement is often called "prosperity theology," and it teaches that we can "speak a word of faith" and have what we would like God to do, be done. The faith movement is sometimes also called the "name it, frame it, claim it" movement.

These teachings are wrong and sometimes presumptuous.

But the truth is that our glass house should prevent us from throwing too many stones. My own Reformed and Presbyterian family does it wrong too. We are so sure that God has quit speaking and has quit acting in supernatural ways that our prayers are often limp. We become Christian stoics and don't believe that God answers any prayers. The faith-movement folks believe he answers all of them.

God probably blushes because of both of us.

Whenever I pray, I have serious doubts. Sometimes I think I'm just pretending. How do I deal with the doubts?

When John Wesley had come to an intellectual understanding of the principles of faith, he went to one of his Moravian friends and asked, "How can I preach faith if I don't have faith?"

This was the answer he received: "Preach faith until you have faith and then, when you get faith, you will preach faith because you have faith." In other words, "Fake it until you make it." That isn't hypocrisy, it is putting legs on the reality that you know.

Ask yourself, "What would I do and how would I pray if I had faith?" Then do it.

If you do that, it won't eliminate all your doubts. Doubt— reaching for and hoping for trust and belief—is, according to the Bible, a part of our relationship with God. It is only the doubt that is looking for autonomy that is sinful. So doubt, and move in the direction of what you hope is true. The father who was concerned about his child and said to Jesus, "I believe; help my unbelief!" (Mark 9:24) was rewarded with an amazing answer to his prayer.

I'm angry at God. I resent all that he has allowed to happen in my life. How can I pray to a God like that?

Tell him what you just told me.

I was once speaking in Pittsburgh and was watching television in my hotel room. I was watching a religious program, and there was a woman crying. I was intrigued and continued to watch.

She said she had grown up an atheist. She had never gone to a church, owned a Bible, or said a prayer. And then her daughter was in an automobile accident and was in the hospital. She talked to the attending physician, who told her the prognosis was not very good. He told her that her daughter could remain in a coma the rest of her life or she could die. "Of course," the doctor said, "she might come out of it. We will just have to watch and wait."

The lady said that she went from the hospital to a bar across the street where she got plastered. Then she got in her car and drove home. It was raining as she drove into her driveway. "I can still see the wipers pushing the droplets from the windshield as I turned off the engine," she said. "Then I began to curse God, and I knew how to curse. For half an hour I poured out my venom and hatred before God. When I was spent, there was silence. In the silence I heard a voice, and the voice said: *That's the first time you've ever spoken to me, and I love you very much.*"

Sometimes I don't feel very spiritual when I pray. I feel like a hypocrite telling God that I love him when I don't. The truth is that the only reason I pray is that I'm afraid not to pray. Should I stop praying?

Of course not.

Just be honest with God. I don't know what it is about us that makes us think that God is unaware of how we feel. You can fake it with your friends and lie about your feelings, but you can't do that with God. Always remember that he is God and there is a necessity of respect when one speaks before a very powerful King. But also remember that he is your Father and that he isn't surprised or offended by you.

I can understand how you can sometimes not feel very spiritual. I can understand not loving God very much sometimes. I visit that place fairly often myself. If I can understand that, I'm sure that God can too, and he loves you a lot more than I do.

In the prayer that Jesus taught us, he said we were to ask forgiveness for our debts "as we forgive our debtors." I'm having trouble forgiving. Maybe that's the reason my prayers aren't very effective. Can you help?

First, remember that forgiveness is more often a process than an act. In other words, don't expect too much too soon. If the sin against you has been a small picayune sin, you can probably forgive it easily; just let it go (which, by the way, is the meaning of the Greek word for "forgive"). But if the sin against you is a big one, you are probably not going to let it go quickly.

However, you can begin, and that is all God requires. Pray, "Father, I'm angry at ____. Praying for ____ is very hard. So I lift ____ before you and ask that you would change my heart."

You will be surprised at how God works in your prayers to allow you to let go. Forgiveness of others is one of the biggest keys to effective prayers, but being in the process is all that God requires.

I don't know about you, but I get irritated when people say to me, "Just forgive and move on." That's easy for them to say. If what had been done to me had been done to them, maybe they could forgive easily and move on. But when it's me, it's not that easy.

And, at the same time, I suspect I'm not altogether that easy to forgive.

God always reminds me of how he forgave me. "I forgave you when you didn't deserve it, and you committed far more grievous sins against me than that person has committed against you." Sometimes it is that reminder that leads to my being able to genuinely forgive.

⤞⟡⤝

My prayers are dead. Could it be because I've committed the "unforgivable sin"?

No.

Jesus talked about the "blasphemy against the Spirit" in Matthew 12:31 as the unforgivable sin. One must consider the business of the Holy Spirit. The Holy Spirit convicts us of sin, teaches us truth, and points us to Jesus. Because the Spirit's business is to convict us of sin, if we continually ignore and turn away from his gentle warnings, eventually we will become calloused and will no longer be able to hear him. At that point we will have committed the unforgivable sin, not because God would not forgive us if we asked, but because we no longer ask.

If you had committed the unforgivable sin, you would never have asked the question. In other words, if you think that you might have committed the sin of blasphemy against the Holy Spirit, you haven't. Not only that, but if you had, you would care nothing about prayer, about God, or about anything spiritual. You do. So you're safe.

⤞⟡⤝

The Bible says that God "hates" divorce (see Mal. 2:16). I have just gone through a divorce, and for months I prayed that it wouldn't happen. Now I don't know what to think. Were my prayers wasted?

No, your prayers weren't wasted. In fact, no prayer is ever wasted.

In a perfect world, there would be no divorce. God's desire was for your marriage to be strong and viable. But people keep getting in the way. That doesn't surprise God, and it isn't outside the purview of his sovereignty; but, nevertheless, it happens. Your prayers reflected God's perfect will. God is pleased with that.

Now go on about your business, lean hard on God, and he will clean up the mess. I'm not worried about you. You are going to be fine.

What is God's "chastening"? When my prayers aren't answered, does that mean that God is chastening me?

The idea of chastening comes from Hebrews 12:5–11 and refers to God's love for his children. He sometimes disciplines us for our good. His discipline is always rehabilitative and never retributive. Retributive punishment is never a factor in the life of a believer. The Bible says there is no condemnation for those who are in Christ. That is what the Cross is all about. However, sometimes God does correct us in the same way that a parent would correct a child who likes to play in the street.

I believe that our sense that God is judging us or chastening us is more often wrong than right. God is probably not chastening you. Most of us are so into guilt that when locusts attack a crop in a Third World country we ask, "What did I do wrong?" Recognizing your guilt was necessary to get you to Christ, but after that it doesn't have a purpose except to remind us of God's grace and forgiveness.

When you feel that God doesn't hear your prayers, it probably isn't chastening. Maybe it's indigestion.

I have really sinned this time. Will God ever hear my prayers again? Will he ever use me again?

Of course God will hear your prayers. After you had sinned, he didn't say, "Oh, my heavens! Look at my child. He screwed it up again. I had such high hopes for him." You didn't surprise God with anything you did. It isn't falling in the mud, but staying there, that is the problem. So go to him. He isn't angry.

We go to God to get saved *and* to get loved. Too many Christians get saved and leave before they get loved. That is why so many Christians are narrow, critical, and judgmental. They should have stayed until they got loved. God doesn't need you. He does fine without your help. I suspect that he won't use you for a while, but that isn't because he is angry at you. He wants you to just let him love you for a while. When you have enough love to give to somebody else, he'll send you back into the field.

And one other thing: God mostly uses wounded healers. As painful as your sin is right now, it is the stuff that God will use to build a monument to his glory. Not only that, you will find great power in your wound.

I don't hear much about repentance in your teaching. Aren't confession and repentance very important parts of prayer?

Of course. My problem is that Christianity is so often used as a means of condemnation that I feel I need to remind people about the Cross, about Christ's imputed righteousness, and about the gospel's essential message of joy.

Repentance is not change. It is God's methodology of change. The Greek word for "repentance" means "to change one's mind." Repentance is the powerful acknowledgment that all change begins in the mind before it ever takes place in actions. Repentance is remembering who you are, who God is, what you have done wrong . . . and telling him about it. With that acknowledgment comes change. However, even if there is no change, he still loves us.

If we have been forgiven for our sins—past, present, and future—why confess?

Because you need to get some things off your chest.

In your prayers on the radio, you always say, "Forgive the sins of the one who teaches, for they are many. We would see Jesus and him only." Why do you pray that?

It's called a disclaimer.

It is dangerous for a Bible teacher to give the impression that he, as the advertisement for a midwestern Bible college said, lives "one hundred miles from any known sin." The truth is that when I teach, I want to be honest about places where I fail and places where I'm reasonably successful. I place myself under the authority of the Bible, just as you do. If I only taught those passages of the Bible where I demonstrated total obedience to God, I would go into vinyl repair.

The prayer is a reminder to you and to me that I need grace as much as or more than anybody else.

I have prayed, and God answered my prayers the way I wanted him to. Now I'm not very happy with those answers. What can I do now?

Not any fun, is it? So what have you learned?

Sometimes God will say, "All right, if that is what you want, I'm going to give it to you. When you realize what a dumb request it really was, come back to me, and we'll see what can be done."

I'm not suggesting that God doesn't filter out the dumb requests. But he does sometimes teach us the hard way. It may be that you have made your bed and you are going to have to sleep in it. That will keep you humble and close to God. It may be that now that you have realized, as did Job, that you spoke without understanding, God will change the situation. Whatever he does, he starts with where you are right now as he redeems the bad prayer or gives you power under pressure.

I'm afraid to go to God. Is that the right attitude?

If you have never been afraid before God, you have probably never been before God. A lot of Bible teachers try to ameliorate those passages in the Bible that speak of fear of God. They say that it doesn't mean "fear." Well, I sometimes wonder what God they are praying to. It is no mean thing to come into the throne room of God. Go read the first verse of Isaiah 6, and you will see what an encounter with the real God solicits from those who pray.

However, don't forget that he is also your Father. As C. S. Lewis had the Beaver say in *The Lion, the Witch and the Wardrobe* about Aslan the lion: "Of course he isn't safe. But he's good."[1]

I keep asking God to guide me, but I still don't know what his will is in my life. How do I know God's will?

Don't worry about it so much. Jesus said that if our will was to do his will, we would know his will (see John 7:17).

Many Christians think of finding God's will as if it were an Easter-egg hunt. God isn't in the business of keeping his will from you. He doesn't say that he wants you to be obedient and then, when you ask him what he wants you to do, say, "Guess." The Bible is clear that some things are always God's will (love, prayer, compassion, gentleness, etc.), and some things are never God's will (murder, dishonesty, adultery, hatred, etc.). If you want to do God's will, do what he says to do and don't do what he says not to do. When you do what he says not to do or you don't do what he says to do, ask forgiveness and get up quickly.

Aside from that, do "whatever your hand finds to do . . . with your might" (Eccles. 9:10). If he wants you to do something else, he'll let you know through circumstances, through your Bible study, through your brothers and sisters in Christ. The Bible says in 1 Thessalonians 4:3, "For this is the will of God, your sanctification." In other words, God is perfectly capable of moving you anywhere he wants, of bringing forth any circumstances, or giving you any relationship. That is his business. Your business is sanctification or staying close to him and being available. If you do that, don't worry about the other.

My late friend Bill Bright used to say that if his children told him they loved him and wanted to be good, he would not tell them that he was glad and then take the car keys away, lower their allowance, and tell them to spend more time in their room. Likewise Jesus said in Matthew 7:11, "If you then, being evil, know how to give good gifts to your children, how much more will your Father who is in heaven give good things to those who ask Him!"

Does God hear my prayers? Does he care? Does it matter?

Yes.

Yes.

More than you could possibly imagine.

Study Guide/ Discussion Questions

THIS BRIEF STUDY AND *discussion guide has been prepared to help you get the most out of* Approaching God. *In the first part of each study—"Looking Back"—you'll see brief excerpts from a single chapter and questions that will help you review some of the most crucial concepts of that chapter and ponder how they impact each of us. In the second part—"Going Deeper"—we'll look into what the Bible says about the topic under review in order to see how we can grow closer to God as we approach him in prayer.*

Chapter One: Prayer 101
LOOKING BACK

I knew a lot about God, but I didn't know God in anything other than the most superficial way.

1. What is the difference in knowing facts about God and knowing him at a personal level?
2. When we learn the truth about who God is, what are some of the personal implications of those truths?
3. What is the next step you need to take to become more "intimate" with God?

There was more than fear that came from my knowledge of God and the truth he had revealed in Scripture. There was a longing.

1. Which feeling seems more prominent in your mind and heart—fear of God or longing for relationship with him? Explain.

2. What changes in your view of God would help you trust him more?

3. Have you ever "faked" relationship with God? Explain.

One of the reasons it took me so many years to find the joy of prayer is that people assumed I already knew about prayer. So at the risk of saying the obvious, let me give you some presuppositions.

1. *Prayer begins with God.* Why is it that our relationship with God must begin with God? Why can't we initiate the relationship?

2. *Before God calls us to a conversation, he calls us to a relationship.* Does God only hear the prayers of believers? What does being a child of God have to do with his listening and responding to our prayers?

3. *If a finite being is going to communicate with an infinite God, there need to be parameters whereby we know that "real" prayer is taking place.* What sources reveal what God is like? What dangers are associated with prayer that we need to know about?

4. *We approach God in helplessness.* Does God invite us to bring our own agendas to him with the expectation that he will fulfill them? Explain.

5. *Form follows and defines function.* What is the most important thing we need to get "right" when we approach God in prayer?

GOING DEEPER

Read Romans 5:6–8.

1. What state were we in when Jesus died for us? How does knowing this change how you go to God in prayer?

2. What is so distinctive about God's love, as portrayed in this passage?

Read Matthew 9:12–13.

1. What kind of person needs a doctor? What kind of person are you?
2. What does Jesus ask us to learn in verse 13? What did you learn?

Chapter Two: *Hugging a Dirty Kid*
LOOKING BACK

Most folks believe that human beings are good and that if they work hard at it, they can become even better.

1. What kind of heart drives us to seek God for relief?
2. What kind of self-image do you have, and what is the basis of your self-image?
3. How does realizing our own condition help us be less critical of others?
4. Why do some believers get angry at the teaching that God is not angry at other people?

They lied to us about who God is. Those who lied thought they were helping, but they weren't. They didn't mean to lie.

1. What did you think of the author's message at the funeral of the person who died of AIDS?
2. The author said he has been called of God to tell people that if they go to God, God won't be angry with them. What have you been called to do?
3. If God loves us so much, why is sin such a big deal to him?
4. How does love in response to goodness differ from love in the wake of disobedience?

A misunderstanding about the purpose of guilt hurts our understanding and practice of prayer.

1. What is good about guilt? What is good about *your* guilt?

2. What happens in our hearts when we become truly aware of our need for God's grace and mercy?

3. What is the difference between a "dirty" kid and a "stiff" kid? What kind of kid are you?

4. What kind of "soil" does our goodness best grow in? What kind of soil is in your own heart?

Stiffness is made up of the agenda we bring to God.

1. What "requests" (aka "demands") have you taken to God lately that might fall into the realm of your own personal agenda?

2. Why do we pray, if not to get what we want?

3. What does trust have to do with the way we pray and what we ask for?

Going Deeper

Read Isaiah 42:3.

1. What do the images in this verse communicate about who you are?

2. What does this verse tell us about God?

Read Romans 5:20.

1. What does this verse say happens when "law" comes on the scene?

2. Does the increase of grace encourage people to do more wrong? Explain.

Chapter Three: Tying the Trusses Down
Looking Back

There is a natural frustration that follows a serious commitment to prayer. Prayer is not easy.

1. Of the things needed to develop a strong prayer relationship with God, which is the hardest for you: commitment, consistency, making the time, or

finding a comfortable "method" of prayer? Why is this difficult for you?

2. Have your emotions ever made you want to give up on prayer? Emotions like depression, anger, disappointment, doubt? Explain.

3. How do "methodologies" help us pursue and stick with prayer even when we run out of "spiritual gasoline"?

Don't increase the time you spend in prayer until it is absolutely necessary.

1. How much time does a committed person devote to prayer? Explain.

2. What false expectations do we sometimes have in regard to prayer? How do these false expectations set us up for failure?

3. How can "overcommitment" derail our commitment to prayer?

4. What about the raccoon story in this chapter might inspire us to be committed to prayer?

Sometimes the most spiritual thing we can do is the practical. If knowledge doesn't have "legs," the knowledge doesn't mean a thing, and not only that—it doesn't matter.

1. What prayer postures have you tried? What works best for you, or do you find that under different circumstances, different postures "feel" right? Explain.

2. What time and place have you set aside for prayer? If you don't yet have a time and place set aside, what time and place might work for you?

3. What "forms" of prayer have you tried or do you most enjoy? The Lord's Prayer, the ACTS method, praying Scripture, prayer list?

4. How could telling others that you will pray for them help you be more consistent in your prayer?

5. In what way is prayer a "natural" part of who you are?

GOING DEEPER
Read John 16:1.

1. Why would Jesus think that telling us ahead of time about possible dangers would help us?

2. How does being aware of potential prayer pitfalls help you?

Read Luke 18:1–8.

1. What have you continually brought before God in prayer?

2. If God knows everything, why is it important that we even ask him—especially, why do we need to ask him more than once?

Chapter Four: Growing Down
LOOKING BACK

The nature of prayer is such that childlikeness is one of the primary requirements. If you get how to be childlike right, even if everything else is wrong, your prayers will soar.

1. What kind of image does the word *father* solicit for you? Even if that image is not very positive, what characteristics of a perfect father can we apply to God?

2. What can we learn about prayer from the author's dog, Quincy?

3. How does Sören Kierkegaard's "leap into absurdity" apply to being childlike?

For so long my prayers were empty and even silly. I thought that if I did it right, I could control God.

1. What do we fear will happen if we are *not* in control?
2. What kinds of promises will God make us regarding what happens in our lives?
3. What does the author mean when he says that God "isn't safe"?
4. What things in life are you *actually* in control of?

Carl Carretto said, The discovery that I was nothing, that I was responsible for no one, that I was a man of no importance, gave me the joy of a boy on holiday.

1. What's wrong with programs that tell us how wonderful, powerful, and successful we will be if we follow certain principles?
2. What benefit is there in understanding that we are truly *helpless?*
3. In what areas of your life is it difficult to face your helplessness?

One of the things I've learned about the "soft place" of prayer is that I can say whatever I need to say, and the Father will still accept me and love me.

1. Have you ever been angry with God? How do you think God feels about your anger?
2. How can it be okay to tell God how we feel, even that we feel negatively about the life he has given us?
3. Why do children—and grownups—feel the need to make sure someone is listening before "screaming"? What does this say about our relationship with God?

Going Deeper

Read Matthew 7:11.

1. What does this scripture tell us about the kind of father God is?

2. How is God a better gift-giver than we are as parents?

Read Matthew 18:3–4.

1. What needs to change in you so that you are more like a little child?
2. What is "great" about being a humble child?

Chapter Five: Going Deeper (1)
LOOKING BACK

For some people there is a call—a drawing—for a deeper and much more intimate walk with God. Most believers do not feel the need to go deeper. There is nothing wrong with that.

1. Do you agree that deeper prayer is a "calling" and that it's okay not to grow deeper in your prayer life? Explain.
2. Are you satisfied with the current depth of your prayer life? Explain.
3. Have you ever been through a season when you naturally yearned for deeper prayer? Explain.

Too often those who begin the road of a more intimate walk with God do so with a hidden agenda.

1. What agendas have you taken to God? How did that work for you?
2. Has anyone ever come to you—on the pretense of praising you or helping you—but really with a "hidden agenda" of their own? How did this make you feel, and how did you react?
3. What important things have you discovered in your walk with Christ on the way to somewhere else?

Most contemporary Christians define themselves in terms of what they "do" rather than in terms of who they "are."

1. How do you define yourself? What, in your eyes, makes you "significant"?

2. What practical things have you striven to accomplish for God? Is this what God really wants from you? Explain.

3. If the author is right that you won't "leave a place" when you die, how does that change your perspective on who you are and your purpose here?

Those who are called to a deeper walk with God should never do it alone.

1. What "dangers" are there in pursuing a deeper walk with God?

2. What about religion makes it subject to great error and harm?

3. How do evil supernatural elements affect us as we move closer to God?

Going Deeper

Read Luke 18:1.

1. What has caused you to want to give up on prayer in the past? Did you overcome that opposition? Explain.

2. How do our own agendas sometimes discourage us as we wait for God's response to our prayers?

Read Psalm 42:1–3.

1. Has your soul ever panted for God? Under what circumstances?

2. What did the psalmist mean when he said, "My tears have been my food day and night"? Have you ever been overcome with sorrow? Explain.

Chapter Six: Going Deeper (2)
Looking Back

Prayer is the realization that I am now moved into another world.

1. Why do we need to "adjust" as we move from this world to the world of prayer? What methods can help us adjust? What methods have you used with success?

2. What "other voices" distract you from prayer as you move into that world?

3. What are some of the differences between these two worlds?

I have always known that God knows me, which, of course, means that if I got what I deserved, I would be destroyed in a moment in his presence.

1. Why are we allowed to come into God's presence—in spite of who we are?

2. How do our personal dysfunctions and insecurities determine how we approach God?

3. How should we view the wall of fear that stands between us and God's love?

Before God's throne is the only place you can tell your secrets without fear of rejection, shame, or derision. It is the one place where you can be honest and know that you will be understood and accepted.

1. What are we afraid of that keeps us from approaching God?

2. Have you experienced complete honesty with God? If not, what is holding you back? If you have, explain.

3. Is there anything that we shouldn't tell God about? Explain.

The parameters of Christian meditation are focused on God's revelation of himself in the living Word and the written Word.

1. What is the difference between Christian meditation and Eastern meditation?

2. What do you think about using "sanctified imagination" during prayer? If you've experienced this, what things have you imagined?

3. How do people sometimes confuse New Age teaching with imaginative prayer?

If prayer is a conversation between two persons (and it is), then it is important that you not only talk and meditate. It is important that you listen too.

1. Do you believe that God talks to us today, in addition to his direct revelation in Scripture? Explain.

2. If we do believe that God speaks to us, does that mean we also believe he imparts new revelations? Explain.

3. If God does speak to us, why would he not speak to everyone in the exact same way?

4. Has God ever spoken to you? What did he say? How did it affect you?

GOING DEEPER

Read Hebrews 4:16.

1. When you come before God's throne, how do you come? Are you timid and fearful or confident and bold?

2. How is it that we are invited to come "boldly" before God's throne when we are so unworthy to be in his presence?

Read Jeremiah 29:13.

1. What does prayer have to do with seeking and finding God?

2. What promise is in this scripture? What kind of heart is required for that promise to be fulfilled?

Chapter Seven: Good for Goodness' Sake
LOOKING BACK

Obedience is far less important to God than you fear and far more important to God than you could possibly know.

1. In what way is "obedience far less important to God than you fear"? What does the author mean by this?

2. What fears do you or others have regarding the connection between our obedience and God's love for us?

3. How can the opposite also be true—that obedience is "far more important to God than you could possibly know"? How do you reconcile these two ideas?

God doesn't have to fix you, because you have already been fixed by the blood of Christ and by the righteousness that has been imputed to your account.

1. What does "imputed" mean?

2. How does Christ's blood negate our need to be "fixed"?

3. In what ways are you "obsessive about being better"? Why do you think that obsessing about getting better often results in the opposite of what we strive for?

4. What is the purpose of prayer, if not to make us better?

When you encounter Christians who are negative, narrow, and critical, you can rest assured that they haven't been spending much time with God.

1. How does spending time with God shape the kind of person you are?

2. Have you ever felt rebellious toward God's laws? Why? How does knowing how much God loves you affect those rebellious feelings?

3. Does fearing that God won't love you if you don't

perform in a certain way help you become better? Explain.

The only people who get any better are those who know that if they don't get any better, God will still love them.

1. What is the difference between a *changed* life and a *changing* life? What kind of life do you have?

2. Do you agree with the author that you can't love until you have been loved? Explain.

3. What is meant by the statement "love allows confession without demanding correction"? How does God's unconditional love aid us in the process of self-examination?

4. How can prayer and God's love free us from the inclination to impose our will on others and release us from the hold that others have on us?

GOING DEEPER

Read 2 Corinthians 5:14–15.

1. How does Christ's love compel us?

2. What does his love compel us to do?

Read Romans 5:6–8.

1. How does knowing that Jesus died for us while we had no strength of our own help us to have a changing life?

2. If Jesus died for us while we were still sinners, what do you think his attitude will be toward us when we approach him in prayer?

Chapter Eight: Invitation to the Dance
LOOKING BACK

When God invites his people to prayer, he invites them to the dance—a celebration of who he is and what he has created, a celebration of life and meaning and forgiveness and heaven.

1. Why and how does an adherence to "prayer rules" affect our prayers and relationship with God?

2. What do you think about the idea of laughing with God in prayer? Does this make you feel uncomfortable? Explain.

3. Is it possible to take prayer too seriously? Explain.

We believers sometimes forget that we have been set free. Freedom scares us, and more important, it scares those religious leaders who are into control.

1. Why does freedom scare us?

2. Why do some religious leaders want to keep us in fear?

3. How are our prayers changed when we recognize and accept our freedom?

We sometimes reason that it is better to be a loser in a righteous cause than to be a winner in an unrighteous cause. It is no wonder that our prayers are so somber and pitiful.

1. Why do we sometimes see ourselves as "losers" in a righteous cause? What's wrong with this viewpoint?

2. Have you ever experienced the presence of God's army, like Elisha did? Explain.

3. How does believing we are victorious affect our prayers?

The breathtaking response of the father to his returned prodigal son is almost too good to be true. He had a party!

1. If the parable of the Prodigal Son is not really about the prodigal—as the author suggests—who is it about? Have you ever reacted like this other character? Explain.

2. What was wrong with the older son's attitude? What "prayer rules" might this attitude create?

3. What do you think about the letter to the author from "A Brother in Christ"?

GOING DEEPER
Read Psalm 18:19 and Psalm 37:4.

1. What is the reason, according to Psalm 18:19, that God delivered the psalmist?
2. What does Psalm 37:4 tell us to do?
3. In light of these two verses, what kind of relationship are we to have with God? Is this the kind of relationship you have with God? Explain.

Read Galatians 5:1.

1. Why does this scripture tell us to "stand fast in the liberty"? Why do we have a hard time claiming our freedom in Christ?
2. What happens to our prayer relationship with God when we become "entangled again with the yoke of bondage"?

Chapter Nine: It's a Family Kind of Thing
LOOKING BACK
Prayer is robbed of its power when its focus is directed only toward an individual and his or her God.

1. If it's important that prayer be with a "bunch," what does this imply regarding contemplative or individual prayer?
2. What is the connection between group prayer and the effectiveness of prayer?
3. What has your experience been regarding praying with others?

You need a friend with whom to pray. You need to spread the load out.

1. How is prayer a load too heavy to carry alone?
2. What does the biblical teaching on the gifts of the spirit have to do with prayer?
3. How can prayer be lonely, and what can we do to get rid of the loneliness?

Of course God hears and answers when one person prays, but there is a phenomenal effect when a bunch pray.

1. Why is there more power in group prayer than in individual prayer?
2. Why do you think people responded so enthusiastically to the healing services that the author conducted at his church?
3. Have you ever witnessed healing as a result of group prayer? Explain.

We are so prone to denial that the only way we can remain honest is to pray together.

1. How does praying with other people prompt us to be honest?
2. What might inhibit us from wanting to pray with others?
3. What masks do you wear that you may be afraid of taking off in group prayer?

If there is no laughter, Jesus has gone somewhere else. If there is no joy and freedom, it is not a church.

1. What do you think about the statement above? How important is joy and celebration to our prayer relationship with God?
2. Are there any limits to what we should laugh and be joyful about in corporate worship and in prayer?
3. Do you believe that you, like the author's missionary friend, have been "called to plant flowers in hell"? What opportunities have you had to do this? How did you respond to those opportunities?

GOING DEEPER

Read Matthew 18:19–20.

1. What promises are contained in this passage? Have you ever seen these promises fulfilled in your own life as a result of prayer? Explain.

2. What opportunities do you have to gather with and pray with other believers? If you don't have opportunities for such prayer, what can you do to create such settings?

Read Galatians 6:1–3.

1. What is our responsibility toward fellow believers who have done something wrong?

2. Have you ever needed and/or received support from fellow Christians when you had done wrong or were burdened? Explain.

Chapter Ten: Signs and Wonders
LOOKING BACK

Let's pose an inappropriate question: How can I get positive answers to my prayers? In other words, how can I get God to do what I want him to do?

1. What is inappropriate about the above question?

2. Have you ever sought answers to questions like the above? What did you learn in your search?

3. When we do ask such questions, how does God respond to us? How did he respond to Peter in Luke 18, when Peter made a self-serving statement?

While it may be inappropriate to ask questions about how to have a more effective prayer life, how to get positive answers to our prayers, and how to have spiritual power—let's ask anyway.

1. What part does faith play in effective, powerful prayer? Where does faith originate?

2. What kind of prayers can you be absolutely certain God will answer positively?

3. What do we learn from the Greek regarding persistent prayer in Matthew 7:7–8?

4. What attitude adjustment might you need to make to ensure that your prayers are *requests* rather than *demands?*

God may not answer the prayers we pray the way we want him to answer them, but he does come.

1. Does it seem like a cop-out to you that God would *come* to us in our pain, but not *take away* our pain? Explain.

2. Have you ever had an experience where—though God did not take away the negative circumstances in your life—you felt his loving presence and peace? Explain.

3. How is God's presence—without a miraculous change of events—a show of "signs and wonders"?

Probably the most important prayer you can ever pray is the prayer of relinquishment.

1. What is a "prayer of relinquishment"?

2. If you relinquish your rights to get a positive response from God, does that mean you will—as a reward— get a positive response from him?

3. What do you think of the concept that God sometimes "checks our willingness"? Have you ever experienced such a check in your life? Explain.

There are some things for which you don't have to pray. Because we are his, certain blessings are always ours, and we don't have to plead for them.

1. What kinds of things do we not need to ask or plead for?

2. Rather than petitioning God for such things, what should we say to God about them?

3. Have you ever had the experience where God simultaneously called you to pray about something and assured you in that call that your prayer was already answered? Explain.

4. How can we build praise into our petitions?

Going Deeper

Read Romans 8:28.

1. Does this verse promise that only good things will come into our lives? Explain.

2. What does this verse promise about the many events of our lives?

Read Matthew 7:7–8.

1. What is our responsibility in this passage?

2. Does this passage assure us that everything will always turn out exactly as we want? Explain.

Chapter Eleven: The Pain of Unanswered Prayer
Looking Back

The question before the house is this: why does God answer some prayers and not others?

1. What experiences have you had with answered and unanswered prayers?

2. Why doesn't our good and loving God always grant our requests?

3. Have you ever had a prayer answered in the dramatic way that God answered the author's prayers for his baby daughter's leg? Explain.

Jesus showed us [in the parable of the tax collector and the Pharisee] that there is no correlation between external acts of goodness and God's positive response to our prayers.

1. Do you agree with the above statement that your goodness—or lack thereof—does not affect God's response to your prayers? Explain.

2. Are you more like the Pharisee or the tax collector in Jesus' parable? Explain.

3. Why does God answer the prayers of "bad" people, like the tax collector? Why does God answer the prayers of any of us?

The nature of one's actions can only be determined by the disposition of one's motivation.

1. Why is it so important to know what God is like before we question how he answers prayer?

2. What are the implications of believing in a God who is loving but not sovereign? What are the implications regarding prayer?

3. What does trust have to do with comprehending God's response to our prayers? Have you had the chance to exercise trust in difficult situations? Explain.

There are great dangers in believing or teaching that God will always do good things for you, if you will only ask him, and if he doesn't, it is because you didn't have enough faith or try hard enough.

1. Even Jesus' prayer in the Garden for relief from the coming torture and death was not answered positively. How do you make sense of this?

2. Have you ever been pressured to take unwise action to prove the power of faith? Explain.

3. What truths about God help you deal with not getting the answer you want from him?

Going Deeper

Read Job 13:15. .

1. Have you ever felt "slayed" in your life? Were you able to trust God, even then? Explain.

2. How have you responded to tragedy in your life? What have you learned since then that might affect how you respond next time?

Read Hebrews 11:13.

1. What promises is this verse talking about? What promises do you hold on to that may not be realized in this life? How do you feel about having to wait for them?

2. Does your faith in heaven affect how you handle disappointments here on earth? Explain.

Notes

Chapter 1
1. John Owen, *Communion with the Triune God,* ed. Kelly Kapic and Justin Taylor (Wheaton, Ill.: Crossway, 2007), 94.
2. Mark Harris, *Companions for Your Spiritual Journey: Discovering the Disciplines of the Saints* (Downers Grove, Ill.: InterVarsity, 1999), 14.
3. A. W. Tozer, *The Pursuit of God* (Camp Hill, Pa.: Christian Publications, 1982), 71.
4. *Things You Never Knew Existed* (Bradenton, Fla.: Johnson Smith).
5. Tozer, *Pursuit of God*, 11–12.
6. O. Hallesby, *Prayer*, trans. Clarence Carlsen (Minneapolis: Augsburg, 1931), 12–13.
7. F. W. Faber, *Growth in Holiness* (Baltimore: Murphy, 1854).

Chapter 2
1. Marvin Olasky, *The Tragedy of American Compassion* (Washington, D.C.: Regnery, 1992), 54.
2. Olasky, *Tragedy of American Compassion*, 54.
3. Ted Peters, *Sin: Radical Evil in Soul and Society* (Grand Rapids, Mich.: Eerdmans, 1994), 3–4.
4. Reprinted from *The Singer* by Calvin Miller, © 1975 by InterVarsity Christian Fellowship of the USA.
5. Blessing given by Brennan Manning, February 26, 1993.

Chapter 3
1. C. S. Lewis, *The Screwtape Letters* (New York: Iversen, 1969), 24.

Chapter 4
1. W. H. Auden, from the poem "September 1, 1939."
2. Carlo Carretto, *Letters from the Desert,* (New York: Orbis, 1972), 17.
3. Carretto, *Letters from the Desert*, 133–34.
4. Christopher Fabry, *Spiritually Correct Bedtime Stories* (Downers Grove, Ill.: InterVarsity, 1995), 4–5.
5. Anthony de Mello, *Awareness* (New York: Doubleday, 1990), 162–63.

6. Evan K. Gibson, *C. S. Lewis, Spinner of Tales* (Grand Rapids, Mich.: Christian University Press, 1980), 134.

Chapter 5

1. Madeleine L'Engle, *Walking on Water* (Wheaton, Ill.: Harold Shaw, 1980), 161–62, 164–78.
2. Carretto, *Letters from the Desert*, 44, 134.
3. Jim Elliot, *The Journals of Jim Elliot*, ed. Elisabeth Elliot (Old Tappan, N.J.: Fleming H. Revell, 1978), 309.
4. St. Teresa of Ávila, *A Life of Prayer* (Portland, Ore.: Multnomah, 1983), 1–2.
5. Thomas à Kempis, *Of the Imitation of Christ* (Boston: E. P. Dutton, 1867), 89–90.
6. Richard F. Lovelace, *Dynamics of Spiritual Life: An Evangelical Theology of Renewal* (Downers Grove, Ill.: InterVarsity, 1979), 41.
7. John Bunyan, *The Pilgrim's Progress* (Philadelphia: Charles Foster, 1895), 75.

Chapter 6

1. J. I. Packer, *Knowing Christianity* (Wheaton, Ill.: Harold Shaw, 1995), 120.
2. Packer, *Knowing Christianity*, 121.
3. Benedicta Ward, trans., *The Desert Christian: The Sayings of the Desert Fathers* (New York: Macmillan, 1975), xix.
4. Henri Nouwen, *The Way of the Heart: Desert Spirituality and Contemporary Ministry* (San Francisco: Harper San Francisco, 1981), 27–28.
5. De Mello, *Awareness*, 5.
6. M. Basil Pennington, *Centering Prayer: Renewing an Ancient Christian Prayer Form* (Garden City, N.Y.: Image Books, 1982).
7. Richard L. Pratt Jr., *Pray with Your Eyes Open* (Phillipsburg, N.J.: Presbyterian and Reformed, 1999), 27, 29–30.
8. Packer, *Knowing Christianity*, 129.
9. Dallas Willard, *In Search of Guidance* (Ventura, Calif.: Regal Books, 1984), 230.

Chapter 7

1. Abraham Kuyper, *Lectures on Calvinism* (Grand Rapids, Mich.: Eerdmans, 1931), 172–73.
2. Nouwen, *Way of the Heart*, 34.
3. C. S. Lewis, *The Weight of Glory and Other Addresses* (Grand Rapids, Mich.: Eerdmans, 1949), 61.

4. Lewis, *Weight of Glory*, 65.
5. Brennan Manning, *Lion and Lamb: The Relentless Tenderness of Jesus* (Grand Rapids, Mich.: Chosen Books, 1986), 96–97.
6. These Luther quotes are from dramatists Charlie and Ruth Jones ("Peculiar People") and their production, *Luther*. The quotes are historically accurate.
7. Philip Yancey, "Be Ye Perfect, More or Less," *Christianity Today*, July 17, 1995, 41.
8. Archimandrite Sophrony, *His Life Is Mine*, trans. Rosemary Edmonds (Crestwood, N. Y.: St. Vladimir's Seminary Press, 1977), 73.
9. Jerry Bridges, *Transforming Grace: Living Confidently in God's Unfailing Love* (Colorado Springs: Navpress, 1991), 108.

Chapter 8
1. Reggie Kidd, Senior Banquet, Reformed Theological Seminary, May 20, 1995.
2. Bunyan, *Pilgrim's Progress*, 222.

Chapter 9
1. Charles J. Sykes, *A Nation of Victims: The Decay of the American Character* (New York: St. Martin's, 1992), 13–15.
2. Francis A. Schaeffer, *True Spirituality* (Wheaton, Ill.: Tyndale, 1971), 174.
3. Richard J. Foster, *Celebration of Discipline: The Path to Spiritual Growth* (New York: Harper & Row, 1978), 163–64.

Chapter 11
1. C. S. Lewis, *Letters to Malcolm: Chiefly on Prayer* (New York: Harcourt Brace Jovanovich, 1964), 59.
2. Rabbi Harold Kushner, *When Bad Things Happen to Good People* (New York: Avon, 1981).
3. C. S. Lewis, *A Grief Observed* (New York: Seabury, 1961), 35–36.

Chapter 12
1. C. S. Lewis, *The Lion, the Witch and the Wardrobe* (New York: Collier/Macmillan, 1950, 1970), 76.

For more from Steve Brown,
you can contact
Key Life Network at
1-800-KEYLIFE
or visit the websites at
www.keylife.org
and
www.stevebrownetc.com

Key Life is a ministry committed to
getting people Home with radical
freedom, infectious joy,
and surprising faithfulness.